Teachers and Teaching on Stage and on Screen

Teachers and Teaching on Stage and on Screen

Dramatic Depictions

EDITED BY

Diane Conrad and Monica Prendergast

First published in the UK in 2019 by
Intellect, The Mill, Parnall Road, Fishponds, Bristol, BS16 3JG, UK

First published in the USA in 2019 by
Intellect, The University of Chicago Press, 1427 E. 60th Street,
Chicago, IL 60637, USA

Copyright © 2019 Intellect Ltd

All rights reserved. No part of this publication may be reproduced, stored in a retrieval system or transmitted, in any form or by any means, electronic, mechanical, photocopying, recording or otherwise, without written permission.

A catalogue record for this book is available from the British Library.

Cover designer: Aleksandra Szumlas
Copy editor: MPS Technologies
Production editor: Faith Newcombe
Typesetting: Contentra Technologies

Print ISBN: 978-1-78938-067-5
ePDF ISBN: 978-1-78938-069-9
ePub ISBN: 978-1-78938-068-2

Printed and bound by Hobbs, UK.

To find out about all our publications, please visit
www.intellectbooks.com.
There, you can subscribe to our e-newsletter, browse or download our current catalogue and buy any titles that are in print.

This is a peer-reviewed publication.

We dedicate this book to Dr. Carl Leggo (1953–2019) whose interest in the dramatic representation of teachers led us to envision this project. Carl was an inspirational mentor, colleague, and friend; he is much missed.

Contents

Editors' Introduction: We Are Therefore We Teach — 1
Diane Conrad & Monica Prendergast

PART I: TEACHER REFLECTIONS/REFLECTIONS ON TEACHERS — 13

1. Three Perspectives on *Freedom Writers*: Considering Teaching Across the Career Span — 14
   Jaime L. Beck
2. Characteristics of a Successful Learner Applied to *Why Shoot The Teacher?* — 23
   Phil Duchene
3. The Roles We "Were Born to Fill": Thinking about Performing Teaching with *Mona Lisa Smile* — 32
   Dorothy Morrissey
4. A Curriculum of Diversity in *Monsieur Lazhar* — 41
   Jenny Osorio
5. Laughing to Learn: Irony in *Election* — 51
   Carl Leggo & Claire Ahn

PART II: TEACHERS AS HEROES OR ANTIHEROES — 59

6. The Light and Dark Archetypes of Teachers: What Can *Matilda* Tell Us about Teacher Identity? — 60
   Angelina Ambrosetti
7. The Problem with Mr. Holland: The Portrayal of Music Teachers in Film Through *Mr. Holland's Opus* — 69
   Nancy Curry & Jeffrey Curry
8. The Politics of Representation of Pedagogues in Nollywood: A Critical Analysis of *Somewhere in Africa: The Cries of Humanity* — 79
   Taiwo Afolabi & Stephen Okpadah
9. An Unlikely Revolution: Portrayals of Teaching in *Strictly Ballroom* — 89
   Anita Hallewas
10. Good Teacher/*Bad Teacher*… Is That All We Are? — 99
    Patricia Jagger

PART III: PEDAGOGIES/PEDAGOGICAL MOMENTS — 109

11. O Brave New World? The Role of Arts Education as Presented in — 110
Hunky Dory
Claire Coleman & Jane Luton

12. "You're Not Hardcore (Unless You Live Hardcore)": Exploring Pedagogical — 120
Encounters in *School of Rock*
Mitchell McLarnon

13. *Harry Potter and the Order of the Phoenix*: A Pedagogy of Misdirection — 130
Matthew Krehl Edward Thomas & Bernadette Walker-Gibbs

14. Playfulness, Relationships, and Worldviews: Indigenous Pedagogy — 138
and *Conrack*
Matthew "Gus" Gusul

15. Bill & Ted's Assessable Adventure: A Frame Analysis of Assessment — 148
Representations in Popular Culture Through *Bill & Ted's Excellent Adventure*
Rachael Jacobs

PART IV: ETHICS AND DESIRE IN TEACHING — 159

16. Teaching as a Moral Act: Reflections on Five Plays Featuring Teachers — 160
and Students (Shaw's *Pygmalion*, Kanin's *Born Yesterday*, Riml's *RAGE*,
Mamet's *Oleanna*, and Russell's *Educating Rita*)
Monica Prendergast

17. Granting "the Wherewithal to Resist": The Erotic as Pedagogical — 170
Supplement in Alan Bennett's *The History Boys*
Ian Tan Xing Long

18. Why are You Doing This? Negotiating the Gift of Education in — 179
Development Work in Nepal through *Kathmandu: A Mirror in the Sky*
Ruth Hol Mjanger, in dialogue with Bibek Shakya,
Reiny de Wit, & Meena Subba Karki

19. Learning with Brecht: Exploring the "Learning to Read and Write" Scene — 189
in *The Mother*
Stig A. Eriksson

20. Teaching, Fantasy, and Desire: Me and *Mona Lisa Smile* — 200
Kate Bride, edited by Elizabeth Yeoman

PART V: DESTABILIZING PERSPECTIVES OF TEACHERS AND TEACHING — 209

21. Wrestling with Vulnerabilities and the Potential for Difference: — 210
The Pedagogy of Drug Use in *Half Nelson*
Diane Conrad

22. The Seductress in the Classroom: The Female Teacher as Erotic Object   218
    and Fantasy in *The Piano Teacher*
    Melissa Tamporello
23. Knowing Where We Came From: An Examination of the One-Act   227
    Play *Education is Our Right*
    Carmen Rodríguez de France
24. *Art School Confidential*: Profound Offence or Just Good Fun?   236
    Anita Sinner & Thibault Zimmer
25. The Emancipatory Reaggregation of the *Irrational Man*: (Im)moral   245
    Possibilities of an Existential, Lived Curriculum
    Sean Wiebe & Pauline Sameshima

Biographies   256

Editors' Introduction:
We Are Therefore We Teach

Diane Conrad & Monica Prendergast

Why This Book?

We began this book project with a shared intrigue in our favourite plays and films that portray teachers and teaching. Ever the drama teachers and teacher educators that we are, we were convinced that a book of discussions focusing on such portrayals would offer a tremendous pedagogical resource. As we began looking at dramatic depictions of teachers and teaching, we were astounded – the more we looked the more we encountered. There are indeed a vast number of such plays and films, not to mention television portrayals, which we do not have the space to explore here. The overwhelming response we received to our call for chapters confirmed that our interest in the topic was shared by others and brought to our attention an even greater variety of relevant works. The phenomenon of dramatized teachers appears to be true across cultures, as evinced by the number and variety of proposals we received from international contributors about current or historical international plays and films. Some of the authors in this collection take up in their chapters the questions of why teacher films abound and what work these portrayals do. Dorothy Morrissey cites Dalton (2010), who "contends that the popularisation of teaching performances in Hollywood movies, not only influences, but constructs our individual and collective perceptions and expectations of teachers."

The plays and films the contributing authors suggested writing about go far beyond what Dalton (2006) calls the Hollywood curriculum of simplistic representations that work to maintain the status quo. On the contrary, the chapters we have gathered critique the Hollywood "good teacher" (Dalton, 2006) repertoire, delve into satiric parodies and alternative representations, and explore issues through analyses of independent and international films as well as several plays. They examine teacher–student relationships, institutional cultures, societal influences, and much more.

Why do so many plays and films portray teachers and teaching? It is not a coincidence that so many such films exist. Taiwo Afolabi and Stephen Okpadah acknowledge the great number of films that incorporate "themes that revolve around the import, status and significance of teachers in the society." They propose that it may be "because it is believed that pedagogues are instrumental to the growth of any society and teachers' intelligence and intellectual capability determine the pace of development in any nation." Angelina Ambrosetti (2016) avers that, "throughout old and new history, teaching is considered to be an honourable profession, one that is complex and involves specific skills and knowledge to be effective. Society has high expectations of teachers as they are entrusted with shaping the future generation" (p. 1). School is one of the iconic settings, along with family home and workplace, where life unfolds for all of us. We have all spent countless hours in schools and other educational settings. Our relationships with teachers are a significant part of our life experiences. Who does not have a story of a memorable teacher? Whether in formal primary, secondary, or tertiary contexts, or in informal educational settings – the soccer coach, piano teacher, girl-scout leader, or driving instructor – teachers were there. They may be remembered because they were beloved or despised, inspiring or boring, hilarious or harsh. Whatever the case, they were there and had an impact on us.

Many of the plays and films analyzed in this collection speak to complex and ongoing educational issues and debates. This suggests the high level of investment that we have in education in society that is in turn reflected in cultural representation on stage or screen. Everyone seems to have a stake in the state of education. As a topic or setting for plays and films, education, the world of teachers and teaching, provides a familiar backdrop to allow for an exploration of cultural issues relevant to the field of education and to society in general. What is worth teaching? How do we know? What are the best ways to teach? How do we teach diverse learners? How do we prepare young people for adult living? What are the challenges of teaching? How does a teacher stay resilient in her chosen profession? What is the cost of living a life in the classroom? Teaching portrayed on stage or on screen provides vivid reflections of the state of education, on how teachers teach, how students respond to school, and where success and failure may be found. These portrayals have an influence on popular opinion. As such, these plays and films do important work, work that demands our serious attention.

What Lies Behind?

There is a small but very engaging body of literature on the topic of educational settings and characters in film (less so on stage representations). Mark Readman's (2016) collection *Teaching and learning on screen: Mediated pedagogies* focuses on how the act of pedagogy is portrayed in film, in both formal and informal educational spaces. Readman describes the intent of his book: "[I]t is an exploration of the imaginative terrain of teaching and learning and is underpinned by the idea that the imaginary is always ideological" (p. 3). This is an understanding shared in our collection, and many chapters here tackle the ideological underpinnings at play in how teachers are depicted in drama.

Melanie Shoffner's (2016) anthology *Exploring teachers in fiction and film: Saviours, scapegoats and schoolmarms* considers that "we learn as much about teachers from the fictional as from the factual" (p. 2). This insight becomes particularly valuable in the context of teacher education, as education students bring with them ideas about teachers and teaching from both fictional and real-life encounters. This is a function we hope this book may serve for our colleagues in teacher education programs. Unpacking preconceptions and stereotypes about who teachers are is an important aspect of teacher training and professional identity formation.

Mary M. Dalton has made these notions the focus of her research and her writing has had a significant influence in the field of education (Dalton, 1995, 2006, 2010, 2013; Dalton & Linder, 2008). Dalton herself is a communications scholar, although she draws from both cultural and curriculum theories (in the latter, particularly those of Dwayne Huebner [1975]) in her investigations of how "good," "bad," "gendered," "gay," and "radical" teacher figures are represented in popular Hollywood films. Dalton's overarching interest is in "how we can use the intersection between the popular and the personal as a place to create new meaning so we can openly challenge the popular culture construction of curriculum and radical teaching" (2010, p. 15). We are inspired by Dalton's foundational work to bring a group of educators and education scholars together in this collection to reflect on dramatic portrayals of teaching from an insider perspective.

Additional scholarship in this area is found in works by sociologist Robert C. Bulman (2002, 2015), sociologist and media studies scholar Susan Ellsmore (2005), critical pedagogy scholar Henry Giroux (2002), critical race theorist Ronald E. Chennault (2006), and Fisher, Harris, and Jarvis' popular culture studies perspectives (2008). We particularly note an early book on this topic by two Canadian education colleagues who investigate how images of teachers and teaching emerge from various kinds of cultural texts (Weber & Mitchell, 1995). Journal articles of related interest include those on narrative myths in education (including filmed narratives) (Gregory, 2007); the personal and professional lives of teachers seen in movies (Trier, 2001); the role of the Latin/x teacher in film dramas (Reyes & Rios, 2003); educational-setting films as ethnographies of otherness (Leopard, 2007); and an examination of the role of English teachers in films (Bauer, 1998). Theses and dissertations on dramatic portrayals of teachers we have found include: the role of the Principal in film (Wolfrom, 2010); how movies affect pre-service teachers' thinking about teachers and teaching (de Gravelle, 2015); the representation of high schools in films (Simenz, 2007); films that portray teachers as romantic rebels (Gazetas, 1992); and the female teacher in film (Gilbert, 2014).

To conclude, our literature review demonstrates a small but robust field of inquiry into the dramatic representations of teachers and classrooms. This book adds to that body of scholarship with an intentional goal to consider both educational and cultural studies perspectives on the films and plays investigated by authors in the chapters that follow.

What Lies Ahead?

The book is divided into five sections around themes that emerged from our collection of contributions. In the first section, "Teacher Reflections/Reflections on Teachers" the authors use the plays and films as sources for reflection on their own educational practices. In Jaime L. Beck's essay, we hear how the findings from her research on teacher experiences relate to the portrayal of real-life teacher Erin Gruwell in the film *Freedom writers* (DeVito, Sher, Shamberg, & LaGravenese, 2007). Next, teacher educator Phil Duchene considers how the film *Why shoot the teacher?* (Hertzog & Narizzano, 1977) reflects the challenges faced by early career teachers, especially when working in remote or rural settings. Dorothy Morrissey's is the first of two chapters in our collection on the film *Mona Lisa smile* (Johanson & Newell, 2003). Morrissey's chapter looks at the performative aspects of teaching in her essay, and the types of roles teachers are expected to fulfill in the profession. Jenny Osorio considers how the French-Canadian film *Monsieur Lazhar* (Déry, McCraw, & Falardeau, 2011) enacts what she calls a "curriculum of diversity." Finally, in this section, Carl Leggo and Claire Ahn look at the use of irony in the film *Election* (Berger & Payne, 1999) as they reflect on their own lived experiences of teaching.

In the second section, "Teachers as Heroes or Antiheroes," our essayists examine the spectrum of teacher portrayals that range from the sympathetic hero figure through to the antagonistic villain. To begin, Angelina Ambrosetti looks at the film adaptation (DeVito, Shamberg, Sher, & Dahl, 1996) of Roald Dahl's (1988) *Matilda* to see how its positive and negative archetypal representations of teachers has an effect on teachers' sense of identity. Music educators Nancy and Jeffrey Curry criticize what they see as an unrealistic and problematic portrait of music education in *Mr. Holland opus* (Duncan, Kroopf, & Herek, 1995). Then, Nigerian scholars Taiwo Afolabi and Stephen Okpadah broaden our perspectives by looking at the politics of teacher representation in a film *Somewhere in Africa: The cries of humanity* (Arase, 2011) from that country. Anita Hallewas' essay on *Strictly ballroom* (Miall & Luhrmann, 1992) shows us how "bad teaching" is rejected in favour of a group of ballroom dance students teaching and supporting each other, all the way to victory. The section ends with Patricia Jagger's essay on the comedy *Bad teacher* (Eisenberg & Kasdan, 2011) that continues the critique of one-dimensional depictions of teachers as either "good" or "bad."

Section three offers a tighter focus on how Pedagogies/Pedagogical Moments are rendered onscreen. Claire Coleman and Jane Luton walk us through the film *Hunky dory* (Finn & Evans, 2012) and consider how it presents arts education, and art educators, in helpful and critical ways. *School of rock* (Rudin & Linklater, 2004) provides author Mitchell McLarnon the opportunity to examine how the reluctant (and unqualified) substitute music teacher Dewey Finn learns to become a good teacher through his encounters with students. Matthew Krehl Edward Thomas and Bernadette Walker-Gibbs draw on the teaching at Hogwarts in *Harry Potter and the Order of the Phoenix* (Barron, Heyman, & Yates, 2007) to support their notion of a "pedagogy of misdirection." Matthew "Gus" Gusul's essay looks at the filmed version of Pat Conroy's memoir *Conrack* (Ritt & Frank, 1974) about his teaching in an isolated island community in South Carolina. Gusul uses the film to consider his own learning about indigenous approaches to pedagogy. Last in this section, while using *Bill & Ted's excellent adventure* (Kroopf, Murphey, Soisson, & Herek, 1989) as her (somewhat surprising) model, Rachael Jacobs traces the forms of assessment drawn from popular culture that are made visible in this film.

Dramatic depictions of teachers become more complex, and one might argue more three-dimensionally human, in the book's fourth section on Ethics and Desire in Teaching. Co-editor Monica Prendergast begins this section with an essay that examines five plays featuring a teacher–student dynamic: Shaw's *Pygmalion* (1916/2005), Kanin's *Born yesterday* (1946), Riml's *RAGE* (2014), Mamet's *Oleanna*, (1992), and Russell's *Educating Rita* (1981). Her focus is on using an important essay by performance theorist Dwight Conquergood as a model of ethical performance that is then mapped onto the five plays she presents. Ian Tan Xing Long next looks at the discomforting portrayal of a history teacher who steps over the ethical line in the play (and film) by Alan Bennett, *The history boys* (2004). Our next essay takes us to Nepal in Ruth Hol Mjanger and colleagues' dialogical essay looking at some of the tensions encountered when working in international development settings in education through the Spanish film *Kathmandu: A mirror in the sky* (Bollaín, 2011). Stig A. Eriksson presents an essay based on a play by Bertolt Brecht, *The mother* (1931/1965), which considers how this great twentieth-century German playwright chose to represent teaching on stage. Finally, Kate Bride's essay is a posthumous one that we were grateful to receive from her former supervisor Elizabeth Yeoman. It is a privilege to publish Bride's work, which was part of her graduate thesis completed shortly before her untimely death. This is the second essay on the movie *Mona Lisa smile* (Johanson & Newell, 2003) that, in this case, focuses on the questions of fantasy and desire that teachers and students risk in their engagement both in and beyond the classroom.

The fifth and final section of our collection considers exemplars that invite Destabilizing Perspectives of Teachers and Teaching. Co-editor Diane Conrad opens with her exploration of the movie *Half Nelson* (Boden, Patricof, Howell, Orlovsky, Korenberg, & Fleck, 2006) and its complex portrayal of a sympathetic teacher who is struggling with drug addiction. This theme of more human portrayals of teachers continues in Melissa Tamporello's essay on *The piano teacher* (Heiduschka & Haneke, 2001) in which the eroticization of teaching is a key theme. Next, Canadian Indigenous playwright Drew Hayden Taylor's one-act play *Education is our right* (1990) offers Carmen Rodríguez de France the opportunity to look at where Canada has arrived along the path of truth and reconciliation with Indigenous communities that suffered through the residential schools era. An essay by Anita Sinner and Thibault Zimmer, looking at the film *Art school confidential* (Hall & Zwigoff, 2006), shows how using films with educational settings and characters may provide student teachers with unsettling portraits of the profession. How might we negotiate and chart our way through these challenging moments when student teachers choose to resist the critical and dramatic portrayals of teachers and teaching? Finally, we close the book with Sean Wiebe and Pauline Sameshima, who consider the possibilities of a different way to think about curriculum that they see in the Woody Allen film *Irrational man* (Aronson, Tenebaum, Walson, & Allen, 2015), with its demanding portrayal of a teacher–student romantic relationship.

How to Use This Book

We are honoured to share this collection, which only scratches the surface of the wealth of dramatic depictions of teachers and teaching that are available and waiting to be roused. Each of the chapters presented in this book offer a threefold pedagogical opportunity: First, the authors' interpretations advance discourses on one of many possible analyses of each work. Second, as works of art, the plays and films themselves are teaching instruments. As Stig A. Eriksson points out in his examination of Bertholt Brecht's work, the playwright created a dramatic genre, which he called the *Lehrstück* or learning-play. In this tradition we encourage readers to seek out opportunities to watch or read the plays and films discussed as educational texts. Third, within the dramatic works, portrayals of the teacher characters and their teaching practices present rare and valuable opportunities for intimate scrutiny of the minutiae of the profession.

We recommend that post-secondary course instructors make use of the five framing themes that organize the contents of this anthology. If the course sits within a teacher education or graduate education programme, there is plenty of opportunity for students to consider how the dramatic representation of teachers intersects with their own lived experience of teaching, and/or their ideas and preconceptions of teachers and teaching. Teacher educators Sean Wiebe and Pauline Sameshima suggest that, "the sheer volume of teacher films available suggests that one way teachers come to understand their classroom role is through film." They cite Clandinin (2013) to surmise that, "through film teachers might question their personal practical knowledge their understanding of the ethics of the profession, or their purposes for wanting to be and remain teachers." Which dramatic portraits do students most recognize as familiar? How truthful are those familiar likenesses? And which portrayals seem more alien and unfamiliar, more distant or strange? What are the responses to these perhaps more troubling or challenging depictions? Students can journal and discuss their responses as they read through the book together. Wherever possible, and mindful of copyright fair use laws, it is ideal for students to be able to watch a scene or two from each film.

In a course that sits either inside or outside of education, such as one in film or cultural studies, we also suggest that instructors invite students to better see the world within which each film takes place. Is this world benign or malevolent? Who holds on to power in this world, and who is seeking power? Where are examples of justice and injustice seen? How are these representations of education indicative of the valuing or devaluing of schooling in our own society? How much voice and agency do the characters in the film possess? How is voice or agency accessed or denied? These kinds of critical questions may deepen student understanding of film as cultural products that are too often intended to support and promote the status quo. Identifying exemplars that do the opposite, which critique or destabilize the way things are, can be powerful tools for learning.

We envision another type of reader who is reading this book for her own pleasure. Perhaps this imaginary reader is a teacher, or has been one? Or perhaps, like most of us, this reader has gone through the typical life path of many years spent in a classroom as a student. We hope this reader may find glimpses of her own story within the essays we have gathered. And we invite this reader to consider how she has thought about the role of teacher in the past, and how these essays might have shifted this thinking towards a more complicated and complex understanding.

This book brings together scholar-educators to reflect upon portrayals of education, teaching, and teachers as presented in the plays and films that have inspired them. We feel that a strength of this collection is precisely in the diversity of voices and perspectives that are presented – from the range of international films and plays selected by contributors to comment upon, to the cultural, gendered, political, etc.

perspectives they bring, to the range of experiences that informs their understandings. The multiplicity of distinct presentations included here serve to enrich our understandings beyond any simplistic interpretations of teachers and teaching. Such breadth of imagination is necessary if we are to envision education in new ways. Our broad-minded contributors are international artists, university faculty, graduate students, practicing teachers, teacher educators, and educational administrators working in the fine arts, education, and the humanities from Canada, the United States, New Zealand, Australia, Ireland, Norway, England, Nigeria, and Nepal. The films and plays they write about are from Canada – including a work by an Indigenous playwright and a Quebecois film – Great Britain, the United States, and Spain (with the narrative set in Nepal), Australia, Nigeria's "Nollywood," Germany, and Austria. We hope the collection engenders boundless reflection and dialogue as the book chapters, and the plays and films they discuss, do for us.

REFERENCES

Ambrosetti, A. (2016). The portrayal of the teacher as mentor in popular film: Inspirational, supportive and life-changing? *M/C Journal of Media and Culture, 19*(2), 1–15.

Arase, F. R. (Director). (2011). *Somewhere in Africa: The cries of humanity* [Motion picture]. Ghana & Nigeria: Raj Films and Heroes Production.

Aronson, L., Tenebaum, S., & Walson, E. (Producers), & Allen, W. (Director). (2015). *Irrational man* [Motion picture]. USA: Sony Pictures Classics.

Barron, D. P., Heyman, D. P. (Producers), & Yates, D. D. (Director). (2007). *Harry Potter and the Order of the Phoenix* [Motion picture]. USA: Warner Brothers.

Bauer, D. M. (1998). Indecent proposals: Teachers in the movies. *College English, 60*(3), 301–317.

Bennett, A. (2004a). *The history boys*. London, UK: Faber & Faber.

Berger, A. (Producer), & Payne, A. (Director). (1999). *Election* [Motion picture]. USA: Bona Fide Productions.

Boden, A. Patricof, J., Howell, L., Orlovsky, A, Korenberg, R. (Producer), & Fleck, R. (Director). (2006). *Half Nelson* [Motion picture]. USA: ThinkFilm.

Bollaín, I. (Director). (2011). *Kathmandu: A mirror in the sky* [Motion picture]. Spain: Savor Ediciones S.A. Trailer retrieved from https://www.youtube.com/watch?v=ktxLyOTAkOQ

Brecht, B. (1965). *The mother* (L. Baxandall, Trans.). New York, NY: Grove Press. (Original work published 1931)

Bulman, R. C. (2002). Teachers in the 'hood: Hollywood's middle-class fantasy. *The Urban Review, 34*(3), 251–276.

Bulman, R. C. (2015). *Hollywood goes to high school: Cinema, schools and American culture* (2nd ed.). Duffield, UK: Worth.

Chennault, R. E. (2006). *Hollywood films about school: Where race, politics and education intersect*. New York, NY: Palgrave Macmillan.

Clandinin, D. J. (2013). Personal practical knowledge: A study of teachers' classroom images. In C. J. Craig, P. C. Meijer, & J. Broeckmans (Eds.), *From teacher thinking to teachers and teaching: The evolution of a research community. Advances in research on teaching* (vol. 19, pp. 67–95). Basingstoke, UK: Emerald Group.

Dalton, M. M. (1995). The Hollywood curriculum: Who is the "good" teacher? *Curriculum Studies, 3*(1), 23–44.

Dalton, M. M. (2006). Revising the Hollywood curriculum. *Journal of Curriculum and Pedagogy, 3*(2), 29–34.

Dalton, M. M. (2010). *The Hollywood curriculum* (2nd ed.). New York, NY: Peter Lang.

Dalton, M. M. (2013). *Bad Teacher* is bad for teachers. *Journal of Popular Film and Television, 41*(2), 78–87.

Dalton, M. M., & Linder, L. R. (2008). *Teacher TV: Sixty years of teachers on television*. New York, NY: Peter Lang.

de Gravelle, E. L. (2015). *Reality check, I am not Hilary Swank: How American teacher-centric commercial films tried and failed to teach me how to be a teacher* [Unpublished departmental honors thesis]. Texas Christian University, Fort Worth, TX.

Déry, L., McCraw, K. (Producer), & Falardeau, P. (Director). (2011). *Monsieur Lazhar* [Motion picture]. Canada: Séville.

DeVito, D., Shamberg, M., Sher, S., & Dahl, L. (Producers), & DeVito, D. (Director). (1996). *Matilda* [Motion picture]. USA: TriStar Pictures.

DeVito, D., Sher, M., Shamberg, S., & LaGravenese, R. (2007). *Freedom writers* [Motion picture]. USA: Paramount Pictures.

Duncan, P. S., & Kroopf, S. (Executive producers), & Herek, S. (Director). (1995). *Mr. Holland's opus* [Motion picture]. USA: Buena Vista Pictures.

Eisenberg, L. (Producer), & Kasdan, J. (Director). (2011). *Bad teacher* [Motion picture]. USA: Columbia Pictures.

Ellsmore, S. (2005). *Carry on, teachers! Representations of the teaching profession in screen culture*. Stoke-on-Trent, UK: Trentham.

Finn, J. (Producer), & Evans, M. (Director). (2012). *Hunky dory* [Motion picture]. UK: Film Agency for Wales.

Fisher, R., Harris, A., & Jarvis, C. (2008). *Education in popular culture: Telling tales on teachers and learners*. Abingdon, UK: Routledge.

Gazetas, A. (1992). *The image of a teacher as a romantic rebel in narrative film* [Unpublished master's thesis]. University of British Columbia, Vancouver, BC.

Gilbert, L. A. (2014). *Cinematic representations of female teachers: A narratological analysis of mise-en-scene in recent Hollywood films* [Unpublished doctoral dissertation]. Northern Illinois University, DeKalb, IL.

Giroux, H. A. (2002). *Breaking in to the movies: Film and the culture of politics*. Hoboken, NJ: Wiley-Blackwell.

Gregory, M. W. (2007). Real teaching and real learning vs narrative myths about education. *Arts and Humanities in Higher Education, 6*(1), 7–27.

Hall, B. A. (Producer), & Zwigoff, T. (Director). (2006). *Art school confidential* [Motion picture]. USA: Sony.

Hayden-Taylor, D. (1990). *Toronto at dreamer's rock and Education is our right: Two one-act plays*. Markham, ON: Fifth House.

Heiduschka, V. (Producer), & Haneke, M. (Director). (2001). *The piano teacher* [Motion picture]. Austria: Kino International.

Hertzog, L. T. (Producer), & Narizzano, S. (Director). (1977). *Why shoot the teacher?* [Motion picture]. Canada: Canadian Film Development Corporation.

Huebner, D. (1975). Curricular language and classroom meanings. In W. F. Pinar (Ed.), *Curriculum theorizing: The reconceptualists* (pp. 217–235). Berkeley, CA: McCutchan.

Johanson, F. (Producer), & Newell, M. (Director). (2003). *Mona Lisa smile* [Motion picture]. USA: Revolution Studios; Red Om Film Productions.

Kanin, G. (1946). *Born yesterday*. New York, NY: Dramatists Play Service.

Kroopf, S., Murphey, M. S., Soisson, J. (Producers), & Herek, S. (Director). (1989). *Bill & Ted's excellent adventure* [Motion picture]. USA: Orion Pictures Corporation.

Leopard, D. (2007). *Blackboard jungle:* The ethnographic narratives of education on film. *Cinema Journal, 46*(4), 24–44.

Mamet, D. (1992). *Oleanna*. New York, NY: Vintage.

Miall, T. (Producer), & Luhrmann, B. (Director). (1992). *Strictly ballroom* [Motion picture]. Australia: M&A Productions.

Mitchell, C., & Weber, S. (1999). *Reinventing ourselves as teachers: Beyond nostalgia*. London, UK: Falmer Press.

Readman, M (Ed.). (2016). *Teaching and learning on screen: Mediated pedagogies*. New York, NY: Springer.

Reyes, X. A., & Rios, D. I. (2003). Imaging teachers: In fact and in the mass media. *Journal of Latinos and Education, 2*(1), 3–11.

Ritt, M., & Frank, H. (Producer), & Ritt, M. (Director). (1974). *Conrack* [Motion picture]. USA: Twentieth Century Fox.

Riml, M. (2014). *RAGE*. In E. Hurley (Ed.), *Once more with feeling: Five affecting plays*. Toronto, ON: Playwrights Canada Press.

Rudin, S. (Producer), & Linklater, R. (Director). (2004). *School of rock* (Motion picture). USA: Paramount Pictures.

Russell, W. (1981). *Educating Rita*. New York, NY: Samuel French.

Shaw, G. B. (2005). *Pygmalion*. Clayton, Germany: Prestwick House. (Original work published in 1916)

Shoffner, M. (Ed.). (2016). *Exploring teachers in fiction and film: Saviours, scapegoats and schoolmarms*. New York, NY: Routledge.

Simenz, C. J. (2007). *Representations of urban high schools in Hollywood motion pictures* [Unpublished doctoral dissertation]. Marquette University, Milwaukee, WI.

Trier, J. D. (2001). The cinematic representation of the personal and professional lives of teachers. *Teacher Education Quarterly, 28*(3), 127–142.

Weber, S., & Mitchell, C. (1995). *"That's funny you don't look like a teacher": Interrogating images and identity in popular culture*. London, UK: Falmer.

Wolfrom, K. J. (2010). *Reel principals: A descriptive content analysis of the images of school principals depicted in movies from 1997–2009* [Unpublished doctoral dissertation]. Indiana University of Pennsylvania, Indiana, PA.

PART I

Teacher Reflections/
Reflections on Teachers

Three Perspectives on *Freedom Writers*: Considering Teaching Across the Career Span

Jaime L. Beck

Based on a true story, the film *Freedom writers* (DeVito, Sher, Shamberg, & LaGravenese, 2007) follows Erin Gruwell's entry into teaching in an urban high school in California. Despite having been on track to be a lawyer, Gruwell chooses instead to become a teacher, a "good teacher": one who is personally involved in the lives of her students, even "at great personal cost" (Dalton, 2004, p. 39). As often happens to beginning teachers (see Anhorn, 2008; Darling-Hammond, 2003; Ingersoll & Kralik, 2004), Gruwell's first teaching assignment is one of the school's most challenging, and she is offered very few resources or supports to meet this challenge.

This chapter presents a multi-faceted examination of *Freedom writers* from the perspectives of three teachers at different stages in their careers. These perspectives serve to highlight some of the core tensions within education the film presents, tensions that might be overlooked in a surface viewing of the film as a "feel-good" teacher story. Drawing on past research I have conducted with beginning teachers (Beck, 2010, 2017; Servage, Beck, & Couture, 2017) and teachers in their mid-careers (Beck, 2016), and framed by a developmental approach to teacher growth (Britzman, 2003; Day & Gu, 2010; Flores & Day, 2006), this chapter examines *Freedom writers* from the monologue perspectives of: a teacher about to enter the profession; a teacher in her third-year confronting the realities of a life in teaching; and a teacher in her mid-career continuing to teach.

Following Leavy's (2011, 2013) arts-based literary approaches to research, I have crafted each monologue, not as a direct representation of a particular research project, but as research-informed creative non-fiction based on my now thirteen years of inquiry into teacher experiences. *Freedom writers* is an authentic touchstone for each of the perspectives as, through the course of my research, I have learned how teachers view these teacher-as-isolated-hero narratives differently, at different career stages. Perhaps most significantly, in my inquiries with teachers I found that teacher experiences continue to be hidden and misunderstood as a teacher's career advances. As a result, I see dialogue and empathy across perspectives as being sorely needed in education. Thus, a primary driver for drawing on fiction is its ability to facilitate a more "empathic understanding" as readers are invited "to vicariously experience events from a different perspective" (Barone & Eisner, 1997, p. 78). Fiction, of any kind, "is uniquely able to draw readers in and express subtlety and connectivity" (Leavy, 2013, p. 36).

Questioning Education's Status Quo

The monologues that follow also serve as critical perspectives on some of the dominant educational imagery of teachers in films. As Barone (2003) articulates, prevailing imagery in these popular films "is, to a large extent, educationally debilitating [...] composed of a cluster of negative stereotypes of public schools, teachers, and students" (p. 202). In *Freedom writers*, two of Gruwell's more senior colleagues represent Education's status quo: a more veteran teacher, Mr. Gelford, and Gruwell's administrator, Ms. Campbell. These colleagues seem unenthused about the new challenges presented by a recent demographic shift at the school. A new "voluntary integration" programme has brought students to the school who seem, to these more veteran educators, a burden. Conversely, Gruwell is drawn to the school *because* of the policy, and therefore the opportunity to make a difference. By the end of the film, despite her successes as a teacher in this context, Gruwell leaves the school, its students, staff, and all of its existing policies behind, and intact.

The end credits tell us that Gruwell did not "quit" teaching full stop, rather she moved on to the same college as some of her students – they "graduated" together, in a sense. This part of the story is one we recognize as "a happy and known ending, one that makes [the story] to leave acceptable" (Clandinin, Downey, & Huber, 2009, p. 146). It becomes easy to "shrug off" the fact that Gruwell leaves high school teaching because she "moved up." We are thus led away from a critical discussion of why this highly skilled and passionate teacher could not continue doing a job she seemed both destined and committed to doing. By the end of the film, we too leave the school's status quo behind, unquestioned as a hopelessly fixed reality. However, if Erin Gruwell is the kind of teacher we want for our students, and I believe she is, then we need to take a more critical look at why too many teachers, both in film and in real life, leave the K-12 classroom.[1] The following offers an opportunity to reframe the *Freedom writers*' narrative, and perhaps to being to imagine a system in which exceptional teachers thrive and are able to sustain their capacities for the course of their career.

Monologue I: Nysa

Nysa

Today I had an orientation at my practicum school. I had to wake up ridiculously early but it wasn't hard, I mean, I barely slept anyways. By the time I got to the school my stomach was kind of a wreck. Practicum feels like Christmas morning, combined with the scariest job interview ever. I'm ready though. Part of me feels like I've been ready my whole life. And, after all the courses I've just taken, I can handle anything.

The programme has been amazing from day one. We started by sitting in a circle and sharing our reasons for being there. There are so many stories I remember. Like Hayden's story of that one teacher who saw past the juvenile delinquency to the university-bound student beneath. Hayden told us, through tears, that success as a teacher means passing that help along, even to just one student. There was Avery too, who just wanted to share her passion for math, and wow, she loves math! We all had other things in common too, like, we all "played school" when we were little, and observed the habits of our best teachers. We also all have our favourite teacher movies.

We were asked at one point to write a paper on our favourite teacher film. I chose *Freedom writers*. I love that movie! Especially because it's based on a true story. I wrote about how it's tough for her at first, for Erin Gruwell. She has practically *no* help from anyone; the other teachers have already given up. One of them even tells her to just bide her time until the students "quit coming," like everyone expects. They obviously don't really care about their students. It's going to be tough to work with teachers like that. But Gruwell sees potential in her students, and tries to understand their lives. Her classroom becomes a safe space, and then she offers them notebooks where they can just write. They write about their lives, and she spends the time it takes to read them all, and to encourage them.

To me, the film just reaffirms my teaching philosophy. It's about creating a safe place for students, and believing in them, seeing their potential, and giving them an opportunity to use their strengths. Gruwell took the time to do that, even though the school practically told her not to and she had to sacrifice a lot to do it, but, many of her students went on to college. She made a difference in so many lives. That's definitely the kind of teacher I want to be, and I'm ready!

Monologues II and III: Brenna

Brenna

November. I've been teaching for three years. It's not quite what I thought it would be. I keep trying to figure out why. One obvious reason: I'm *still* teaching dance. That was, and continues to be a pretty big curve ball! When I started teaching I had a bit of a dance on my CV, and they told us in Teacher Ed., "Take the job, put whatever you can on your CV, and then take the job!" So I did. Most of the job is teaching English, which is my teaching area. I thought, after a year or two, once I'm no longer the newbie, I'll transition out of dance and teach strictly English. What I didn't realize is, that even with just one class, I was *the* dance teacher at the school. That means, "The drama production this year is a musical, can you help us with our choreography?" and "We want to start a dance club, can you be our sponsor teacher?" I thought it was a great idea – not choreographing the musical, that was tough for a first year teacher to fit in, especially one with zero experience choreographing musicals – but the dance club. It was a GREAT idea, and I couldn't say no to students.

Fast-forward two years and I'm so established as the dance teacher that I see I can't really transition out. But also, I am not sure that I want to. Yes, it adds a lot to the already heavy English teacher workload: in-school events, weekend field trips, after school practices, dance meetings with the students, guest instructors, and of course, taking more dance classes myself. But it's really where I connect with students, where I am most able to become a meaningful part of their lives. Yet, it's still not what I thought it would be. Why? Because I'm always drowning in paperwork? Or, because I did report cards wrong the first time? Why do I let those things get to me?

My students keep telling me I should watch that new movie, *Freedom writers*, apparently I remind them of her. I've been avoiding it. I used to love movies like that but now, I don't really want to compare myself to a "good teacher" in some Hollywood film. Sure, I *know* I'm a good teacher sometimes, with the dance club, in my English classes, but most of the time I *feel* like I have no idea what I'm doing, and I don't feel supported. At the end of each day, there's still so much left undone, and I'm exhausted. I'm exhausted but I can't sleep, I keep losing weight but I'm not hungry, not that I really have time to eat anyways. I am starting to worry about these things, about what my health will be like a few years down the road. There are only so many nights of sleep or meals you can miss, right? Most days, I just don't feel *well*. There's even a tiny part of me thinking about doing something else…

June. I finally watched *Freedom writers*. I had to. My principal gave me the book as my farewell gift. It was meant as a nice gesture, but it didn't feel that nice. During our last staff meeting she made this farewell speech; it started with that long list of the things I have done since starting at the school. Some of the things I didn't even remember, and hearing it all at once like that – it was a bit surreal. She listed all the levels of English I have taught, the English Language exchange I organized, etcetera, etcetera. Then of course, she talked about dance. She shared some notes written by my dance students – those were also stories full of time, all the time I put in, all the things we had worked on together. I was touched. But, I still don't feel "successful." I mean, here I am, getting a farewell speech after only *three years* of teaching. But, I need a break. It's not normal, right, to faint at work for no reason? Anyways, I'm at the staff meeting and I'm having all of these mixed feelings, and then the principal ends her speech by saying, "So, now that we've burnt her out, she's heading back to grad school." Her tone was slightly sarcastic, and many people laughed. I guess it was funny? Now that they've burnt me out? Is that what's happened? I just felt kind of stunned, I didn't even hear what she said after that, I just shook her hand and took the copy of *Teach With Your Heart* that she gave me, and went home and watched that damn movie.

The film is, well, my students were right, it *is* my story, right there, in plain sight. And in some ways that's a good thing and I'm honoured to be compared with this dedicated and talented new teacher. But in other ways, it's not a good thing. This is a heavy story to bear. Here is this amazing teacher, who works a second job to buy her students supplies, who spends all her time and energy working for and with her students. Her husband leaves her because she's so dedicated. Then, at the end of the movie, she's leaving the classroom, after all that she's invested, after all that she's lost. The reason? Well, they say it directly: "her methods are impractical, impossible to implement with regularity." Her principal asks, "Do you honestly think you can create this family in every classroom, for every grade, for every student?" I didn't have to hear Gruwell's answer. I can't keep this up. So what does that mean? Leaving? I mean, shouldn't "good teachers" be the ones who stay?

Monologue IV: Dara

Dara

This year, I'm not taking a student teacher, and I'm not going to feel guilty about it either. It's about self-preservation. Every year, I take a student teacher, and I do my best but, it's challenging. I mean I know that kind of teaching, that all-consuming-I'm-going-to-change-every-single-student's-life type of teaching, it's just not sustainable. And I try not to be discouraging, to offer gentle guidance. But even the smallest suggestions I make are met with that critical look, that look says, "Oh, you're just jaded or old school or burnt out, make room for me!" And I remember, you come in, you're raring to go, your head's full of students standing on desks for you and – I get it. You want to experience that. But as you continue to teach, like I have, you start to realize that going the distance means keeping things in perspective, in balance, and I wish I could somehow prepare them for this. But balance is definitely not the message you get from Hollywood films.

The latest, *Freedom writers*, was a little hard to watch. I could see where Gruwell was coming from, I mean, those students deserved better. It's hard to stomach the idea of turning your back on students just to save some energy for next year. But you have to make tough choices. It's a tough system.

That principal Gruwell has, Ms. Campbell, I can tell she is trying to be helpful. I see the gentle way she tells Gruwell to consider scaling back her lesson plans, and maybe don't wear those pearls to class. It's not bitterness, it's experience. Later, she spells out the real dilemma: "We have millions of children," she says, "to get through the education system [...] and we need a means of accomplishing that which allows as many students to benefit as possible." She's right. There's only so much you can do when you have as many as forty students in a class, and you have four of those classes back-to-back! At some point, you have to look at the practicalities, or you just don't survive. You have to make choices, or you break.

I don't want you to get the impression that it's easy; it comes with a lot of guilt. Of course, I still want the best for my students. I still have this teacher ideal in mind. It's just that, well, we all have limits, and there is always going to be so much more you could be doing, so much left undone at the end of each day. Gruwell's husband, in the film, reminds me of my own partner. He watches Gruwell work herself practically to death and doesn't know what to do. Finally, he tries to explain how he feels: "What you're doing is noble, and it's good," then he adds, "I just want to live my life and not feel bad about it." What's wrong with that? This year, that's me. That means no student teacher scrutinizing the corners I've cut. I'll just teach and let teach, and maybe I'll live my life just a little, while trying not to feel bad about it.

Discussion

As someone who wanted to be a teacher from an early age, I loved watching movies like *Freedom writers*. The teachers portrayed in these kinds of films defined what it meant to be a "good" teacher. These narratives also contributed to the "culture shock" (Britzman, 2003) or "praxis shock" (Kelchtermans & Ballet, 2002) I experienced. The reality of teaching is so much more complex than these films depict, and so much more challenging than our "apprenticeship of observation" (Lortie, 1975) as students in schools prepare us. Yet, I often wonder what I would have really *heard* if someone had tried, as Dara tries with her student teachers, to prepare me for the overwhelming amount of paperwork in teaching, or for just how much of an impact the bureaucracy of teaching can have. I believed that any hoop I would have to jump through would be worth it, if I could make a difference. I did not consider the shape I would be in on the other side of the hoop.

As I began to listen to the stories of teachers who stay in teaching (Beck, 2016, 2017), I gained new insights. Many teachers who stay walk the line of compromise between wanting to be the teacher they have in mind, and needing to save enough energy for themselves, their families, and for the years of teaching ahead. This space between ideals and daily realities is one that too is devoid of dialogue. The conversations about the challenges of teaching, however, are tricky to have. We might imagine how, for Dara, revealing the ways in which she "cuts corners" to survive a "tough system" would leave her vulnerable, open to scrutiny. We might also imagine how Erin Gruwell's enthusiasm reminds Ms. Campbell of the teacher she once wanted to be, but found impossible in the context of the public school system in which she worked. Dalton (2004) describes the relationships between the "good" teachers who enter as outsiders, and the "stodgy" administration, and how in Hollywood films, "the goals of these teachers and administrators are so completely different that they engage in their own respective diatribes without ever conveying one to the other what they really mean" (p. 36). Dalton explains that this void of *real* communication is what allows the status quo to remain; it becomes "unthinkable to viewers that these teachers might actually unite one with another to form a bloc together with students to displace the educational bureaucracy" (p. 41). If we can break this Hollywood spell, perhaps we can reimagine our real-life educational spaces as changeable. We need to have conversations, across perspectives and with empathy, about what we might collectively do differently in order for good teaching to thrive. Some of this might involve acknowledging our *selves* in teaching and allowing for more "professional self-care" (Newell & MacNeil, 2010) in our daily practice. Other changes might involve advocating for better structural conditions for teaching and learning. Whatever the action, it begins in dialogue, and beyond the Hollywood film.

REFERENCES

Anhorn, R. (2008). The profession that eats its young. *The Delta Kappa Gamma Bulletin*, 74(3), 15–26.

Barone, T. (2003). Challenging the educational imaginary: Issues of form, substance, and quality in film-based research. *Qualitative Inquiry*, 9(2), 202–217.

Barone, T., & Eisner, E. (1997). Arts-based educational research. In R. M. Jaeger (Ed.), *Complementary methods for research in education* (2nd ed., pp. 72–116). Washington, DC: American Educational Research Association.

Beck, J. L. (2010). *Breaking the silence: Beginning teachers share pathways out of the profession* [Unpublished master's thesis]. University of British Columbia, Vancouver, BC. Retrieved from https://circle.ubc.ca/handle/2429/27689

Beck, J. L. (2016). *Teachers' experiences of negotiating stories to stay by: A narrative inquiry* [Unpublished doctoral thesis]. University of Alberta, Edmonton, AB. Retrieved from https://era.library.ualberta.ca/items/01a3f73c-acb4-4de1-9ddb-ed403484c6f6

Beck, J. L. (2017). The weight of a heavy hour: Understanding teacher experiences of work intensification. *McGill Journal of Education*, 52(3), 617–638.

Borman, G. D., & Dowling, N. M. (2008). Teacher attrition and retention: A meta-analytic and narrative review of the research. *Review of Educational Research*, 78(3), 367–409.

Britzman, D. (2003). *Practice makes practice: A critical study of learning to teach* (Rev. ed.). Albany, NY: State University of New York Press.

Clandinin, D. J., Downey, C. A., & Huber, J. (2009). Attending to changing landscapes: Shaping the interwoven identities of teachers and teacher educators. *Asia-Pacific Journal of Teacher Education*, 37(2), 141–154.

Dalton, M. M. (2004). *The Hollywood curriculum: Teachers in the movies*. New York, NY: Peter Lang.

Darling-Hammond, L. (2003). Keeping good teachers: Why it matters, what leaders can do. *Educational Leadership*, 60(8), 6–13.

Day, C., & Gu, Q. (2010). *The new lives of teachers*. London, UK: Taylor & Francis.

DeVito, D., Sher, M., Shamberg, S., & LaGravenese, R. (2007). *Freedom writers* [Motion picture]. USA: Paramount Pictures.

Flores, M. A., & Day, C. (2006). Contexts which shape and reshape new teachers' identities: A multi-perspective study. *Teaching and Teacher Education*, 22(2), 219–232.

Gruwell, E. (2008). *Teach with your heart: Lessons I learned from the freedom writers*. New York, NY: Broadway Books.

Harfitt, G. J. (2015). From attrition to retention: A narrative inquiry of why beginning teachers leave and then rejoin the profession. *Asia-Pacific Journal of Teacher Education*, 43(1), 22–35.

Howes, L. M., & Goodman-Delahunty, J. (2015). Teachers' career decisions: Perspectives on choosing teaching careers, and on staying or leaving. *Issues in Educational Research*, 25(1), 18–35.

Ingersoll, R. M., & Kralik, J. M. (2004). *The impact of mentoring on teacher retention: What the research says* (pp. 1–23). Denver, CO: Education Commission of the States. Retrieved from https://www.gse.upenn.edu/pdf/rmi/ECS-RMI-2004.pdf

Kelchtermans, G., & Ballet, K. (2002). The micropolitics of teacher induction: A narrative-biographical study on teacher socialisation. *Teaching and Teacher Education*, 18(1), 105–120.

Kelly, S., & Northrop, L. (2015). Early career outcomes for the "best and the brightest": Selectivity, satisfaction, and attrition in the beginning teacher longitudinal survey. *American Educational Research Journal*, 52(4), 624–656.

Leavy, P. (2011). *Low-fat love* (Vol. 1). Rotterdam, NL: Sense Publishers.

Leavy, P. (2013). *Fiction as research practice: Short stories, novellas, and novels.* Walnut Creek, CA: Left Coast Press.

Lortie, D. C. (1975). *Schoolteacher: A sociological study.* Chicago, IL: University of Chicago Press.

Newell, J. M., & MacNeil, G. A. (2010). Professional burnout, vicarious trauma, secondary traumatic stress, and compassion fatigue: A review of theoretical terms, risk factors, and preventive methods for clinicians and researchers. *Best Practice in Mental Health*, 6(2), 57–68.

Servage, L., Beck, J. L., & Couture, J. C. (2017). Foundations for professional growth: A longitudinal look at induction practices in Alberta. In B. Kutsyuruba, & K. D. Walker (Eds.), *The bliss and blisters of early career teaching: A pan-Canadian perspective* (pp. 335–350). Burlington, ON: Word & Deed Publishing.

NOTE

1. Exact attrition figures are difficult to track (Harfitt, 2015). However, there is consensus in the research that a large portion of early career attrition is "unhealthy" (Borman & Dowling, 2008). That is to say, the teaching profession does not effectively "weed out" those for whom teaching is a poor fit, rather, teachers of all skill levels and abilities are lost to early career attrition (Howes & Goodman-Delahunty, 2015). One study estimates that "highly selective graduates have an 85% greater likelihood of leaving the profession than less selective graduates in the first three years" (Kelly & Northrop, 2015, p. 648), implying that teaching loses some its "best and brightest" professionals. Regardless of the figures, we must also consider the impact that early career experiences have for the individuals who choose to become teachers, the students they teach, and the school communities of which they are part. Whether they leave or choose to stay in the profession, these early experiences can have lasting personal and professional consequences (Beck, 2010, 2016; Servage et al., 2017).

Characteristics of a Successful Learner Applied to *Why Shoot The Teacher?*

Phil Duchene

Do you want to see our calf? We had two but one of them died. Dad says it was just as well because there wasn't enough feed, anyway.

(Hertzog & Narizzano, 1977, *Why shoot the teacher?*)

Introduction

Some years ago, in a kinder, gentler world than Max Braithwaite's, I had a small part in a University of Victoria's Faculty of Education–based research project with professors Robert Anthony, Terry D. Johnson, Alison Preece, and fellow graduate student, Susan Smith. The brief was a little intimidating: namely, it asked if it was possible to point to *universal* learner characteristics, both processes and outcomes that could promote learning and create personal change.

After at least two years on the work, it was decided that, yes, these characteristics might be identified. Named the "Characteristics of a Successful Learner," it is a broad-brushed tool but lends itself particularly well to story-based examples and is essentially a proactive cross-curricular evaluation tool.

It was deemed that the successful learner is: Thoughtful, meaning curious and enjoys reasoning, inferential thinking and critical judgment, and who is reflective and insightful; Industrious, meaning persistent and hard working in adversity and initial failure; Generative, being creative and productive with the ability to produce unique and original solution or apply ideas and solutions of others in order to achieve a satisfactory end; Empathetic, that is, with an aware of awareness of, sensitivity to, concern for, and willingness to act on behalf of others, be collaborative, and who values the importance of interdependence; a Risk Taker, meaning someone who attempts new ventures with a sense of calculating that distinguishes it from foolhardiness or recklessness; and Strategic, that is, a resourceful, planning learner with a capacity to identify and to bring personal resources to bear on a problem, with an organized capacity to select and deploy resources to effect a satisfactory solution. These five characteristics are processes. The outcomes are Knowledge, both procedural – an understanding of processes and how to apply knowledge – and propositional knowledge, a general knowledge gained from experience, and Self Esteem, that is, the ability to realistically appraise oneself and accept strengths and weaknesses. These headings took on the memorable acronym, TIGERSKS.

The real goal of the study was to focus on the characteristics' possible implementation for students of all ages, their teachers, and their schools. To that aim, we research team members talked through characters from countless movies, dramas, and stories; from children's novels, for example, *Charlotte's web* (White, 1952) or *The wizard of Oz* (Baum, 1900), to elementary and middle school students' own family members, checking for possible matches for what we considered successful learners. And it became a little like playing with Joseph Campbell's *The hero with a thousand faces* (1949) for the first time. If this is familiar to you, perhaps you found that it is something of a challenge to choose a story with a strong protagonist who does *not* follow most of the hero's steps. The critical difference for us was that Campbell's heroes could not control their fates. It was like looking fixedly backwards in a car mirror as you drive. The Hero's Journey is a staggering monomyth based on Campbell's forty years of painstaking story analysis. It is a commentary on the universal need for storytelling that crosses all cultures. It is not, though, a recipe for problem solving.

Our personal reflective model made it possible, we thought, to *change* outcomes for the learner, and if widely enough adopted, perhaps the learning environment itself. We ran a number of pilot models in British Columbia classrooms. On reflection, and looking from 2018 with many similar projects now online, it was all a bit evangelical. The model did require a determined paradigm shift away from the intellectual bankruptcy of letter grading that is still very much an elephant in staffrooms today. Teachers needed some skill as writers since the commentary was delivered through anecdotal prose characterized by reason. Innovation in Education is never introduced with the carrot of "If you take this on, you're excused these duties and expectations," and consequently some of the pilot teachers eventually put up boundaries due to the simple need for self-preservation. However the model remains a simple, elegant tool that I will use to frame my discussion of *Why shoot the teacher?* (Hertzog & Narizzano, 1977) supported by some of Braithwaite's autobiographical notes. Having never seriously seen the light of day, TIGERSKS has kept its lustre well and I am still happily explaining the premise and framework in my own classes as though it had been devised last semester.

Why Shoot the Teacher?

The movie *Why shoot the teacher?* is a Canadian prairie gem. The modestly celebrated highest grossing Canadian movie for 1977 is an adaption of Stephen Leacock Award winner Max Braithwaite's account of his first year of teaching in the Dirty Thirties. This retrospective piece is set in the ironically named community of Willowgreen, Saskatchewan. Max Brown (Bud Cort) a young graduate of Normal School (not from university it is worth noting) can aspire only to teach in the Elementary system. In his case it is in a one-room schoolhouse. And there are no jobs in any but the remotest of communities. Our hero, from Saskatoon, offers his services in over one hundred letters of application, eventually for just $400 year. He enters an isolated world of very hard times and accompanying barter, "Course, we can't pay you in cash" says School Trustee, Lyle Bishop (Chris Wiggins). The wry community support, prairie weather, loneliness and emotional survival, and featured students are sharply drawn with affection and realism.

The film is a chronological flicker through scenes that shape Max Braithwaite's memory of his first teaching school year. Some scenes are four-in-the-morning excruciatingly self-critical; others, rather happier, like the frenetic schoolhouse dance scene recorded with the sense of a Caravaggio painting – all light, shadow, and animal energy. What makes the work so accessible for teacher candidates is that Max is a *tabula rasa*, as they are; and like all good dramas, *Why shoot the teacher?* is one that allows them to vicariously experience a sharply focused position, in this case that of a beginner teacher.

Max's life in his one room school in the "dirty thirties" bore few similarities to his own upbringing in the city of Saskatoon, sharing the same prairie climate but not the grinding hardship of rural communities. However, he is not an immigrant and recognizes and embraces the resilience and self-reliance of the traditional Canadian character, from the singular virtue of hard work to a love of amateur dramatics, to the absolutely no-quarter hockey game. And it is still a very tough assignment.

I would like to frame the learner characteristics theoretical model described above over our hero Max's experience to better understand his role and the story's place and time settings.

Thoughtful

The term "thoughtful" is not to be confused with empathy. Simply, it is being curious, reflective, and insightful together with a broader identification of learning patterns. First, for Max, we are given both a wide vision of geographical emptiness and also his highly focused personal experiences, and here I am reminded of Andrew Wyeth's (1948) masterful painting *Christina's World*. Everything in Max's tight universe is examined and pondered over: political socialist under currents that were to become the Canadian Pension Plan and Healthcare for All. As highly vocal mentor Harris Montgomery (Gary Reineke) says to Max of their witnessing a family's pathetic eviction and foreclosure on an impoverished farmstead, "What's the bank want this house for, anyway?"; the importance of the Saskatoon berry in the prairie diet; hellish blizzards ironically captioned as "Spring," and worse dust storms; infamous practical jokes (with their always accompanying touch of sadism); the intense nature of a briefly domesticated coyote, Raffles, who became his closest friend. "I have never forgotten him. He was a worthy representative of a tough, uncomplaining, resourceful fun loving prairie breed." All are teased out and made some sense of by our young hero.

Industriousness

The sheer difficulty of many new teachers, from any era, of facing the challenges of their first classrooms should be over-emphasized. In the early twenty-first century it is the breadth of those challenges that has changed since the 1930s – not that inherent challenge. By way of offering an example of the importance of sheer hard work in any professional calling, I like to share with my teacher candidate students that Mozart put in sixteen-hour days on composition and was, effectively, a music teacher-on-call for six years before his first appointment in Salzburg. In the film, Max survives teaching a Grade One to Grade Ten class, made up from the damaged, hungry, and marginalized, to the few children whose parents have the basics to embrace middle class expectations. He does so with a set of stolen encyclopaedias, eight months Normal school training, his memory of the best teaching examples from his own school days, and by sheer grit. His teacherage is the basement space below the schoolhouse, since no one in the community is able or willing to board him in these difficult times. He has a bed, a table, a stove, and chairs and is fortunate to have a chemical toilet. He is expected to cope and he is reminded, remote location or not, that another teacher could be found in a heartbeat.

Generative

Max's creativity is always needed both to elicit his students' involvement and the following of the ideas of a new curriculum that promoted Dewey's (1938) humanistic ideas of education. The curriculum guides of the day were short on detail about how those ideas might be accomplished by brand new teachers in one-room schoolhouses in the midst of rural poverty. His own self-esteem, which needs to intellectually grow and explore, is, of course, inextricably linked to professional creativity. Further, the arts are a luxury in the community and unknown for most children outside the schoolhouse. A few fortunate farmhouses have radios that serve as concert halls, sports arenas, public forums, and newspapers. Max has a happy, informal drama background in which he takes pride. He relishes this experience in his role of bringing the curriculum to life. From "The little red hen" (the perfect Prairie story with guts and truth: those that don't work don't deserve to eat) to Shakespeare's *Blow, blow thou winter wind* with the grade nines – from the vicissitudes of Rosalind back to those of the little red hen. Public performance at school is restricted to the Christmas concert by which, he says, all teachers were judged. In the classroom, we have glimpses of students performing poems and play scenes in one corner of the full schoolroom. He is given a partly domesticated coyote by an itinerant farm hand. The animal becomes the unwilling subject of hands-on scientific study by the children who learned, "the first lesson about *Canis Latrans* is that he has very sharp teeth. When I came up from (the teacherage) painting my wound with iodine I stood Raffles on a bed sheet and we examined him. Things went better. We ascertained he measured forty five inches from tip of tail to tip of nose, stood two feet tall at the shoulder […] his eyes were slanted, his cheek bones high, the end of his nose snubbed. We also learned that standing on a sheet on a desk to be examined had an adverse effect on bowel control."

Empathy

Max's personal education in coming to understand his role as a teacher and caregiver is filled with poignant examples. He has children who fall asleep through fatigue and hunger and he notes that the school may be one place that some can sleep alone and undisturbed. A number of children are sewn into their underwear in the fall and Max's only caveat is the need to know how to be upwind during interactions. Through the simplest gestures of humanity he starts to regularly give hungry girls part of his own lunch only to be confronted angrily by a shamed father for his presumption. By the time the school inspector (Kenneth Griffiths) arrives during a gopher hunt – one hundred tails means a dollar paid by the province and is real money – Max realizes his base as a teacher now firmly sits with the welfare of his students. "When he (the inspector) left I was sad to think of what his visit might have been had I not been so numbed by solitude and he so unbendingly official. Of how we might have sat and talked of education and the problems peculiar to these ragged but valuable children. Of how we could have opened their minds with tales of places he had been and they would never be; some concept of the great land they were part of but didn't know. Instead, he'd carped on details and I'd acted the bumpkin."

It is worth stating that beginner teachers may be reminded that they will, in time, best know their own students' needs.

Risk Taking

Max's teaching assignment constitutes considerable risk at a number of levels. To begin with, it is a test of his suitability for the teaching profession. At least there was a shred of hope for work in education at the time, unlike for engineers who were famously unemployable. At a small political meeting organized by Harris Montgomery (Gary Reineke) Max tells a popular story of an engineer who fell into the South Saskatchewan River. A would-be rescuer asks him what he does and where he works. On learning the details the rescuer leaves the engineer to his fate and goes to the factory to apply for the upcoming vacancy. Max knows his own training to be inadequate, though, and he has so little confidence in new curricula ideas that his first reaction is to teach in a completely traditional manner as he himself was taught. He is uncertain of his ability to simply care for himself and, indeed, the community mothers initially take pity on his obvious worldly ineptitude by cleaning the basement teacherage and by providing the most basic of groceries: a bushel of oats and a quarter of a hog. The nature of his position as teacher means he is by definition ascribed only formal, distanced relationships in the community. The night of the dance at the schoolhouse sees him offered a shared drink from a flask. He feels some acceptance at last, until the offer is rebuked by another: "What are you thinking? That's the teacher!" (Gary Reineke). Max's only close friendship is with an English war bride and parent, Alice Field (Samantha Eggar), which simply underlines his loneliness. She runs away from her family on the night of a blizzard to shelter first in the schoolhouse barn and then in the teacherage. As Evelyn Ellerman (2012) puts it in her movie commentary; "Their attraction is born from a mutual desperation at finding themselves marooned in Willowgreen. Both of them appreciate music and literature. They talk and laugh in the little schoolhouse like survivors on a cultural life raft. Alice feels trapped in a marriage to an uncommunicative veteran of World War I. Like many women of her background in that era, she is desperate enough to run away from home, children, husband; her life is a drab, endless round of drudgery." On finding her the next day, Alice's husband, Bert (Michael J. Reynolds) warns Max he will break his back if he ever mentions her stay at the schoolhouse even as necessary as it was. In a sense, he is risking his whole self; physical, intellectual, and emotional.

Strategic

Max is handed a planning task that very few teachers face today, namely to prepare and deliver a curriculum to nine grades. He uses an "each one teach one" mentoring approach so the one room class is effectively broken up into three or four activity areas. Literacy and numeracy for primary grades are his first concern. The newfangled Social Studies subjects take second place to beginner reading and writing; the non-reading students take a quarter of all his time. There are three books in the classroom when he arrives, one of which is on white slavery, initially being shared in a scene by a grade-ten student with primary children. It is immediately confiscated, leaving two. His saving grace is that he has brought with him a set of encyclopaedias to take care of the other subjects, through a monitor system where older students read to younger ones. And he has plasticine for students to make the animals featuring in primer stories and to teach Canadian geography.

It is his organization and capacity alone that can bring personal and material resources to bear on problems including everything from accessing water for the school and his personal needs – after strapping a boy for cutting up a book Max is told, "Pa says I don't have to bring water no more," to manipulating end-of-year tests to help students move on and to more fairly showing student improvement.

Knowledge and Self-Esteem

Max initially realizes his own inadequacies, but he takes strength from the stoicism of the community. He is changed, in a blacksmiths' term, case-hardened, by the prairie experience. He learns that without a closely supportive society the individual will be condemned to soul-destroying loneliness. It is, perhaps, easily forgotten that both mental illness and real hunger stalked the prairies in the Depression era. The author of the book upon whom the film character is based, Max Braithwaite, was one of eight siblings. So he was never alone before this teaching assignment, thus making his situation even more of a personal trial. His students' families are living in poverty in the world's harshest habitable climate. He becomes increasingly aware of his self-worth, and that means knowing truly what his students need over what is deemed important by a schools' inspector, or indeed, educational innovators who presume teachers can accommodate new ways of knowing and delivering new approaches with only short-term theoretical training. Max's new self-knowledge also sees him realize there are limits to his own acceptance of a lack of intellectual and social stimulation.

Interestingly, the movie credits roll with caption notes saying that Max returned for a further contract, but Braithwaite's autobiography sees him fleeing the rural prairies to teach in small town communities. My own experience in working in more needy teaching assignments seems to have followed, like Max's, three distinct phases. One: you may be initially resented as an outsider for various reasons. For example, you do not know the culture, or the children, or perhaps your predecessor was particularly liked. Two: through hard work and without expectations on your part you show your worth and are accepted; and three: the community does not want to let you go. I guarantee this last one may even be a surprising revelation; the request to stay likely coming from parents and students with whom you may have had some friction. In Max's final autobiographical words: "There was an annoying pull backwards, a definite reluctance to leave, despite the loneliness, frustration and poverty. Was it the attraction of habit (a released prisoner might miss the cell for a day) or was it something more? Had this place and happenings become a part of me, affecting to some extent my thoughts and actions for all time?" are simplified into "I knew I'd be returning to Wintergreen in the fall for another year." As Evelyn Ellerman (2012) puts it, "not because he has to but because they know him there. And, now, he knows them."

Conclusion

The outstanding virtue of *Why shoot the teacher?* is its mirroring of the ongoing concerns of all beginner teachers; knowledge, control, and acceptance (with a little wistful romance included). Most important of all, Max endures and embraces the profession in his own terms discovering in teaching terms the old adage that the universe is what we say it is.

The screenplay speaks to the goodness and toughness of the rural community and its neatly understated support for the newcomer who has proved his worth. That Max is a figure of fun, when they so choose, is part of his initiation. Yet, it is his ability as a teacher, the parental appreciation for the care of their children – "I just want to thank you. Rosie done good this year" (Hertzog & Narizzano, 1977), and his resilience, that sees him win his prairie spurs.

REFERENCES

Baum, F. L. (1900). *The wizard of Oz*. Chicago, IL: George M. Hill.
Braithwaite, M. (1965). *Why shoot the teacher?* Toronto, ON: McClelland & Stewart.
Campbell, J. (1949). *The hero with a thousand faces*. Princeton, NJ: Princeton University Press.

Dewey, J. (1938). *Experience and education.* Indianapolis, IN: Kappa Delta Pi.

Ellerman, E. (2012). *Canadian film online.* Alberta, VI: Athabasca University.

Hertzog, L. T. (Producer), & Narizzano, S. (Director). (1977). *Why shoot the teacher?* [Motion picture]. Canada: Canadian Film Development Corporation.

White, E. B. (1952). *Charlotte's web.* New York, NY: Harper.

The Roles We "Were Born to Fill": Thinking about Performing Teaching with *Mona Lisa Smile*

Dorothy Morrissey

Introduction

Katherine Watson, the lead character in *Mona Lisa smile* (Johanson & Newell, 2003), performs teaching in ways that repeat the portrayal in popular culture of the "good" teacher as "hero" or "saviour" (Dalton, 2006; Fisher, Harris, & Jarvis, 2008). Watson's performance reflects the tendency in Hollywood to dichotomize teaching (and teachers) into *either* good *or* bad; a dichotomy that serves to exalt the notion of teacher as saviour (Dalton, 2006, 2010). For, as Fisher and colleagues (2008) suggest, the heroic teacher has the power to impress not just students, but audiences as well. Dalton (2010) argues that the popularization of teaching performances in Hollywood movies, not only influences, but constructs our individual and collective perceptions and expectations of teachers. I contend, moreover, that these popular either/or performances serve to obscure the more complex "realities" within which teaching is "actually" performed. In this chapter, I seek to uncover something of these complexities by reflecting on the context in which I began my own performance of teaching in Ireland – in a career that has spanned more than thirty years. Towards this end, I engage in dialogue with Katherine Watson's "heroic" performance of teaching in *Mona Lisa smile*. In the film, we see Watson (played by Julia Roberts) teaching a number of lessons and, in this chapter, the first two of these lessons provide the springboard for my reflections.

Performing Teaching in Mona Lisa Smile

Mona Lisa smile (Johanson & Newell, 2003) presents the story of Watson's "heroism," as a beginning teacher at "the most conservative college in the nation"

(Johanson & Newell, 2003) over the course of an academic year. Told from the perspective of one of her students, Watson's story is presented in the form of a linear narrative and condensed into 119 minutes. For, as Dalton (2010) asserts, "The medium of film [like all media, including this book chapter] operates under many constraints, including time" (p. 24). Set in 1953, the film opens with Watson, a graduate of UCLA, moving from California to take up a post as an art history teacher at Wellesley College; a prestigious New England college for women. Watson, as stated in the opening voice-over, "didn't come to Wellesley because she wanted to fit in. She came because she wanted to make a difference" (Johanson & Newell, 2003). So, from the beginning, she is positioned as an outsider. She, nonetheless, sees her mission and that of Wellesley as one and the same: to "turn out tomorrow's leaders." This congruency is confirmed for her in the opening ritual of the academic year:

> Who knocks at the door of learning?
> I am every woman.
> What do you seek?
> To awake my spirit through hard work and dedicate my life to knowledge.
> (Johanson & Newell, 2003).

In her very first class, about which she is apprehensive and for which she has obviously prepared, Watson, like many (if not most) novice teachers, is focussed on her own performance; on "surviving" (Bartell, 2005). As a beginning teacher, she is ill-equipped to respond to the unexpected. Positioned at the front of the lecture theatre behind the podium, she proceeds to dispense her textbook knowledge of art history to her students. When, however, her students anticipate her slides – having familiarized themselves with the course textbook, she does not know how to respond. Her helplessness is exacerbated by the performative presence (revealed at the end of the class) of a member of the Wellesley establishment, who glances disapprovingly in her direction and who, in a subsequent meeting, cautions her to have "better discipline next class." His regulatory presence signals the institutional codes and conventions Watson is expected to repeat. At this stage, however, Watson, an outsider, is not yet fully cognisant of these codes.

Teaching as Performative

Each time I view the scene described above, I am reminded of my own beginnings as a novice primary school teacher. Inevitably, the meanings I make about my experiences now are not the meanings I made then. Nor are they the meanings I might make if I was thinking with a text other than *Mona Lisa smile*. Inevitably, my meaning making is (implicitly) informed by the many theories I have encountered over the years as well as (more explicitly) by those that preoccupy my current thinking. Indeed, I see theory (after Clandinin & Connelly, 2000) as integral not just to the process of meaning making but to experience itself, which is always interpreted (Greene, 1995). In this chapter, Greene's (1995, 2001) writings on aesthetic education and theories of teacher development (Bartell, 2005; Berliner, 1994; Fessler & Christensen, 1992) are integral to my narrative of experience. For, after Greene (1995), I see my life as a "narrative in the making" (p. 1), composed of multiple interlocking narratives, also in the making. Thinking with the work of Schechner (2013) in performance studies and Butler (2007a) on gender, I understand teaching and teacher identity as performances; as composed of repeatable behaviours that people train for and rehearse. These repeatable behaviours pre-exist the individuals performing them and are held in place by repetition and regulation; by performativity (Butler 2007a, 2007b; Lyotard 1984; Pineau 2005). Teaching (and, as Butler contends, gender) is, therefore, performed within pre-existing codes and conventions, though these may vary within and across cultures as well as over time (Pineau, 2005; Schechner, 2013). Many of these codes are explicit and may even be subject to mechanisms of bureaucratic control (Lyotard, 1984). Others, nevertheless, remain implicit and may take longer (particularly if one is an outsider) to learn or decode. However, since these behaviours "can be recombined in endless variations" (Schechner, 2013, p. 30) and in an endless variety of contexts, no performance of teaching is the same as any other. So, for me, to conceive teaching as a performance is to open spaces for destabilizing the performative imperatives regulating it. In this chapter, the narrative I present (though composed of multiple strands) is but one possible narrative among many possible narratives in the making.

My Performance of Teaching

In 1982, I graduated as a primary school teacher. I was 20 years old. (Watson is 32.) In college, I had been introduced to Freire's (1970) *Pedagogy of the oppressed*, so I knew that I did not want to repeat the performances of teaching I had experienced as a student in secondary school and in college. I wanted to perform in ways that did more than just deposit knowledge into my young charges. I wanted to engage (after Freire) in dialogue with the children I was teaching; to engage with them in reflecting and acting upon the world so as to transform it. The knowledge transmission model was the norm in the school in which I got my first job as a teacher. The performative imperative to repeat it weighed heavily on me, so I tried to be a depositor teacher. The result: frustration and exhaustion on my part and disengagement and "indiscipline" on the part of the children. Like Watson, I felt inadequate and ashamed; I experienced myself not as a beginning, but as a "bad" teacher. Like Watson too, who is set apart from the other teachers at Wellesley by her lack of "pedigree," her "bohemianism," and her inexperience, I felt isolated from the other teachers in my school. I was separated from them by my inexperience and by my silently articulated non-Catholic status. In a Catholic school (90% of Ireland's primary schools are still Catholic), teachers were expected not just to teach Catholic religious education but to "be" Catholic as well.

As part of my undergraduate (BEd) degree, I chose an elective course in drama education. Drama, perhaps more than any of the other arts, is a social art form. Drama pedagogy – like Freire's approach to dialogic inquiry, requires teachers to perform in ways that do not rely solely on the transmission of knowledge. However, the transmission model that had infused my training as a teacher also infused the context in which I found myself as a beginning teacher. This model was at odds with the rhetoric (if not the "reality") of Ireland's child-centred *Primary school curriculum* (1971). It was at odds too with my own experience as a primary school student, and it was at odds with the demands of both drama and dialogic inquiry. As a beginning teacher, I struggled with these competing demands, feeling compelled to conform to what was expected on the one hand and yearning to trouble those expectations on the other. If my attempts to transmit knowledge led to student disengagement and indiscipline, however, my attempts to engage students in any sort of dialogue resulted in complete chaos. Slowly but surely, I honed my teaching skills. It took many years, however, to develop the range of techniques, strategies, and approaches required to facilitate dialogic inquiry. Gradually, I learnt to negotiate the tensions between the either/or poles within which I was teaching (and living) and to embrace both. Occasionally, as I was negotiating these tensions, I would experience what Csikzentmihalyi (1997) calls "flow"; the feeling when things are going well of an "almost automatic, effortless, yet highly focused state of consciousness" (p. 110; see also Morrissey, 2014). These experiences tended to occur by chance, when the children and I were focussed on complex and confusing "problems" and often as we engaged aesthetically with the arts. For example, one day, as we were exploring a poem about the stoning of an old woman by a group of children, a nine-year-old girl remarked that the stones were like words and could hurt just as much. Gradually, I began to see that I did not have to choose between knowledge transmission and dialogic inquiry; between the curriculum and children's lives. It is, however, only in retrospect that I can articulate all of this. As a beginning teacher, gaining experience (and, thereby, skills), necessarily, took precedence over articulation (Bartell, 2005; Berliner, 1994). My "survival" depended on it.

Troubling Performative Imperatives

In her second lesson, we see Watson, having failed to "survive" the first lesson, abandon the transmission model in favour of dialogic inquiry. She appears, after just one lesson, to have acquired the knowledge, competence, and insight to shift from a performance of teaching concerned with cultural transmission to one promoting active co-performance on the part of her students. This shift, from a stage of teacher development concerned with survival to one involving conscious choices about both content and pedagogy is a shift that in "reality" (and, indeed, in my experience) takes many years (Bartell, 2005). In *Mona Lisa smile* (Johanson & Newell, 2003), it is presented as one that can be made "overnight," which ignores the experience, competence, and insight required to make such a shift. This rapid transformation, however, places Watson in the mould of Hollywood's "good" teachers, who seek to connect with their students' lives (Dalton, 2010). In this second lesson too, I see parallels between Watson's approach to aesthetic education and my own; the latter developed over many years and informed by many experiences (including theoretical ones). In my aesthetic education classes, I choose (after Greene, 1995) works of art that might leave my students "somehow ill at ease" (p. 135) and "prod" them "beyond acquiescence" (p. 135). Watson, likewise, projects an image of Soutine's expressionist painting, *Carcass of Beef* for her students to consider. In this, she poses a direct challenge to the validity of Wellesley's traditional art history syllabus (unusual for a "good" teacher) (Dalton, 2010). As her students frantically search their textbooks to tell them what to think, Watson challenges them to think for themselves. She also moves from behind the podium and sits among them. In the performative space of the classroom, "space" and the positioning of bodies in it "speak" (Dunlop, 1998). Watson's use of space signals her intention to engage in dialogue with her students, to explore with them an alternative syllabus: "What is art? What makes it good and who decides?" (Johanson & Newell, 2003) Her use of space also disrupts the teacher–student relationship assumed by the spatial organization of the lecture theatre itself. In this scene, Watson, in terms of both lesson content and teaching approach, disrupts the performatives attached to teaching at Wellesley. In this scene too, she encounters student resistance, most especially from the editor of the college magazine, Betty Warren (played by Kirsten Dunst), the daughter of one of Wellesley's most powerful alumni.

While in *Mona Lisa smile*, Watson's shift from novice to competent teacher is presented as uncomplicated, the film signals – albeit in simplified form, the complexities within which teachers perform; it signals the complexities attached to institutional codes in the first lesson scene and those attached to student–teacher relationships in the second. For the remainder of the film, Watson's performance of teaching is situated in the interstices and intersections of these complexities and the broader cultural context in which they are enmeshed.

Making Choices

Gradually, the chasm between Wellesley's mission and Watson's becomes apparent. The College's primary purpose turns out to be that of preparing its (white) female students for their roles as wives of America's elite males and mothers of the nation's most privileged children. Watson on the other hand is intent on getting them to question accepted values and (gender) roles. She even gives a "C" grade to a student who normally gets straight "A"s, berating her for regurgitating others' opinions and counselling her, as she offers her a second chance, to trust her own. While at the end of the second lesson, described above, Watson gives a nod to Wellesley's art history syllabus, asking her students if they have read chapter three, she gives no such nod in the lessons that follow. She holds the next two classes outside the confined space of the lecture theatre and its performative imperatives, in an art gallery and in an art studio. When she rubs up against the newly wed Betty Warren by refusing to make allowances, in terms of attendance and course requirements, for her newly married status, she finds herself classified as "subversive" in the college magazine. Her transgressions, now public, are noted by the college administrators, among whom is Betty's mother. So, as is the custom with Hollywood's "good" teachers, Watson finds herself at odds with the administrators and, at the end of the film, she decides to leave Wellesley rather than to kow-tow to their demands to conform. As soon as she realizes that she is fighting a losing battle, Watson (in the vein of the "good" Hollywood teacher) puts her efforts into "saving" one particular student, Joan Brandwyn (played by Julia Stiles), persuading her that she can go to law school *and* marry: "You can bake your cake and eat it too […] you can study and get dinner on the table by five" (Johanson & Newell, 2003). Joan, however, decides to elope, choosing marriage and children over a career. She explains to Watson that,

> It was my choice not to go. He [her new husband] would have supported it […]. You are the one who said I can have anything I want […]. You didn't come to Wellesley to help people find their way. I think you came to help them find *your* way.
>
> (Johanson & Newell, 2003)

Here, as Fisher and colleagues (2008) write, Watson, the feminist, "is forced to confront her own prejudices and the implications of choice" (p. 41). Ultimately, choice, in Schechner's (2013) terms, is performed in the context of the conventions (or performative imperatives) in which our lives are lived.

The Broader Cultural Context

When I left school, my mother persuaded me to choose teaching as a career. She herself had left school at 14 and saw teaching, which would accommodate time for housework and childcare, as an ideal choice for a woman. My mother's understanding of teaching, and of a woman's career, undoubtedly impacted my "choice." It was circumscribed too by the dominant (Catholic) understanding – still enshrined in Ireland's Constitution (1942), of a woman's primary vocational role: as wife and mother (Inglis, 1998). In 1980s Ireland, teaching was both Catholicized and feminized.

In *Mona Lisa smile*, as in many Hollywood movies featuring a "good" teacher protagonist, the institutional structures of Wellesley College remain intact, despite Watson's attempts to challenge them (Dalton, 2010). For, as Dalton writes:

> The elements of the Hollywood model of the good teacher are constructed in the movies in ways that are intended to symbolize the radical or progressive teacher on-screen, but these elements may also be read as constraints that lock these same teachers into the role of fostering social conformity instead of organizing opposition [...]. By pitting the individual good teacher against the institutions of education in symbolic rather than in meaningful action, the imbalance of power makes it impossible for the teacher [...] to win [...] [m]aking the teacher an outsider precludes involving him or her in collective action with other teachers and also eliminates the possibility of dialogue between the good teacher and the representatives of educational bureaucracies.
>
> (p. 42)

Conclusion

Unlike Watson, and Hollywood's (usually young) "good" teachers, it was many years before I would feel secure enough to challenge any of the custodians of the institutions in which I taught directly. As a beginning teacher in a Catholic school, in a time of high unemployment, I did not dare to divulge that I was not a Catholic (though I had been brought up as Catholic). Around the time I started teaching, a secondary school teacher, Eileen Flynn, was dismissed from her post in a Catholic convent school. She was in a relationship with a married man and had a child with him. Four years later, I married in a Catholic church. In Ireland in the 1980s, teaching – and primary teaching, in particular, was governed not so much by competency standards as it is today, but by the Catholic Church, which provided the system's administrators. In my classroom, however, as I honed my craft, my classroom became (and continues to be) a performative space in which the students and I co-performed, unsettling certainties, experimenting and fashioning and refashioning ourselves in the "always, emergent, contingent, and powerladen" (Spry, 2011, p. 39) context of the classroom (Pineau, 2005). I am far from certain about the impact of such co-performances. For, like Watson's performance, they do not involve collective action and are contained and controlled by the performative imperatives regulating teaching and learning in schools (Pineau, 2005). I see them, however, as performances of possibility, having the potential to reach beyond themselves. For, as Greene (2001) asserts, our achievements as teachers may be incremental rather than immediate: "We […] achieve what we hope to achieve (strangely enough) when our students leave us and make their choices in the open world, and often times, we never know or can know what we have done" (p. 61). Katherine Watson could never have known that she would one day "save" Betty Warren – that, citing Watson's influence, she would go to law school, when her dreams of domestic bliss were shattered.

REFERENCES

Bartell, C. (2005). *Cultivating high quality teaching through induction and mentoring.* Thousand Oaks, CA: Corwin Press.

Berliner, D. C. (1994). Expertise: The wonders of exemplary performance is performance. In J. N. Mangieri, & C. B. Collins (Eds.), *Creating powerful thinking in teachers and students* (pp. 141–186). Ft. Worth, TX: Holt, Rinehart & Winston.

Butler, J. (2007a). *Gender trouble: Feminism and the subversion of identity* (2nd ed.). London: Routledge.

Butler, J. (2007b). Performative acts and gender constitution: An essay in phenomenology and feminist theory. In H. Bial (Ed.), *The performance studies reader* (2nd ed.) (pp. 187–199). London: Routledge. (Original work published 1988)

Clandinin, D. J., & Connelly, F. M. (2000). *Narrative inquiry: Experience and story in qualitative research.* San Francisco, CA: Jossey-Bass.

Csikzentmihalyi, M. (1997). *Creativity: Flow and the psychology of discovery and invention.* New York, NY: Harper Collins.

Fessler, R., & Christensen, J. (1992). *The teacher career cycle.* Needham Heights, MA: Allyn & Bacon.

Dalton, M. M. (2006). Revising the Hollywood curriculum. *Journal of Curriculum and Pedagogy, 3*(2), 29–34.

Dalton, M. M. (2010). *The Hollywood curriculum* (2nd ed.). New York: Peter Lang.

Dunlop, V. (1998). *Looking at dances: A choreological perspective on performance*. Bath, UK: Verve.

Fisher, R., Harris, A., & Jarvis, C. (2008). *Education in popular culture: Telling tales on teachers and learners*. Abingdon, UK: Routledge.

Freire, P. (1970). *Pedagogy of the oppressed*. New York, NY: Continuum.

Greene, M. (1995). *Releasing the imagination: Essays on education, the arts and social change*. San Francisco, CA: Jossey Bass.

Greene, M. (2001). *Variations on a blue guitar: The Lincoln Centre Institute lectures on aesthetic education*. New York, NY: Teachers College Press.

Inglis, T. (1998). *The moral monopoly: The rise and fall of the Catholic Church in Ireland* (2nd ed.). Dublin, IE: UCD Press.

Irish Government Publications. (1945). *Bunreacht na hÉireann: Constitution of Ireland*. Dublin, IE: Oifig an tSoláthair.

Irish Government Publications. (1971). *Curaclam na Bunscoile: Primary school curriculum*. Dublin, IE: Browne and Nolan.

Johanson, F. (Producer), & Newell, M. (Director). (2003). *Mona Lisa smile* [Motion picture]. USA: Revolution Studios; Red Om Film Productions.

Lyotard, J. F. (1984). *The postmodern condition: A report on knowledge*. Manchester, UK: Manchester University Press.

Morrissey, D. (2014). An autoethnographic inquiry into the role of serendipity in becoming a teacher educator. *International Journal of Qualitative Studies in Education, 27*(7), 124–134.

Pineau, E. L. (2005). Teaching is performance: Reconceptualizing a problematic metaphor. In B. K. Alexander, G. L. Anderson, & B. P. Gallegos (Eds.), *Performance theories in education: Power, pedagogy and the politics of identity* (pp. 15–39). Mahwah, NJ: Lawrence Erlbaum Associates. (Original work published 1994)

Schechner, R. (2013). *Performance studies: An introduction* (3rd ed.). New York, NY: Routledge.

Spry, T. (2011). *Body, paper, stage: Writing and performing autoethnography*. New York, NY: Routledge.

A Curriculum of Diversity in *Monsieur Lazhar*

Jenny Osorio

Introduction

Immigrating to another country is not an easy decision to make, whether it is for security reasons or because of the need and desire of a better future for one's children – realities that might not be possible anymore in the home country. Immigration is often the last choice, as no one likes to be forced to leave their country. While the decision itself is not easy, neither is the travel the most difficult part. What comes after is the real challenge: arriving to an unknown country and culture, of which the environment, language, and customs are usually very different. As an immigrant myself, I know the challenges experienced by families when trying to understand the new environment and build rapport with personal and official spheres, such as the education, health, and legal systems. This path towards adaptation is often accompanied by judgment and stereotypes about and from both the newcomer and the host communities. Artistic representations such as literature and film are ways of expressing the complexities of this reality, from diverse perspectives and experiences. They allow us to gain an understanding from the other's point-of-view.

In this chapter, I will analyze the film *Monsieur Lazhar* (Déry, McCraw, & Falardeau, 2011) from my own sensitivities as an immigrant through the perspective of a curriculum of diversity, explaining how linguistic, cultural, and education system differences are portrayed, and how the teacher and the students navigate these spaces in the film. Additionally, I will explore how the topic of death and bereavement is dealt with in contradictory ways by the school administration and by the teacher and students.

The Film: Monsieur Lazhar

Monsieur Lazhar (Déry et al., 2011) is a Canadian French language movie released in 2011, directed by Philippe Falardeau. The film is an adaptation of *Bashir Lazhar*, a play by Évelyne de la Chenelière (2010). In a Montreal private elementary school, a teacher, Martine Lachance, commits suicide in her classroom, where Simon, one of her students, finds her. In need of a substitute teacher, the school hires Bachir Lazhar, an Algerian immigrant, to teach the class for the rest of the academic year.

Throughout the movie we follow the relationship between Bachir and his students, particularly with Alice, with whom he develops a special connection. We also see the cultural differences he experiences as a newcomer and as a new teacher. Moreover, we witness Bachir's personal struggle, as he is claiming refugee status after his wife and children were killed in Algeria. Bachir helps his students to cope with their teacher's death and their bereavement and to express their feelings. Towards the end of the film, the school principal fires Bachir as she can no longer hide that he is not a teacher and never was one in Algeria, where he worked as a functionary and later, as the owner of a restaurant, while his wife was a teacher. Bachir is allowed to teach his class one last day so he can say goodbye to his students.

A Curriculum of Diversity

According to Hurren (2003) curriculum is considered as "the medium in and through which generations struggle to define themselves and the world" (p. 111). Such processes of defining our identities are the results of comparisons between personal experiences and the experiences of other's. In the film, we see how the students' and the teacher's definitions are conceived and developed through the experiences they live and the interactions through which they engage with others.

Linguistic differences: "Voulez-vous un lift?"[1]

The film contains many references to the language and the diverse relationships students, the administration, and M. Lazhar have with it. During the interview of M. Lazhar with Mme. Vaillancourt, she confuses his first name and last name, calling him M. Bachir and then, correcting herself. In a similar way, when taking class attendance for the first time, M. Lazhar struggles writing the names of his French-Canadian students, names such as *"Camille Soucy,"* but he has no problem writing *"Abdelmalek Merbah,"* a name that would be familiar to him in his home language.

Although Bachir speaks French fluently, his rapport with the language is not the same as his students'. He had learned French at school as part of the colonial heritage of his country, whereas his students learn the language from the perspective of the power of the colonizer. The film presents the irony of Bachir teaching the language he was once taught as a product of colonization. An example of this relation can be seen when M. Lazhar explains the components of a sentence to his students. When he refers to an "adjective," one student corrects him saying that, "adjectives do not exist anymore." However, in Abdelmalek's mother's and Bachir's grammar they do exist, as they were taught the language from the same perspective of the colonies.

Nevertheless, M. Lazhar always displays respect and admiration for the language: He not only learned French as a product of colonization, but he was also taught to respect and to admire the language that had brought "culture" and "civilization" to his "uncivilized" country. This admiration might have valued French over Arabic as part of the relations of power and prestige between these languages. On the other hand, the students and the other teachers take the language for granted. So when M. Lazhar expresses his desire to take the kids to see *Le Malade Imaginaire,* the fact that the students do not know the French literary masters, and the mocking attitude of the teachers, are surprising to him.

Cultural differences: Bachir Lazhar - "what origin is that?"

The film is set in Montreal, a city where multiple cultural identities live together. Differences cause curiosity, and are usually raised by the physical appearance of people, or by their names or linguistic accents. When the origin of these differences is unfamiliar, Taylor refers to the experience as encountering a "distant place" – a place "which a group judges to be distant, in that it is outside their 'normal' experience" (2014, p. 276). The understandings people have with distant places depend on their direct experiences with the places and the level of familiarity between their local reality and the reality of the distant place (Taylor, 2009). Moreover, Taylor points out the difficulty to teach about distant places because of a teacher's lack of "in-depth knowledge to challenge generalizations" often received from mass media (2014, p. 277). This conception of distant place generates stereotypes and an oversimplification of the unknown, as it is portrayed in the film.

In a scene, the students are playing a game called "King of the Hill" in which each one has to defend the snow hill in order to become king. Claire, a teacher, asks the students to stop the game. M. Lazhar intervenes:

Bachir: "A boys' game."
Claire: "It is a bit violent."
Bachir: "Rough, perhaps."

The concept of violence from Claire's occidental perspective is very different to Bachir's concept of violence. For her, pushing and playing rough is violent; from the perspective of Bachir, a person who had experienced war as the everyday reality and suffered its consequences, the term has a stronger connotation and cannot be compared to the children's behaviour in the playground.

With respect to gender differences related to culture, Bachir is confronted not only with the preconceived stereotypes about Arabs, but he is also surrounded by a feminized space in the school, or what his male colleagues call: a "womanocracy." Any movement of his is watched and any comment questioned, looking for traces of macho attitude. An example of this can be seen when M. Lazhar stops in the corridor, observing the way his colleague Claire teaches. Gaston, the Physical Education teacher sees him and asks him if she is his favourite and if he is interested. Gaston relies on his knowledge of distant place portrayed by the mass media, assuming the stereotype that it is a common practice for men from Middle East to pick and choose their wives.

Stereotypes about physical interaction are also raised: In one scene, M. Lazhar pats Simon on the head after seeing him sending a paper ball to a classmate. The teacher then asks him to apologize to his classmate. Marie-Frédérique, another student, asks M. Lazhar to apologize to Simon; when asked why, she replies, "We are not in Saudi Arabia here," alluding to the fact that physical violence is not tolerated in Quebec as it probably is, she assumes, in Bachir's home country.

Differences arise as well when it comes to food. At a school party, a teacher is puzzled when Bachir names the desserts he has brought. Minutes later, he asks about Rice Krispies squares, and Gaston, the Physical Education teacher explains, "It's like baklava, but from Quebec." Bachir, not sure how to take that translation, chooses the safest road, and eats a baby carrot.

Citizenship status: "You left Algeria because of terrorism?"

The multicultural environment of Montreal is reflected in M. Lazhar's classroom; we see Abdelmalek, who speaks Arabic, and Victor, whose grandparents were from Chile. Alice's nanny and the employee from the post office are also from different cultural backgrounds. In one of the scenes, Bachir goes to the post office to pick up a parcel. The employee sees the box and tells Bachir, in Arabic, that it is his favourite jam. Bachir replies that it is his favourite too, but speaks in French. The linguistic choice Bachir makes indicates that while he does not deny his origins, he is committed to adapting to this new environment and abiding by its customs.

Citizenship was defined by Marshall as "a status bestowed on all those who are full members of a community. All those who possess the status are equal with respect to the rights and duties with which the status is endowed" (1950, p. 28). In this sense, M. Lazhar considers himself a citizen, by being an active member of the education system and serving the greater good of society. However, this sentiment of equality is not shared by everyone. At a teacher–parent meeting, M. Lazhar meets Marie-Frédérique's parents. When he talks about her behaviour in class, her parents react arguing that she is "strong, not rigid." Moreover, they imply that M. Lazhar, being from a different cultural background, cannot grasp all the nuances of the society and the current situation. To the teacher's surprise, Marie-Frédérique's parents express that "[they] prefer that [he] teach [their] daughter, not try to raise her."

One evening Bachir is invited to Claire's place for dinner. She talks about her travels – visiting Africa before coming to Montreal and how she considers herself an immigrant too, like Bachir. Then, she asks Bachir if he shared his culture with his students:

Claire: "What about your culture?"
Bachir: "It's not in the curriculum."
Claire: "But exile is another kind of journey."
Bachir: "No, Claire. For most immigrants, it's a trip without papers uprooted to a country whose culture is foreign."

Bachir's response expresses the complexity of immigration and exile, which cannot be compared to a pleasure trip, or moving to a different country for the sake of adventure as implied by Claire.

Education system differences: "That's not how it works, M. Bachir"

The need for following the rules of the Montreal school board is emphasized throughout the film and contrasted with the educational procedures and traditions that M. Lazhar attempts to implement, with which, presumably, he is familiar from his past and home culture. In the scene when M. Lazhar first meets with the school principal, he offers his services as a schoolteacher and expresses his availability to start immediately, and to work "part-time, full-time, overtime... ." The school principal explains that there are specific procedures to follow when hiring teachers and that despite the urgent need, things have to be done following the procedures. Later in the film, we see Bachir studying the provincial curriculum after class, and trying to make sense of the abstract goals of the curriculum. Moreover, When M. Lazhar asks Mme. Vaillancourt, the principal, to publish the controversial but powerful text written by one of his students in response to their teacher's suicide, she refuses immediately. Her priority is the school performance:

"The class is doing well, grades are good, miraculous, considering what you ask. I don't want any waves, ok?"

The education system differences shown in the film include the ways in which *space* and *physical contact* are dealt with in the school. An example with respect to differences in the arrangement of space is seen at the beginning of the film, when M. Lazhar asks the students why the desks are organized in a semi-circle, to which a student replies that Martine decided to do so to foster team spirit in the class. M. Lazhar asks students to rearrange the desks in straight rows. This causes surprise amongst other teachers who express that they had not seen such layout in years. To M. Lazhar, discipline and order are the bases of a good education, and it starts by a direct visual contact between students and teacher.

On the other hand, M. Lazhar is surprised by the administration's rationale when dealing with classrooms. There was no extra classroom into which to move the students after the death of their teacher, so the school administration decided to paint the classroom walls and to remove all the objects related to the previous teacher, in an effort to erase the incident. Seeing how this situation affected the students, M. Lazhar asks the principal to switch rooms with another class, to which she replies that it would be "like dumping your snow in a neighbour's yard." According to the principal, Martine's death is no one's fault, but someone has to live with the consequences, in this case, M. Lazhar's students.

Another difference pointed out in the film is about physical contact. As one of the teachers notes, "Today, you work with kids like with radioactive waste." This idea of needing to maintain distance is portrayed throughout the film in the diverse interactions teachers have with the children. In the beginning of the film we see Gaston using his whistle to call the students' attention. Later, he expresses his frustration through the example of when his son came back from summer camp with serious burns on his back, because his instructor was not allowed to touch him to apply sunscreen. Moreover, Boris, a student who suffers with migraines, is usually excused because, as another student states, it is "forbidden" to give him a headache relief pill.

Towards the end of the film M. Lazhar discovers that Martine Lachance had a problem with one of her students, Simon. She offered him a hug, after which he accused her of kissing him. This caused a scandal throughout the school and there is some suggestion that it may have played a role in her mental instability and suicide. In the last scene of the film, Alice comes to the classroom to say goodbye to M. Lazhar. They hug each other in search of comfort, defying the rules of "no contact." This scene is very powerful and meaningful, as it is this same gesture for which Martine Lachance was criticized as having made an "error of judgment."

Healing and Education

Monsieur Lazhar (Déry et al., 2011) addresses a very difficult topic, not only in the educational setting, but in life in general: death. In a way, death can be seen as the "distant place" described by Taylor (2014), in that one cannot access it. The school administration and M. Lazhar respond to the situation in diverse ways, based on their understandings of this distant place. In the film, M. Lazhar deals with two different deaths: on the one hand, the deliberate, self-inflicted death of the teacher Martine Lachance; and on the other, his wife and children's deaths, resulting from the lack of freedom of expression in Algeria. M. Lazhar travels between these two spaces as he supports his students through their grief.

According to Heath and Cole (2012) "children's perceptions of loss are greatly impacted by their level of understanding and ability to comprehend the meaning and permanence of death" (p. 245). These perceptions are formed in students as they are exposed to different situations involving *silences* and *conversations* in the film.

Silences: "It's life that's violent, not the text"

From the adults' perspectives, no one wants to talk about or engage in conversations of death. After the suicide incident, the principal struggles to find a substitute, and the school administration's goal is to carry on as if nothing had happened. The only measure the administration takes is to provide the services of a psychologist in case students want to talk with her; they have one thirty-minute session per week with her as part of a group therapy. The principal does not allow M. Lazhar to publish the text written by Alice in response to the suicide because she finds the text "violent" and believes it is not healthy to bring up the topic of death again. In the same way, Bachir does not talk about his personal experiences to anyone, except for the mandatory requirements of immigration.

Conversations: "Why do we talk about suicide? You are a teacher, not a psychologist"

There is a desire and a need to talk about death, from the students' perspectives. When students had to prepare a presentation about violence, Alice prepares a text, in which she talks about her love for school and the role of school in children's lives. She explains how her love for school is tainted by her teacher's death, and interprets her teacher's suicide as a violent act: "Sometimes I wonder if she wasn't sending a violent message. When we're violent, we get a detention. But we can't give Martine Lachance a detention, because she's dead." In her analysis and comprehension of the school system, she associates "detention" as the solution for violent behaviour; however, she realizes this cannot be applied in life. Afterwards, when meeting with the principal to show her Alice's piece, Bachir refers to the students' reaction as "troubled," but in a positive way, because it shows the desire and the need to communicate and to talk about death.

When Simon can no longer hold his emotions – his feelings of guilt over the part he may have played in his teacher's suicide, he has a breakdown in the classroom. He expresses that the whole school blames him for Martine's death, and he repeatedly asks, "It's not my fault. Is it?" He confesses that the teacher never kissed him, only hugged him to comfort him. M. Lazhar, using a strategy to address challenges children face following a family member's death (Heath & Cole, 2012, p. 246), reassures him that, "It's not your fault. Martine hadn't been well."

According to Haine and colleagues (2008) (as cited in Heath & Cole, 2012, p. 250), children typically follow five stages after a loved-one's death. We can observe these stages at different times during the film, and experienced by different students:

1. The experience of emotions like anger, fear, and anxiety: In the playground, students wonder why Martine committed suicide.
2. Blaming themselves and feeling guilty: Alice blames Simon, and he blames himself for Martine's death.
3. A desire to talk about the deceased: Alice writes a text about violence, and Victor tells a story about his grandfather's death.
4. They dream about them: Simon asks Alice if she can sleep at night after what happened.
5. They do not to want to forget them: Simon keeps a picture of Martine with him.

All these instances reveal the students' need to talk about the incident and to share their feelings that goes beyond the thirty-minute therapy session allocated by the school administration.

Storytelling as healing: "After an unjust death, there is nothing to say. Nothing at all"

According to Cacciatore, Thieleman, Killian, and Tavasolli (2015), experiential death education provides opportunities for students to share feelings around death; it "aims to explore students' personal stories and experiences of loss, to provide reflective activities and open discussions, and to utilize other teaching methods to facilitate an engaging learning environment" (p. 93). Towards the end of the film, M. Lazhar asks his students to write a fable, and in an effort to make it a fair task, he agrees that he will also write one that students will correct. His fable talks about the relationship between a tree and a chrysalis, a metaphor of what he calls "an unjust death." M. Lazhar makes use of experiential death education to explore death and to open the space for conversation. His act of storytelling illustrates the different approaches of M. Lazhar and the school administration in responding to the students' need to grieve and heal their losses. Each one addresses this according to their knowledge and degree of familiarity with death as a distant place. For the administration, the situation being uncommon, while for M. Lazhar, very personal and traumatic.

Conclusion

As explained in this paper, *Monsieur Lazhar* (Déry et al., 2011) can be seen as a film that shows the educational environment through a perspective of diversity and difference. Topics like immigration and cultural differences, the education system, violence, and healing are addressed through different lenses: those of the students, the teachers (from Quebec and from Algeria), the parents, and the administrators. Each group or individual provides particular insights into the same situations, building on the layers of the lived curriculum. Further analysis on this film could focus on areas such as the creation of identity through the political discourse of immigration; the root metaphors associated with the hierarchical structures and patterns in school between the administration, teachers, students, and parents; the curriculum of death and grief; and the question of authority and credentials to impart knowledge.

REFERENCES

Cacciatore, J., Thieleman, K., Killian, M., & Tavasolli, K. (2015). Braving human suffering: Death education and its relationship to empathy and mindfulness. *Social Work Education, 34*(1), 91-109.

de la Chenelière, E. (2010). *Bashir Lazhar: Théâtre* (1st ed.). Montreal, QC: Leméac.

Déry, L., McCraw, K. (Producer), & Falardeau, P. (Director). (2011). *Monsieur Lazhar* [Motion picture]. Canada: Séville.

Haine, R. A., Ayers, T. S., Sandler, I. N., & Wolchik, S. A. (2008). Evidence-based practices for parentally bereaved children and their families. *Professional Psychology: Research and Practice, 39*(2), 113–121.

Heath, M., & Cole, B. (2012). Strengthening classroom emotional support for children following a family member's death. *School Psychology International, 33*(3), 243–262.

Hurren, W. (2003). Auto•geo•carto•graphia: A curricular collage. *Counterpoints: Curriculum Intertext - Place/Language/Pedagogy, 193,* 111–121.

Marshall, T. H. (1950). *Citizenship and social class.* Cambridge, UK: Cambridge University Press.

Taylor, L. (2009). Children constructing Japan: Material practices and relational learning. *Children's Geographies, 7*(2), 173–189.

Taylor, L. (2014). Diversity between and within: Approaches to teaching about distant place in the secondary school curriculum. *Journal of Curriculum Studies, 46*(2), 276–299.

NOTE

1. The quotes in the subtitles throughout the chapter are taken from the film. I translate "Voulez-vous un lift?" as "Do you want a ride?"

Laughing to Learn: Irony in *Election*

Carl Leggo & Claire Ahn

To include irony and play is never necessarily to exclude seriousness and purpose.

(Hutcheon, 1988, p. 27)

Irony shows awe at subject matter that cannot easily be tamed.

(Woodruff, 2001, p. 189)

Carl and Claire have collaborated on several projects focused on teacher identity, life writing, and Hollywood films about school experiences. In this essay, we both ruminate on the film *Election* (Berger & Payne, 1999) from our unique perspectives as former secondary school English teachers who are now privileged to pursue wide-ranging academic research projects, including the ways that teachers and students are presented in films, and how those depictions might be useful for informing teacher education. We have braided our writing in this essay in order to create a kind of two-voiced or dialogic writing where our different voices both converge and diverge.

Carl

Before Stephen Leacock (1931) graduated with a Ph.D. in economics and spent many years as a university professor, he was a school teacher. With caustic truthfulness he reflects on his school teaching experience as "the most dreary, the most thankless, and the worst paid profession in the world" (pp. xiv). Leacock makes many readers laugh because he writes about experiences and views in ways that most of us are not brave or funny enough to confess or profess. Teacher education needs more irony, more humour, more honest recognition of the tangled complexity and haunting impossibility that shapes the lived experiences of teaching and learning.

For Linda Hutcheon (1988) "the subversive potential of irony" (p. 19) promotes questioning and wonder. Jonathan Culler (1997) explains that "irony juxtaposes appearance and reality; what happens is the opposite of what is expected" (p. 73). With irony, there is always an incongruity or discordance between surface meaning and underlying meaning. Irony is an eminently postmodern trope because it is deconstructive and unsettling. So, while Claire and I teach new teacher candidates how to prepare lesson plans, how to design engaging units for teaching the different genres of literature, and how to support students in learning to write expository essays as well as a host of other kinds of writing, we also invite teacher candidates to investigate their understanding of teacher education with an ironic perspective steeped in creativity and imagination. Above all, we invite teacher candidates to ask questions, to inquire about issues of identity, representation, meaning, and agency in the processes of becoming teachers.

In this essay Claire and I focus on the use of irony in the film *Election* in order to invite teachers, teacher candidates, and teacher educators to question "appearance and reality," to ask questions that can challenge our taken-for-granted views and perspectives, and guide us in imagining new possibilities. *Election* pokes fun at clichés, ethics, fantasies, school culture, and teacher identities. The film is a dark comedy, but in the spirit of irony, the darkness reminds viewers to attend to the light with more tempered hope than many sentimental Hollywood films about teachers' lives.

Claire

Irony and humour are often used as vessels to deliver an element of truth to the reader or viewer. *Election* provides an intricate but humorous view into the process of electing a student council president at Carver High School. As I watched, I could not help but wonder if there was ever such a high level of competition within the election process at the school where I taught, or even at my high school when I was a student. The film provides a clever parallel and satire of any political system, but at the same time, because of the plot surrounding an election process within a school, it also beautifully showcases the intricate, complex relationships between teacher and student.

As a seasoned high school English teacher, I could relate to so many of the events seen in *Election*. As I was laughing and shaking my head at some of the scenes in the film; I found myself being drawn back to my own experiences as an educator.

Film, as Giroux (2008) argues, is an incredibly powerful, pedagogical tool: "Hollywood films about schools not only play an influential role in mobilizing particular meanings [...] but also play a crucial role in legitimating the purpose of schooling, the definition of teaching and learning" (p. 7). Utilizing Hollywood films as a text in teacher-education classrooms or viewed in sessions for professional development can provide profound moments of reflection for teachers of all ranks of experience. Films have a magical way of impacting a teacher's understandings about teaching and learning, and (whether conscious of it or not) can help shape an educator's beliefs and values about teaching (Giroux, 2001).

The film *Election* can provide opportunities for teacher candidates, and even veteran teachers such as myself, to explore our identities as teachers, and to consider how this might affect our pedagogy, our interactions/relationships with our students, and also our values and beliefs of the education system. What really struck me while watching *Election* was the theme of appearance versus reality. There are many examples of this in the film, as the use of voiceovers, montages, and irony underscores this theme. I was specifically drawn to the idea of how students often have a very prescribed understanding or vision of their teachers.

Carl

Like Claire, I am keenly interested in how teacher candidates and experienced teachers create, challenge, and re-create the possibilities of teacher identities. Both Claire and I have extensive teaching experience. We can compare the characters in *Election* to the many colleagues and students we have known in our school teaching, and we can recall many school events, including assemblies and elections, that are similar to events in *Election*.

I recently read an intriguing book, *The way of the teacher: A path for personal growth and professional fulfillment* by Sandra Finney and Jane Thurgood Sagal (2017). According to Finney and Sagal, "To respond well to the intellectual, physical, social, cultural, and economic diversity of our students, we need to be aware of how we have been shaped and of our attitudes to human differences" (p. 7) because "our teaching flows from the quality of our inner life" (p. 8). Regarding issues of identity, I am always concerned that teacher candidates are often fearful about how their identities might need to be subsumed, even consumed, in the expectations of the traditional teacher's identity. Learning to compose our stories, especially as a way to compose creative and courageous understandings of our identities, is tough and demanding work. According to Finney and Sagal (2017), "the profession of teaching is one that calls us to be lovers of wisdom, to love learning new things, to more deeply understand old ideas we hold, and to ignite this spark of curiosity and wonder in our students" (p. 107). Regarding Socrates, the teacher with countless questions, Paul Woodruff (2001) notes that, "Socrates hides his meanings in inaccessible places" and "twists and turns away from the role of a teacher" (p. 188). If Socrates "has answers to the questions he asks, he seldom allows them to be unveiled. Socrates' companions call his behaviour 'irony'" (p. 188). Like Socrates, *Election* works ironically to open up questions, imaginations, and new possibilities. The world of *Election* is dark. Nothing works out in the ways characters hope they might, but in some strange way, there is still a sense that everything has worked out. *Election* is full of the clichés that characterize typical Hollywood films about schools, teachers, and students. Nevertheless, while *Election* builds on Hollywood traditions, it also represents an insightful parody of those traditions. Ultimately, for all its darkness, the film succeeds in raising many significant questions about school culture and experience.

Claire

Indeed, as Carl notes, there are many clichés about the school environment that are evident in *Election*. From a teacher's perspective, these stereotypes can provide moments of reflection, to consider our teacher identities, no matter how many years of experience a teacher may have. Take, for instance, the title teacher character, Mr. McAllister (played by Matthew Borderick). He appears to be a passionate teacher, who always has a smile on his face, who is knowledgeable, who is able to make his lessons relatable, and who genuinely cares for his students. Mr. McAllister even states at various points in his opening voice-over monologue that he loves his job, that he could not imagine doing anything else and how he looks forward to and wants to get his students excited about the world, to help prepare them for life outside of school. Throughout this scene, I was nodding my head in agreement, for I too love teaching, and I could not imagine doing anything else. I too wanted to get my high school students excited about reading Shakespeare. Or now, getting my teacher-candidate students excited about creating innovative and engaging lesson plans on Shakespeare. Teaching is in my blood.

As I continued to wrap myself in warm memories of my teaching career, the happy nostalgic moment came to a very abrupt halt with the introduction of Tracy Flick in the classroom (played by Reese Witherspoon). She is the stereotypical over-achieving student. At first my skin just crawled because we teachers have all had "that" student in our class. The student whose hand is always raised, the know-it-all (sometimes the one who *thinks* s/he knows it all), sometimes s/he may "politely disagree," and who often causes the rest of the class to roll their eyes or groan silently. It was not Tracy's character in particular who snapped me out of my nostalgia, but what she said when she talked about Mr. McAllister: "I feel sorry for Mr. McAllister. Anyone who's stuck in the same little room, wearing the same stupid clothes, saying the exact same things year after year for his whole life" (Berger & Payne, 1999). At the same time, there is a montage of Mr. McAllister repeatedly teaching the same concept, with the same diagram, shifting his position ever so slightly, and wearing "the same stupid clothes," but of different colours. I paused the movie at this point and wondered out loud: If Tracy Flick came to this realization, is this what my students thought of me as well? I taught the same subject year after year, with the same notes, with the same emphasis on certain literary tools, and with, for example, the same diagram outlining the love triangle and different plots in William Shakespeare's *A Midsummer Night's Dream*. I could probably do it again right now, even in my sleep. I went through moments of denial, but then came to realize: I am Tracy's description of Mr. McAllister.

Carl

Claire's poignant identification with Tracy's view of Mr. McAllister highlights the spirit of *Election*. While the film addresses significant issues of school life with the barbed hook of irony, *Election* mostly mocks instead of shocks. Anyone who has ever gone to school will recognize the sardonic send-up of school culture and politics. Early in the film, Jim McAllister teaches a class about ethics and morals. Several students offer simplistic explanations of the difference between ethics and morals, but the difference is never completely spelled out. Instead, the whole film is a commentary on ethics and morals. According to Gregory Orr (2002) irony is "that mode in which the head mocks the heart and bares its intellectual teeth at what it sees as a hostile world" (p. 128). While the heart is definitely mocked in *Election*, the "hostile world" is never really that hostile. Instead, the world of *Election* is full of foibles, illusions, and silences. In *Election* the teacher is human – earthy, erotic, fallible. The good teacher is good, but not necessarily always good. Even the good teacher can make big mistakes. *Election* represents a kind of cautionary tale. We all need to question the complex nuances of the teacher's life.

Like Tracy Flick, Jim McAllister is a keener. He explains in a voice-over how in a decade of teaching at Carver High, he had received the Teacher of the Year Award three times, a school record. Schools are places of competition, but competition does not serve ethical living well. *Election* makes me laugh. The film is full of mishaps, mistakes, misery, and misanthropy, all rendered with a biting wit, scalpel-sharp satire, and twisted irony. Without doubt, Tracy Flick is a stereotypical keener. I see much of myself in her and in Jim McAllister. Schools encourage the kind of self-focused competitiveness that Tracy and Jim exhibit. While their eagerness to win is unbalanced, it is simply the product of a school system that promotes winning, even when the stakes are relatively insignificant. In the case of the election in *Election*, Jim McAllister does not care who is elected the class president as long as Tracy Flick does not win.

Claire

While Carl was able to see himself in characters like Tracy, for me her character took me back to my own teaching experience. Tracy, like many of my high school students, may often see their teachers as just a figurehead, doing nothing more than teach day-in-day-out, leading seemingly boring and monotonous lives. They might see us as nothing more than teachers, someone who should be there for them, teaching them "stuff they need to learn," and do not really consider that we have lives outside of school. I recall a time when I was a little behind in my marking, one student grumbled and complained that it was taking so long to get his assignment back, and then he said: "Because isn't it your job? What else do you have to do?" I remember thinking: Wow. Seriously? Does this student not know I have a life outside of school? But then it struck me: Why should he? Why should any of my students? My students saw me every day for a good chunk of their adolescent lives, in a specific role that shaped their definition of who I was. They saw me in an environment that was familiar and comfortable for them. I remember whenever I saw my students outside of school, especially at places like the movie theatre that were much more "fun" than school, they were always a little jarred. I am not sure if it was because my students did not want to see me or talk to me at the theatre. At the same time, I wonder if seeing their teacher outside of the regular setting of the classroom/school disturbed their notion of who I was, that perhaps they did not even consider nor could even admit that I, their teacher, liked to engage in the same activities as they did. I recall, as a young student, working behind the counter at a chocolatier in a mall, when my grade 10 English teacher would come in with her partner. It felt very awkward seeing my teacher outside of the classroom, walking around the mall like a "normal" person.

In the film, Mr. McAllister is dealing with his own issues: his friend/colleague who had an affair with Tracy Flick; Mr. McAllister and his wife trying to have children, but failing, partly because he fantasizes about his cheating friend's wife and eventually does have an affair with her. While these events are exaggerated in the film, I would argue that some of the situations Mr. McAllister experiences are not far from reality. Teachers are human beings. We have to juggle many different responsibilities and also deal with our own personal issues. We are trained to put all that aside, and walk into our classrooms with a big smile on our faces and be there for our students. Teachers are always performing, we are always "playing the teacher" in the classroom. So it is no wonder that students can develop a very limited view of who and what we are.

The question that remains is: how do teachers learn to cope with these situations? These kinds of situations and scenarios cannot really be taught in a classroom through the use of a traditional textbook or lectures, but can be something teachers reflect upon when they watch films. Yes, Hollywood depictions of teachers in film are often exaggerated, perhaps even to an extreme that impacts society's often stereotypical view of teachers. At the same time, can these not also be teachable moments? Can we not pause to ask teachers to think about what they have viewed? How can films such as *Election* encourage teachers to think about their identities as teachers for themselves, and how they might be viewed by their students? What impact can this have on their teaching and also on the development of professional, but personal relationships with their students?

Carl

Like Claire, I have questions, too. What sustains the teacher's spirit? What sustains the student's spirit? Many Hollywood films about school experiences are full of sincerity. I like the dark humour of *Election* with its satire and irony, but when I view *Election*, I understand that irony does not supplant sincerity. Irony subverts appearances in order to call attention to the raw, human, erotic, messy emotions, desires, and dreams that lie under the surface of appearances, but irony does not only poke fun. Irony questions. Irony challenges sentimentality. An ironic perspective does not need to be dismissive and cynical. An ironic perspective can contribute to a more realistic view of experience. What shocks in *Election* is that the teacher cheats. Jim McAllister is clearly a good teacher, but driven by an unhinged competitiveness, or bent with a creeping middle-age crisis, or goaded by the keen enthusiasm of Tracy Flick, which reminds him of who he was, Jim McAllister cheats. When the ballots are counted, Tracy Flick has won by one vote. McAllister disposes of two ballots cast for Tracy Flick, and declares that her competitor has won the election. The school janitor finds the ballots in the trash, and alerts the school principal. McAllister resigns. While *Election* presents an ironic version of the teacher as hero story that Hollywood has popularized for decades, *Election* still depends on the motif of the teacher as hero. There is swift justice in the film. The teacher cheats; the teacher is fired. *Election* presents a sly send-up of ethics and morals while still promoting competition and the letter of the law. *Election* does not take sides. Tracy Flick will do whatever it takes to be successful in her bid to be elected the class president. She is a keener, but her keenness is part of the way that politicians are elected. Jim McAllister is a good teacher who carries a growing frustration like a heavy sack on his back. It is inevitable that he will eventually break. The good news of *Election* is that while everybody can be the object of an ironic vision, most experiences still end happily, or at least with some semblance of happiness. Ultimately, while *Election* is a dark comedy, it is still predominantly humorous and humane.

REFERENCES

Berger, A. (Producer), & Payne, A. (Director). (1999). *Election* [Motion picture]. USA: Bona Fide Productions.

Culler, J. (1997). *Literary theory: A very short introduction.* Oxford, UK: Oxford University Press.

Finney, S., & Sagal, J. T. (2017). *The way of the teacher: A path for personal growth and professional fulfillment.* Lanham, MD: Rowman & Littlefield.

Giroux, H. A. (2001). Breaking into the movies: Pedagogy and the politics of film. *A Journal of Rhetoric, Culture, & Politics, 21*(3), 583–598. Retrieved from http://www.jaconlinejournal.com/archives/vol21.3/giroux-breaking.pdf

Giroux, H. A. (2008). Hollywood film as public pedagogy: Education in the crossfire. *Afterimage, 35*(5), 7–13. Retrieved from https://transformativeteaching.files.wordpress.com/2010/08/hollywood-film-as-public-pedagogy-giroux-h-a.pdf

Hutcheon, L. (1988). *A poetics of postmodernism: History, theory, fiction.* New York, NY: Routledge.

Leacock, S. (1931). *Sunshine sketches of a little town.* Toronto, ON: McClelland & Stewart.

Orr, G. (2002). *The blessing.* Tulsa, OK: Council Oak Books.

Woodruff, P. (2001). *Reverence: Renewing a forgotten virtue.* Oxford, UK: Oxford University Press.

PART II

Teachers as Heroes or Antiheroes

The Light and Dark Archetypes of Teachers: What Can *Matilda* Tell Us about Teacher Identity?

Angelina Ambrosetti

Introduction

The 1996 cinematic adaptation of Roald Dahl's children's novel *Matilda* (Dahl, 1988) brings to life a wicked fictional struggle between children and adults. The central character is a young girl called Matilda and the film divides its time focusing on the adult–child relationships that Matilda engages in; those with her teacher, the headmistress of the school, and her parents. In both the film and novel, and more recently in the stage show, Matilda is portrayed as both a heroine for children and an unforgiving trouble-maker for adults (Pope & Round, 2015). In the film's storyline, Matilda is cast by DeVito, Shamberg, Sher, and Dahl (1996) as a gifted child genius with superpowers who creates mischief for the adults around her. What lies beneath this innocent description, however, is the key focus on the power that adults seemingly wield over children. Her mischief is thinly disguised as revenge on those whom she perceives as disrespectful of both herself and her friends (Pope & Round, 2015).

Given the theme of the struggle between children and adults throughout the film, what is of interest in this chapter in particular are the teacher–student relationships that the film depicts. The story of *Matilda* (DeVito, Shamberg, Sher, & Dahl, 1996) incorporates the portrayal of two teacher archetypes: one who is positive, kind, loving, and supportive, and one who is mean, nasty, and terrorizing. The relationships that are represented, although wickedly exaggerated, reinforce stereotypes and perceptions of teachers. As noted by Dalton (2007), the point-of-view "about the relationships between teachers and students, knowledge beyond the scope of the personal or anecdotal, is created by constructs of popular culture played out in the mass media" (p. 2). In this respect the film highlights constructs of teacher identity that are often portrayed in popular culture.

In this chapter, I examine teacher identity through the lens of popular culture; what it is, how it is developed, and how interactions with others help to shape a teacher's identity. I make links to scenes within the film to help describe the conception of teacher identity and the impact it can have on the students within a teacher's care.

Teaching and Teachers: Stereotypes within the Film Matilda

Teaching is regarded as an honourable profession and teachers are often viewed as having the potential to be influential figures in students' lives. There are specific cultural expectations that society places on teachers, and society in general expects that a teacher be compassionate, empathic, caring, personable, motivational, and knowledgeable. Thus, in film, teachers are often portrayed as playing an important role in their students' lives: that of a role model, an influential other, and in many respects, a mentor (Ambrosetti, 2016). Popular culture, however, has constructed the image of teachers into two types: one that is caring, accepting, and reflective, and one that is bitter, spiteful, and egocentric (Connell, 2013). Put simply, teachers are portrayed in film as light or dark with very little in between.

Stereotypes are often based on perceptions of identity. Identity is an "understanding of who we think we are and who we think other people are" (Danielewicz, 2001, p. 10). A person's identity reflects their personality, and their character traits, values, and beliefs. Our identity is developed and situated within symbolic boundaries that are both figurative and physical (Wadham, Pudsey, & Boyd, 2007). Identity is not a fixed state, but one that changes as a person grows and transforms. The development of one's identity is influenced by culture, family, society, and others with whom we interact (Danielewicz, 2001). It is also "a process of interpretation and reinterpretation of experiences" (Sutherland, Howard, & Markauskaite, 2010). We develop several identities and move between them; these identities often stem from the context in which we find ourselves in and the experiences we have encountered within that context (Gee, 2000; Wadham et al., 2007). Teachers, like many professionals, have both a personal identity and a professional identity (Gee, 2000). Each identity is signified by "identity markers," those aspects that highlight similarities and differences such as the way we speak, the way we dress, or the way we behave (Wadham et al., 2007, p. 13).

Researchers such as Day (2012) argue that personal and professional identities are explicitly linked. Day (2012, p. 15) explains that a teacher's professional identity is "influenced by biography and experience – life outside of school – and reflects social and policy expectations of what a good teacher is, workplace conditions and relationships, and the educational ideals of the teacher." In this respect, Day (2012, p. 15) argues "it matters enormously what kind of person the teacher is." Hence it can be said that a teacher's identity or "reputation" consists of such markers as behaviour, relationships, and the ways that they interact with others in a school context. It is these identity markers of what is perceived to be a teacher that are often stereotyped within popular culture. In this chapter, the interactions and the associated behaviours of the two teacher archetypes that play out with Matilda and her classmates are used to illustrate teacher identity and the stereotypes associated with it.

In *Matilda* (DeVito et al., 1996), we are exposed to both teacher archetypes in the form of the characters Miss Trunchbull, the headmistress of the school, and Miss Honey, the classroom teacher. Although cast as an administrator rather than a teacher, The Trunchbull, as she is referred to by the children within the film, is presented as an imposing character who is unattractive, big, and masculine in stature, and mean in attitude. She strides around the playground thumping her riding crop looking for a child to intimidate and pick on in her very first scene. We watch her as she terrorizes and makes fun of the youngest children, and we watch as they react by complying with her rules. She is portrayed as mean-spirited, child hating, and egocentric: the dark archetype. In contrast, we are introduced to Miss Honey as she gently and lovingly comforts the child who had been terrorized by Trunchbull. Her soft voice, feminine clothes, and caring attitude are in vast contrast to the headmistress. We see Miss Honey in the classroom gently teaching and encouraging her charges, showing kindness and compassion: the light archetype.

Theoretical Underpinnings

Critical theory encourages the questioning of what we know and believe. The examination of interactions between social groups and identities provides us with the starting point to question or contest traditional knowledge (Hesse-Biber, 2010). This examination of the light and dark archetypes in *Matilda* (DeVito et al., 1996) is framed by the work of Bernstein (2000), in that I use his concept of pedagogic practices to take a deeper look into power and control between adults and children, and in turn examine the construct of teacher identity. I also use Bernstein's (2000) metaphor of boundaries and the significance of such boundaries in terms of power and behaviour. The question that frames this examination is: To what extent do the power relations between teacher and student impact upon the development of teacher identity?

Pedagogic practice in this respect is "a fundamental social context through which cultural reproduction-production takes place" (Bernstein, 2000, p. 5). The analysis of the interactions and associated behaviours of the teachers (Miss Honey and Miss Trunchbull) will be framed by the social context of schooling, the relationships that occur between teachers and students, as well as the relationships between the two adults, and how cultural reproduction of those expected behaviours produce the archetypes portrayed. When examining relationships, particularly those involving adults and children, the power relations that are embedded within must be acknowledged as impacting upon the interactions and thus the communications that occur between them. Power relations, according to Bernstein (2000), "create boundaries, legitimise boundaries, reproduce boundaries between different groups, gender, class, race, different categories of discourse, different categories of agents" (p. 5).

Boundaries can move and change, but a boundary, as conceptualized by Bernstein (2000), becomes the "tension between the past and possible futures" (p. xiii). Our identities are influenced by our experiences in past and present times, and the way that we define ourselves aligns to existing and known boundaries (Wadham et al., 2007). Boundaries therefore can be the result of power balances (or imbalances). Foucault's original conceptualization of power in post-structural ideologies can lead us towards understanding these power relationships particularly in respect to adults and children, and teachers and students. Power is explicitly linked to knowledge (Foucault, 1980), and as highlighted by Wadham et al. (2007), "to have knowledge is to have power and to have power you must have knowledge" (p. 27). Different systems of knowledge give particular groups power. Consequently, we can identify that teachers, due to their knowledge of how school should be and children should behave, hold power over their students and thus create the boundaries that exist (Wadham et al., 2007).

The role of a teacher is to "teach both knowledge and skills to their learners in order to prepare them as citizens of the future" (Ambrosetti, 2016, p. 1). A teacher's identity, however, will influence the extent in which this occurs and the boundaries that it occurs in. Consequently, if a teacher's identity is constructed by one's own belief systems, values, and practices that influence actions inside and outside of a classroom (Walkington, 2005), and that teacher identity is "an important melding of personal histories and professional engagement" (Morrison, 2013, p. 9), the insights into the background story of the teachers becomes key.

What Can Matilda *Tell Us about Teacher Identity?*

I now examine teacher identity in *Matilda* (DeVito et al., 1996) by delving into the background stories of Miss Honey and Miss Trunchbull and the interactions they have with Matilda and her classmates as a result of their developed identities. I refer to particular scenes that involve these key characters and examine the background stories presented in order to provide insights into these teacher identities. I also examine the power relations that occur as a result of the developed identities.

Throughout the film we are tantalized by the outrageous antics of the Trunchbull, particularly as she threatens and punishes the children in her care. We are horrified at her bullying of Miss Honey and also revel in the revenge tactics of Matilda and her classmates. In this respect the film reinforces the overarching cultural stereotypical power struggle between adults and children. The key scene that reveals the background stories of Miss Honey and Miss Trunchbull occurs towards the second half of the film, and explains the interactions that occur between the two adults, between the adults and the children, and how who they are has influenced the development of their teacher identities.

This key scene begins with Miss Honey inviting Matilda home for afternoon tea after a particularly harrowing incident involving a newt, "the chokey,"[1] Miss Trunchbull, and Miss Honey's class. On the way to Miss Honey's house, they pause by a big house with a swing. Miss Honey reveals that this is where Miss Trunchbull lives. Matilda asks about the swing and Miss Honey tells Matilda a "fictitious" story of a little girl who grew up in the house. She recounts that it was a happy home until the little girl's mother died and that her mother's stepsister was invited into the home to look after her. The aunt was mean and treated her badly. When her father died, the aunt became her guardian until she was old enough to move out on her own. Miss Honey tells Matilda that the aunt assumed the house and its possessions as her own, leaving the girl with nothing. It is at this point that Matilda guesses that the story is Miss Honey's and she realizes that Miss Trunchbull is the aunt. It is also revealed that Miss Trunchbull still controls Miss Honey through her job at the school and her payment as a teacher. Matilda is outraged by the treatment of Miss Honey; however, Miss Honey herself seems to be accepting of her fate in life. This scene justifies the boundaries that Miss Honey operates within and power imbalance that she experiences throughout the film.

The scene described above reveals a key insight into the development of Miss Honey's teacher identity and how it subsequently influences the interactions that occur between the key characters. First, it is implied through this scene that Miss Honey is able to connect to Matilda (and her other students) due to her own treatment as a child. It also provides context as to her protective nature and her fulfilment of her role as a teacher and why she is willing to operate within a boundary where she has little power. The scene also provides key insights into Miss Trunchbull's (specifically referred to in the dialogue as the child's mother's "stepsister") disconnection to anyone else's needs apart from her own, and her need to stay in control and have power over others. The scene also implies that Miss Trunchbull, as a younger woman, was inherently mean and nasty, but that Miss Honey made the best of the situation in which she found herself. These traits of the two characters are clearly portrayed in the ways that they interact with the children throughout the film.

Miss Trunchbull is an interesting study of teacher identity, particularly with respect to her values and belief system. Early in the film we learn that she is a celebrated Olympian in the javelin, hammer throw, and shot-put. We hear the children discussing her strength and how she uses her strength to punish children. In fact, we witness a scene where the Trunchbull swings a little girl around by her pigtails simply because she does not like little girls with pigtails! We see a dartboard on the back of her office door with pictures of the children on it at which she throws darts. We also hear about "the chokey," a room that the children are terrified of being sent to. There are many scenes such as the above that show us that Miss Trunchbull despises children and uses her power as the headmistress to punish them and justify her treatment of them. In this respect she uses her position of power to create boundaries and then legitimize these boundaries. The boundaries, however, are positioned so that they meet her needs rather than others' needs. This becomes clear when she makes the following statement: "I'm going to punish you because I am big and you are small, I am right and you are wrong, and there is nothing you can do about it" (DeVito et al., 1996). The teacher identity that Miss Trunchbull has created for herself is based on knowledge as power.

Miss Honey, portrayed as a loving and warm teacher, is also subtly positioned as a passive unassuming individual who Dalton (1995, p. 27) describes as someone "involved with students on a personal level, learns from those students, and does not usually fare very well with administrators." Her background story of being bullied by her aunt as a child enables us to accept this aspect of her personality. We see her gentle personality mocked and overpowered by Miss Trunchbull on several occasions. At one point we hear Miss Trunchbull telling Miss Honey that "one day you will see that everything I do is for your own good and the good of the children" (DeVito et al., 1996). Miss Honey's warm and loving teacher identity, however, also provides the context for when she defends the children in her class. We watch her protect Matilda and her classmates from Miss Trunchbull, and comfort them when she has been unable to provide the protection needed. In turn, we see how the children in her class love her and protect her, particularly Matilda, who uses her telekinetic powers to disempower Miss Trunchbull on several occasions as revenge for Miss Honey.

In many respects, Miss Honey is embroiled in two sets of boundaries that eventually interact and cross over with interesting outcomes. It could be said that Miss Honey is "caught between past and future possibilities" (Bernstein, 2000, p. xiii). First, she is bound by and operates within the boundaries created by Miss Trunchbull. Within Trunchbull's boundaries, she is both passive and proactive, willing to speak up on behalf of her students, but not herself. Second, and just as important, Miss Honey has her own set of boundaries in which she takes charge, and these are focussed on the children, their learning, and their protection. Within the boundaries created by Miss Honey, the roles of the participants are collaborative and interchangeable, and this occurs because of her openness and morality, and the values and beliefs that underpin her teacher identity. Miss Honey in this respect does not hold power through knowledge over the children, but instead uses her knowledge to fulfil her role as a teacher.

Interestingly we see a change occurring towards the end of the film whereby Miss Honey is influenced by Matilda in her interactions and behaviour. In one particular incident, Matilda takes control of the situation involving the repossession of Miss Honey's childhood home, thus reversing the power relations between herself and Miss Honey. In this instance, Matilda becomes the power broker and thus alters the existing boundaries. Consequently, we observe the reproduction of boundaries, in that the roles between the adults and the children are reversed. It is here that we see a change in Miss Honey's identity as the social context is renegotiated and experiences are reinterpreted (Sutherland et al., 2010).

Conclusion

The film *Matilda* (DeVito et al., 1996) reinforces the stereotypes of two types of teacher identities that are regularly played out through popular culture. This chapter examined teacher identity by delving into personal aspects of the light and dark teacher archetypes portrayed throughout the film. Traits, values, and beliefs, as well as relationships, interactions, and social behaviour, were examined though Bernstein's (2000) conceptualization of pedagogical practices. Although this examination has occurred through a fictitious context, several key insights have emerged about teacher identity and its impact upon power balances and imbalances between teachers and students.

Boundaries in which interactions occur are determined by those who assume the power in any given situation. In this example, the dark archetype was dominant and assumed the role of power, thus creating the rules within (or legitimizing) the space. However, as we observed, the boundaries can change as the roles (or power) between participants change. In this respect, the boundaries were reproduced and the shift in power produced a dislocation in roles (Bernstein, 2000). As we observed the roles changing, we saw a corresponding change within the associated identities. We could assume that the change in role was not necessarily a change in identity, but rather we saw "the kind of person the teacher is" emerge (Day, 2012, p. 15).

It is clear that one's personal values, beliefs, and experiences impact on and have the potential to shape a professional identity. However, identities can grow and change, and the shifting of boundaries through interactions and experiences can enable this to occur, as illustrated in the film by Miss Honey. Or, as demonstrated by Miss Trunchbull, an identity can remain stagnant by the legitimization of the boundaries that reflect who you are and how you interact with others. Teacher identity is truly a reflection of who we are, is individual, and can be shaped into what you want it to become (Sutherland et al., 2010).

Matilda (DeVito et al., 2000) has illustrated the stereotypical light and dark archetypes of teachers portrayed so often in film. We observe a positive, kind, loving, and supportive teacher who has the children at the heart of her actions, and a mean, nasty, terrorizing teacher who only has her own interests at heart. We see a battle of good versus bad and kind versus mean that is disrupted by a young heroine who highlights that who we are is reflected in what we do.

The background stories of the teachers in this film provide both insight and explanation into how professional identity is influenced by the person, their experiences, and the interactions in which they participate. As the power relations change so do the interactions and the shaping of identity. The extent to which the power relations between the teacher and student impact the development of teacher identity is significant. Although this examination of teacher identity has occurred through a fictional story, it illustrates that the interactions that occur between teachers and students and the impact they have cannot be underestimated.

REFERENCES

Ambrosetti, A. (2016). The portrayal of the teacher as mentor in popular film: Inspirational, supportive and life-changing? *M/C Journal*, 19(2), 1–2.

Bernstein, B. (2000). *Pedagogy, symbolic control and identity*. Lanham, MD: Rowman & Littlefield Publishers.

Connell, R. (2013). Teachers. In R. Connell, A. Welch, M. Vickers, D. Foley, N. Bagnall, D. Hayes, H. Proctor, A. Sriprakash, & C. Campbell (Eds.), *Education, change and society* (3rd ed.) (pp. 261–275). Melbourne, Australia: Oxford University Press.

Dahl, R. (1988). *Matilda*. London: Jonathan Cape.

Dalton, M. M. (1995). The Hollywood curriculum: Who is the "good" teacher? *Curriculum Studies*, 3(1), 23–44.

Dalton, M. M. (2007). *The Hollywood curriculum: Teachers in the movies*. New York, NY: Peter Lang Publishing.

Danielewicz, J. (2001). *Teaching selves: Identity, pedagogy and teacher education*. Albany, NY: State University of New York Press.

Day, C. (2012). New lives of teachers. *Teacher Education Quarterly*, 39(1), 7–26.

DeVito, D., Shamberg, M., Sher, S., & Dahl, L. (Producers), & DeVito, D. (Director). (1996). *Matilda* [Motion picture]. USA: TriStar Pictures.

Foucault, M. (1980). *Power/knowledge: Selected interviews and other writings 1972-1977*. (C. Gordon, Ed.). New York, NY: Pantheon Books.

Gee, J. P. (2000). Identity as an analytic lens for research in education. *Review of Research in Education, 25*(1), 99–125.

Hesse-Biber, S. N. (2010). *Mixed methods research: Merging theory with practice.* New York, NY: The Guildford Press.

Morrison, C. (2013). Teacher identity in the early career phase: Trajectories that explain and influence development. *Australian Journal of Teacher Education, 38*(4), 91–107.

Pope, J., & Round, J. (2015). Children's responses to heroism in Roald Dahl's *Matilda*. *Children's Literature in Education, 46,* 257–277.

Sutherland, L., Howard, S., & Markauskaite, L. (2010). Professional identity creation: Examining the development of beginning preservice teachers' understanding of their work as teachers. *Teaching and Teacher Education, 26,* 455–465.

Wadham, B., Pudsey, J., & Boyd, R. (2007). *Culture and education.* Frenches Forest, Australia: Pearson Education Australia.

Walkington, J. (2005). Becoming a teacher: Encouraging development of teacher identity through reflective practice. *Asia-Pacific Journal of Teacher Education, 33*(1), 53–64.

NOTE

1. The chokey is a tiny cupboard in the headmistress' office where children are locked as punishment.

The Problem with Mr. Holland:
The Portrayal of Music Teachers in Film Through *Mr. Holland's Opus*

Nancy Curry & Jeffrey Curry

When the film *Mr. Holland's opus* (Duncan, Kroopf, & Herek, 1995) was released, many friends approached us, both of us being music teachers, and asked how we liked the film. "Isn't it great?" they gushed, expecting that we would share their enthusiasm for a film that portrays the challenges of teaching music in a public high school. They found the film to be uplifting and inspiring, painting the teacher as a hero who sacrifices his dream of a musical career for his students and family. We, on the other hand, were appalled at the negative attitude towards teaching demonstrated by Mr. Holland, the lack of authenticity in the musical repertoire, and the absence of skilful, effective teaching in the portrayal.

Our friends were taken aback – how could we not like a film that celebrated music teaching? This chapter asks that question through the lens of a praxial philosophy that has arisen in music education in the twenty years since the film was released, changing the paradigm for music curriculum design. We also use *Mr. Holland's opus* to problematize the portrayal of music teachers in film – an important consideration in light of the frequent use of this and other films in pre-service teacher education (Brand, 2001; Pyett, 2014; Raimo, 2002). Finally, we offer an assessment of Mr. Holland's teaching and suggest ways in which this film can start a discussion of expertise, methodologies, and pedagogy with pre-service music education students.

Mr. Holland's Opus: *The Story and the Critics*

The storyline of *Mr. Holland's opus* follows the career path of a young idealistic pianist who dreams of composing a magnificent symphony, but who is struggling to make a living, playing in a band at weddings and bar mitzvahs. Taking advantage of a fast-track licensure system for music teachers, available in the mid-1960s when this story begins, Glenn Holland obtains a position as a high-school music teacher and regards it as a short-term solution for his money woes while he continues to work on his composition projects. When Holland's wife announces that she is expecting a baby, the teaching job becomes a permanent necessity and his other musical work is set aside.

Initially at a complete loss in the classroom, Mr. Holland (as everyone calls him) searches for a teaching approach that will reach his students, and brings rock and roll into class discussions over the objections of his principal. The film depicts several challenges faced by this novice teacher: unsupportive administrators, an infatuated singer, a rhythmically challenged athlete, and a despairing clarinetist. The greatest challenge he faces, however, is the discovery that his son is profoundly deaf and will never share his love of music.

As the years pass, Mr. Holland devotes increasingly more time to his job, thus avoiding the tension at home arising from his refusal to learn sign language and communicate with his son. The death of his idol John Lennon jolts him into the realization that life is short and that he must mend his relationship with his family. His career ends abruptly after thirty years of service when budget cuts eliminate the music programme at his school, causing him to retire and bow out gracefully. As a retirement gift, his students and former students join to perform his American Symphony at the year-end concert, presenting to him his magnum opus.

When *Mr. Holland's opus* was released, it was regarded by critics as a sentimental but moving portrayal of a dedicated teacher. Roger Ebert (1996) described Mr. Holland as a composer who "realizes gradually that [teaching] is his destiny" (para. 2). Janet Maslin (1996) of the *New York Times* praised the script for its wit and "yuppie nostalgia" (para. 9), declaring that Mr. Holland's "real opus is a generous life" (para. 7). A month later, William Grimes (1996) of the *New York Times* investigated the longevity of the movie's popularity, noting that the film had already earned twice its production budget and showed no signs of losing momentum at the box office. He attributed the popularity to a carefully orchestrated marketing campaign that had touched a nerve with "music groups, teachers' organizations, civic groups and political leaders" (para. 7), particularly with its emphasis on music education's vulnerability to budget cuts.

Mr. Holland's Opus: *The View from the Professional Perspective*

As music teachers looking at a supposed exemplar of our profession, we were not alone in our dismay at the public enthusiasm for this film. In a viewer response study, researcher Peter de Vries (2004) recorded and analyzed the reaction of a seasoned high-school music teacher as he viewed the film for the first time. His analysis revealed three themes in the viewer reaction: (1) issues and concerns about education in general; (2) unrealistic depictions of music education in action; and (3) the difficulty of maintaining professional activity as a musician when working as a teacher full time. The teacher pointed out a number of examples of unrealistic framing of music education, such as the high-school orchestra attempting the opening of Beethoven's Fifth Symphony on the first day of class, commenting, "It's dumbing down music and music education" (p. 163).

We, too, were disappointed with the lack of skilful music teaching grounded in thoughtful pedagogy in this portrayal of a music teacher. In the classroom scenes, Mr. Holland conducts by vaguely waving his hand about, lectures his students from a textbook, and demonstrates a lack of familiarity with the instruments he is expected to teach. We saw the film as the portrait of a man who is dissatisfied with his life, who responds eagerly to a student's adoration and ignores his family, who yells at his students when they do not understand what he assumes they do, and sees himself as a martyr. Yet, to this day the film is generally regarded as a portrayal of a heroic, self-sacrificing, and dedicated teacher. So why the conflict between a music teacher's response to the film and the public reception?

Music Teaching in the Movies: Finding Drama at the Expense of Reality

It is admittedly difficult to encapsulate the work of a music teacher in a feature-length film, which needs a linear narrative and a conflict-driven plot, when in real life musicianship skills are developed through years of scaffolded instruction. Recent films that include music education, from *Fame* (De Silva, Marshall, & Parker, 1980) to *Whiplash* (Brill, Reitman, Samuelson, Walters, & Chazelle, 2014), tend to focus on inter-personal relationships instead, drawing from dramatic archetypes to create stereotypical portrayals of music teachers.

In a study conducted with pre-service teachers in music education, Brand (2001) presented a sample of seventeen movies about music teachers to his students and invited their analyses of the portrayals. The students found twelve broad themes that described music teachers and music education in the sampled films:

1. Anyone can teach music
2. Incompetent music teaching
3. Music teacher as friend/quasi-parent/counsellor
4. Powerless music teacher
5. Eccentric/demanding private music teacher

6. Music teacher and sex innuendo (jokes)
7. Music teacher as a love object
8. Music teacher as spinster
9. Immoral/dishonest music teacher
10. Low process/high product, no rehearsals required
11. School music vs popular music
12. Music teacher as generator of greater good

(Brand, 2001, p. 9)

A few of the themes noted above are particularly familiar. The trope of the tyrannical, authoritarian music teacher has most recently been seen in the jazz band director Terence Fletcher in *Whiplash* (Brill et al., 2014) and the piano professor Erika in *The piano teacher* (Cren, Gozlan, Katz, & Haneke, 2001) – both chilling portrayals of obsession and the demand for perfection. Likewise, the eccentric spinster is a well-known stereotype – Greta Vandemann in *The competition* (Pine & Oliansky, 1980) is a concert pianist who sees no problem with entering her student in an international competition by recording and submitting the audition tape herself, and the title character of *Madame Sousatzka* (Dalton & Schlesinger, 1988) seizes an opportunity to achieve the success she never knew herself through the experiences of a talented student, to whom she becomes closely (too closely?) attached. Also popular are the "low process/high product" stories, in which the music teacher seemingly works miracles: Sister Mary Clarence's small group of high-school students becomes a formidable gospel choir (*Sister act 2: Back in the habit*, Iscovich, Mark, Meledandri, & Duke, 1993), the Barden Bellas somehow master complex a cappella arrangements without rehearsals or a director (*Pitch perfect*, Banks, Brooks, Handelman, Niemeyer, & Moore, 2012), and on television, the William McKinley High School glee club (*Glee*, Brennan, Buecker, Falchuk, & Murphy 2009) managed to produce Broadway-worthy production numbers every week for several seasons.

Brand (2001) suggests that *Mr. Holland's opus* is more realistic than these stereotypes, commenting that "to some extent there is a degree of focus on the actual teaching and learning process, and the audience is even treated to glimpses of great teaching" (p. 10). The authors of this chapter, on the other hand, find several stereotypical themes in this film, including "Incompetent music teaching," "Music teacher as friend/quasi-parent/counsellor," and "Music teacher as love object," and fail to find the "glimpses of great teaching" that Brand praises. By examining the teaching demonstrated by Mr. Holland through the lens of critical theory and praxial philosophy, we can begin to understand the cognitive dissonance in the public versus professional perceptions of the film.

Aesthetic Education, Critical Theory, and Music Teaching

Music education theorist Thomas Regelski (2005) uses critical theory to deconstruct the philosophy of aesthetic education as applied to music, an approach based on the work of Leonard Meyer and Bennett Reimer (Reimer, 1989a, 1989b, 1989c; McCarthy & Goble, 2002). Meyer, whose *Emotion and meaning in music* (1956) set out the idea that music is an art object comprised of tone that creates an aesthetic experience in the listener, developed his philosophy in an effort to explain the affective impact of tonal functional harmony. Reimer took that philosophy further, detailing an aesthetic foundation for music curriculum design in *A philosophy of music education* (1989c), first published in 1970. Reimer proposed that "[a] constant interaction between conception about expressive qualities of music, and perception of those qualities, should pervade every aspect of musical study" (1989c, p. 117). To Reimer (1989c), the technical and analytical study of music is secondary to the aesthetic experience, and his approach became known as Music Education as Aesthetic Education, or MEAE.

A close reading of *Mr. Holland's opus* reveals a strong bias towards MEAE in the depiction of his teaching. In a scene in which Mr. Holland's struggling clarinet student announces that she is quitting band, his response is firmly rooted in aesthetic philosophy:

> Mr. Holland: You know what we've been doing wrong, Miss Lang? We've been playing notes on a page [...]. There's lots more to music than notes on a page [...] playing music is supposed to be fun. It's about heart. It's about feelings and moving people and something beautiful and being alive, and it's not about notes on a page. I could teach you notes on a page – I can't teach you the other stuff.
> (Duncan et al., 1995)

When challenged by a bored and disruptive student who declares that he knows all the course content already, Mr. Holland again shows his bias toward Reimer's (1989c) philosophy:

> Stadler: I know this stuff. I can give you all the names and dates you want. I know all the scales, the modes, counterpoint –
>
> Mr. Holland: So what? The name of this class is Music Appreciation. I don't see you appreciating anything. [...] You think you are real smart, don't you? Okay. Prove it. I want a paper on my desk by the end of term. I want it to be single-spaced. I want it to be annotated. I want the name of this report to be "Music: The Language of Emotion."
> (Duncan et al., 1995)

Critical theory "seeks to expose and minimize rationalizations, legitimations, and taken for granted assumptions at the roots of paradigms, ideologies and orthodoxies" (Regelski, 2005, p. 9), thereby allowing us to problematize the portrayal of Mr. Holland and the philosophy of MEAE in three important ways.

First, it questions instrumental reason, the human tendency to understand and accept reality in terms of received wisdom and empirical data, which leads to conceiving of education as learning "how the world is, not how it ought to be" (Regelski, 2005, p. 8). This is the case when music teachers blindly follow dictums such as "only the truly talented should study music," or "you must be able to *read* music to be a *real* musician," giving them the rationale to justify a methodology regardless of its results (emphasis original).

Second, critical theory argues that "traditional theory [...] is Idealistic [*sic*]," and the emphasis on the Ideal in traditional theory results in a tension between theory and practice. In Regelski's (2005) view, "any theory – and this includes music theory – that doesn't inform practice, or that impedes it, is at best false and at worst an ideology" (p. 9). Reimer's (1989c) assertion that aesthetic experience is the primary goal of music education separates theory from practice, creating consumers of music rather than practitioners.

Third, critical theory identifies "legitimation crises [...] where the very legitimations advanced in rationalizing an institutionally created reality become crises for the institution when they are used as the criteria by which the social failing of the institution are pointed out" (Regelski, 2005, p. 9). In other words, when public taste and institutional priorities dictate the aesthetic value of music education, it is vulnerable to attacks on its legitimacy and funding.

While Regelski (2005) focuses his studies on the differences in general philosophies of music education, David Elliott has focused on the philosophy underpinning the work of the music teacher. In his seminal work on music education, *Music matters* (1995), Elliott describes his philosophy of music teaching as a *reflective musical practicum*, taking inspiration from Donald Schön's *The reflective practitioner* (1983) and Howard Gardner's *Frames of mind: The theory of multiple intelligences* (1983). Rather than following the long-standing practice of MEAE, Elliott advocates for a "curriculum-as-practicum," which is "meant to approximate authentic music cultures" (1995, p. 270), in which students enter into a master–apprentice relationship with the music teacher as they learn the technical, musical, and collaborative skills necessary to be a fully-functioning musician.

Elliott argues for a definition of teaching as "a matter of intentional thinking-in-action" while relating to students, in which "a teacher's knowledge-in-action is what gives meaning to the teaching-learning situation" (1995, p. 251). He describes teaching expertise as "fundamentally procedural and situational" (p. 251) and breaks down the definition of expertise as (1) to possess a working understanding of teacher–student interactions; (2) to possess a high degree of musicianship and musical knowledge; (3) to possess the "educatorship" to choose the appropriate teaching strategy in the moment as a lesson or rehearsal is progressing.

Thus, to counter the "how-to" method books and aesthetics approaches to music education (the ancient Greek concepts of *techne* and *theoria*), Regelski (2005) and Elliott (1995) advocate an approach that puts theory into practice, or *praxis*. We, the authors of this chapter, have each developed a praxial pedagogy in our own teaching practice.

Mr. Holland's Praxis

If we deconstruct the portrayal of Mr. Holland's teaching through the lens of Elliott's (1995) praxial philosophy, the reasons become clear for our discomfort with the perception of Mr. Holland as a "great" teacher. Our deconstruction uses Elliott's three-fold definition of expertise: teacher–student interactions, musicianship skills, and "educatorship" or knowledge-in-action.

In his communications with the students, Mr. Holland uses condescending language with individual students, yells corrections at the band, berates the general music class for their poor test results, and covers his ignorance of the various instruments with sharp attempts at humour. For example, in the middle of rehearsal, he tells a trumpet player that, "it is not considered… as they say… 'couth'… to empty your spit valve during a performance… especially not on the foot of the person sitting next to you" (Duncan et al., 1995).

Trumpets do, in fact, accumulate condensation that must be released frequently, so Mr. Holland's little joke demonstrates his lack of familiarity with the instrument, which he disguises with sarcasm. A praxial approach is strengths-based and student-centred, acknowledging what the students *can* do and determining the next steps needed to develop the students' musical ability.

In terms of musical expertise, there is no question that Mr. Holland is a well-trained musician, capable of playing the piano at an advanced level, and knowledgeable about music theory and history. He starts his career in the classroom, however, with no training in conducting, teaching methods, fundamentals of instrumental technique, or even lesson planning. We do see him learning as he progresses through his career, but too often the lack of music education expertise results in resorting to authoritarian tactics or vague feeling-talk. A praxial approach would impel the teacher to seek out professional development, but we see Mr. Holland spending his free time writing music at the piano and his summers giving driving lessons.

Finally, music education expertise includes the quality Elliott calls "educatorship," or the ability to assess the student's music making and determine the next appropriate teaching strategy during the flow of the lesson. This is best demonstrated by Mr. Holland's efforts to teach a rhythmically challenged student how to keep a steady beat. His ideas are good – clapping along to a recording, marching in place – but he "teaches" by imposing motor responses *on* the student, not by finding ways to encourage the motor response *in* the student. For example, he holds the student's hands and claps them himself, grabs the student's shoelaces to tap the foot to the beat, and snatches away the drumsticks to demonstrate when the student fumbles. A praxial approach would apply knowledge-in-action, devising strategies that would lead the student to discover the somatic sensation of a steady beat, such as becoming aware of his heartbeat and matching it by tapping his chest.

Conclusion: Deconstructing Mr. Holland

The contrast between Bennett Reimer's (1989c) aesthetic education and David Elliott's (1995) praxial philosophy parallels the contrast between the public enthusiasm for *Mr. Holland's opus* and some music teachers' (including our) dismayed response to the film (de Vries, 2004). It is not difficult to understand Mr. Holland's preference for an aesthetic education approach. It was the dominant pedagogy in the 1960s, when even the prevalent public-school music textbooks were edited by Bennett Reimer.

As a piano and composition student, Glenn Holland had received years of instruction grounded in the MEAE philosophy, and had no reason to question it. The concept of music as an aesthetic object and a language of emotion is likely that which inspired his passion for composition, and the piano became the tool for his own creative work. For the majority of the film's audience, this was a familiar style of music education that they themselves experienced in school. They recognized Glenn Holland's struggle to communicate his passion for the art and craft of music, even though the students were disinterested or unskilled. They admired his dedication, his determination, and his willingness to defend the value of music education to dubious administrators.

If *Mr. Holland's opus* were to be shown to a group of pre-service music teachers, we suggest it should be as part of a discussion of the various approaches to music education (McCarthy & Goble, 2002) to illustrate the philosophy of music education as aesthetic education. The pre-service teachers would be asked to observe the development of Mr. Holland's teaching style, and to prepare to engage in a discussion of the effectiveness, priorities, and skill set shown by the aesthetic education approach. Similarly, a music education methods class would be best served by using this film to investigate the problems that Mr. Holland encounters in the classroom and propose solutions based on a praxial approach.

Clearly, the intention of the film's creative team was to show a teacher who learns from his students and is determined to find a way to reach them, but the strategies he uses go directly against the praxial philosophy that we advocate as practitioners. Instead of thinking about challenges in his classroom as a challenge to his praxis, Mr. Holland insists that his way is the only way, and therein lies the heart of his problems with his students and our problem with the film.

REFERENCES

Asmus, E. (1999, Spring). The increasing demand for music teachers. *Journal of Music Teacher Education, 8*(2), 5–6.

Banks, E., Brooks, P., Handelman, M., & Niemeyer, S. (Producers), & Moore, J. (Director). (2012). *Pitch perfect* [Motion picture]. USA: Universal Pictures.

Brand, M. (2001). Reel music teachers: Use of popular films in music teacher education. *International Journal of Music Education, 38*, 5–12.

Brennan, I., Buecker, B., Falchuk, B., & Murphy, R. (Executive producers). (2009–2015). *Glee* [Television series]. Hollywood, CA: 20th Century Fox Television.

Brill, J., Reitman, J., Samuelson, C., & Walters, G. M. (Executive producers), & Chazelle, D. (Director). (2014). *Whiplash* [Motion picture]. USA: Sony Pictures Classics.

Cren, Y., Gozlan, C., & Katz, M. (Executive producers), & Haneke, M. (Director). (2001). *The piano teacher (La pianiste)* [Motion picture]. Austria, France, & Germany: Arte France Cinéma; Les Films Alain Sarde; MK2 Productions; Wega Film; Österreichischer Rundfunk (ORF); Kino International (USA); Alliance Atlantis Motion Picture Distribution (Canada).

Colwell, R. (2015). A challenge from Bennett Reimer. *Philosophy of Music Education Review, 23*(2), 117–141.

Dalton, R. (Producer), & Schlesinger, J. (Director). (1988). *Madame Sousatzka* [Motion picture]. UK & Canada: Cineplex-Odeon Films; Universal Pictures.

De Silva, D., & Marshall, A. (Producers), & Parker, A. (Director). (1980). *Fame* [Motion picture]. USA: Metro-Goldwyn-Mayer; United Artists.

de Vries, P. (2004). Reel music teaching: A classroom music teacher reflects on the portrayal of music teaching in *Mr Holland's opus*. *Asia-Pacific Journal of Teacher Education, 32*(2), 159–167.

Duncan, P. S., & Kroopf, S. (Executive producers), & Herek, S. (Director). (1995). *Mr. Holland's opus* [Motion picture]. USA: Buena Vista Pictures.

Ebert, R. (1996, January 19). Mr. Holland's opus. *The Chicago Tribune*.

Elliott, D. (1995). *Music matters: A new philosophy of music education*. New York: Oxford University Press.

Gardner, H. (1983). *Frames of mind: The theory of multiple intelligences.* Philadelphia, PA: Basic Books.

Goble, S. (2003). Perspectives on practice: A pragmatic comparison of the praxial philosophies of David Elliott and Thomas Regelski. *Philosophy of Music Education Review, 11*(1), 23–44. Retrieved from http://www.jstororg/stable/40327196

Grimes, W. (1996, February 21). "Mr. Holland" succeeds, almost despite itself. *The New York Times.*

Iscovich, M., Mark, L., & Meledandri, C. (Executive producers), & Duke, B. (Director). (1993). *Sister act 2: Back in the habit* [Motion picture]. USA: Touchstone Pictures; Buena Vista Pictures.

Maslin, J. (1996, January 19). A teacher who once had dreams [Film review]. *The New York Times.*

McCarthy, M., & Goble, S. (2002). Music education philosophy: Changing times. *Music Educators Journal,* (89)1, 19–26.

Pyett, K. (2014, Fall). Movies, music, and mind: What does Hollywood know about music teaching? *Canadian Music Educator,* 31–34.

Pine, H. (Producer), & Oliansky, J. (Director). (1980). *The competition* [Motion picture]. USA: Columbia Pictures.

Raimo, A. D.-S. (2002). Learning about teachers through film. *The Educational Forum, 66*(4), 314–323.

Regelski, T. (2005). Critical theory as a foundation for critical thinking in music education. *Vision of Research in Music Education, 6,* 2–24. Retrieved from http://www.rider.edu/~vrme

Reimer, B. (1989a, February). Music education as aesthetic education: Past and present. *Music Educators Journal, 75*(6), 22–28. Retrieved from http://www.jstor.org/stable/3398124

Reimer, B. (1989b, March). Music education as aesthetic education: Toward the future. *Music Educators Journal, 75*(7), 26–32. Retrieved from http://www.jstor.org/stable/3400308

Reimer, B. (1989c). *A philosophy of music education* (2nd ed.). Englewood Cliffs, NJ: Prentice-Hall.

Schön, D. (1983). *The reflective practitioner: How professionals think in action.* New York, NY: Basic Books.

Shuler, S. (1996, Sep/Oct). Assessing teacher competence in the arts: Should Mr. Holland have gotten the gig? Introduction to the Symposium on Teacher Evaluation. *Arts Education Policy Review, 98*(1), 11–15.

The Politics of Representation of Pedagogues in Nollywood: A Critical Analysis of *Somewhere in Africa: The Cries of Humanity*

Taiwo Afolabi & Stephen Okpadah

Introduction

Media representation is an essential example in discourses on the politics of representation because it reifies the notion that meaning is constantly changing. Power consistently uses media to fix meaning to support its agenda. Media, collective communication outlets, or tools that are used to store and deliver information or data inform the way in which we perceive the world. Since media assists in the construction of meanings in the world, it is imperative to critically interrogate the meanings of media representations (Hall, 1997).

Structuralist and post-structuralist scholars have argued that signs and systems of language frame our reality about the world and reality is believed to be encoded through media such as film (Culler, 1976; Hall, 1997; Ousmane, 1975). Representation and meaning-making processes have been influenced by mimetic and constructionist approaches. A mimetic approach considers art and language as mirrors reflecting the world (Hamilton, 1997). Such an intentional approach holds that it is the speaker or the author who imposes his or her own unique meaning on the world through language, while in a constructionist approach meaning is constructed using a representational system. Stuart Hall (1997), a renowned cultural theorist, believes that the constructionist approach is a theory of pictorial apprehension and representation that advances public and social characters of language. Furthermore, there is recognition that signification systems play a central part in conveying meaning, a notion grounded in semiotics, the study of how signs are used as representations of meaning. Semiotics is a science and system of language, which considers the creation and deciphering of meanings through signs and signification systems embedded in language. That is, how the structure of language frames our thought about the world forms the basis of representation. Politics of representation are concerned with what it means to be seen and heard – visibility and audibility, the politics and ethics of presence.

The politics of representation recognize the role an individual plays when it comes to receiving and making meaning and appropriates sociocultural and political nuances that influence meaning-making process, hence meaning is constantly changing. Since the society is not fixed, the role of the pedagogue also changes. In the context of this chapter, we are concerned with how pedagogues have been represented through film content in Nigeria.

Pedagogies, Pedagogues, and Representation in Films

Discourses on pedagogues are predominant in popular culture. In fact, the representation of pedagogues in film is not a recent phenomenon. Film cultures, such as Hollywood, Bollywood, and Nollywood,[1] have incorporated themes that revolve around the importance, status, and significance of teachers in the society. Perhaps, this is because it is believed that pedagogues are instrumental to the growth of any society, and teachers' intelligence and intellectual capability determine the pace of development in any nation. Corroborating the above statement, Angelina Ambrosetti avers that,

> throughout old and new history, teaching is considered to be an honourable profession, one that is complex and involves specific skills and knowledge to be effective. Society has high expectations of teachers as they are entrusted with shaping the future generation.
>
> (2016, p. 1)

Contextualizing this discourse, Nollywood films have attempted to explore activities of teachers in society. Nollywood films, among other themes, have discussed teachers' attitudes, training, sociocultural reception to western education, teachers' identities, the impact of language of instruction on students, and the overall pedagogic process in disseminating information to learners. The films offer both constructive and destructive critiques of teachers; hence, the politics of representation of pedagogues in Nigerian films varies. For instance, Ambrosetti (2016) observes that Nigerian popular films often portray teachers as inspirational figures, pillars of society, and those who can have a major influence over the development of the students in their care. Within the brief story that a film provides, teachers are more often than not positioned as "mentor type" figures to students entrusted in their care, who guide and support them to become who they want to be. This mentor and protégée relationship is pivotal in the acclimatization and assimilation of the ideology of the teacher by the student(s).

There are also many negative representations of teachers in Nollywood films, which include: the comic teacher with his baggy trousers; the uncultured headmaster with his old and rickety bicycle; the sexy female teacher who overawes her male students with her mini-skirts and makeup; the young and handsome male teacher who indulges in sexual relationships with his female students; the university lecturer who takes his female students to bed in return for good grades; and so on. Beyond these awkward representations, the role of the teacher in revolutionary discourse has been sparsely discussed in Nigerian films. These films counter negative representations of teachers, and instead call for the need for revolution, the pedagogue's role in revolution, and the need for appropriate representation of pedagogues' identities. In light of the above, we examine how pedagogues have been represented in film content in Nigeria by critically examining Frank Rajah Arase's (2011) film, *Somewhere in Africa: The cries of humanity*.

Examples of Representation of Pedagogues in Films

From the inception of film in popular culture, there have been explorations of the role of teachers in child development, cultural construction and reconstruction, societal development, revolution, and so on. Films have always projected teachers as mentors to students. For instance, in other cultures, films such as *Bulletproof monk* (Roven, Chang, Woo, Segal, Hunter, & Hunter, 2003) and *First blood* (Feitshans & Kotcheff, 1982) show that teachers play important roles in the life of the protagonist. The influence of the teacher, consequently, has rippling effects on the society. In *First blood*, Colonel Sam Trautman (Richard Crenna), a former commander, is instrumental to the brave and heroic adventure of John Rambo (Sylvester Stallone). This narrative is also repeated in *Bulletproof monk*, in which a nameless monk (Chow Yun-Fat) is not only a mentor and teacher to the young protagonist, but he acts as a guardian angel to Young Kar (Seann William Scott). Similarly, in many Asian movies, protagonists are trained and mentored by masters who are committed wholeheartedly to the wellbeing of their students.

In Nollywood, films that depict teachers and their role in the society are few in number. However, on the Nigerian television terrain, one of the foremost and most popular teacher-focused dramas is *The village headmaster* (Lewis, 1958–1988). Some films that portray teachers as dominant characters portray them in a negative light. Films such as *Nwa teacher* (Igwe, Enech, & Chidebe, 2003) and *Adams goes to school* (Chidebe, 2003) portray teachers as clowns; *SS3 students* (Chidox, 2014) depicts teachers as sex perverts who defile students for marks; and some Nollywood films represent university male lecturers' sexual assaults on female students.

The role of teachers in staging revolution has been only sparsely examined in the Nigerian film compendium. Of the films that do look at teachers in this role, some represent teachers as facilitators and agents of change in the country's politics and economy. Such films show that there is a relationship between education and revolution. Hence, Sunny Ododo (2014) argues that, "the importance and linkage of education to the development of any society is a settled matter" (p. 49). In fact, for any society to attain liberty from economic and political oppression and suppression, a teacher must be involved because pedagogues "play some significant roles in sustaining democracy and setting the agenda for national development" (Ogungbe, 2016, p. 602).

Assertions about the importance of teachers are buttressed with Lancelot Oduwa Imaseun's 2014 film, titled *Invasion 1897*. This film is a critical discourse on history. It brings to the fore the attendant effect of imperialism and the rape-exploitation of the Benin Empire by the British colonial masters. In this film, the university professor (Rodolph Walker) is the originator of the revolutionary act of one of his students, Igie (Charles Chucky Venn). He is represented as a mentor, supporter, and facilitator of the revolution necessary for the next generation. Through his knowledge, he challenges his students to search for historical truth and reclaim their identities. In the film, teachers are represented as the backbone for revolution.

One film that fully captures the representation of pedagogues and their role in societal development in Nollywood is *Somewhere in Africa: The cries of humanity* (Arase, 2011). This film is not about teacher-driven revolution alone, it situates pedagogues as central in the quest for positive change in the society. Using the notion of representation, we interrogate how media content (cinema) represents pedagogues through an analysis of the film.

Synopsis of Somewhere in Africa: The Cries of Humanity

Somewhere in Africa: The cries of humanity (Arase, 2011), a conjunctive production of Heroes Films and Raj Films, is a creative, artistic, and fictional rendition, set in Kimbala, of numerous historical coups that had occurred in Africa. Heads of state, such as General Olemba, had been killed and their governments toppled. A civilian government led by President Gabiza emerged, but is ousted by General Mombasa. Thus, President Gabiza alongside other political stalwarts, such as the Minister for Finance, Christopher Archibong, was assassinated. There is an uprising as rebels emerge from various facets in Kimbala, canvassing for the removal of General Mombasa as Head of State. Frank Luema, a journalist, goes to Kimbala in the guise of a Reverend Father, named Francis Jackson. He meets the widow of the late finance minister, Mrs. Archibong, a teacher, and they plan to overthrow General Mombasa. However, Luema's luggage is ransacked at the hotel by the government and he is subsequently arrested. The late finance minister's widow is arrested as well and killed by General Mombasa in the presence of her students, who later indulge in a revolt. Some of them are killed and others arrested, molested, and raped. Frank Luema's arm is cut off, while student Nivera's left ear is chopped off. Sanity returns to Kimbala when power is coercively wrestled from General Mombasa in a countercoup.

Representation of Pedagogues

The disobedient pedagogue

Hall's (1997) theory of representation seeks to interrogate two questions: "Who or what is to be represented and who or what is to be the representative" (Political Representation, 2005, para. 2). "The first question revolves around the description of constituencies [while] the second concerns the method of selection by which the representative is determined" (Political Representation, 2005, para. 2). From the sage village storyteller, to the westernized village headmaster and the sophisticated city-trained teacher, it is not far-fetched that pedagogues are portrayed and represented as prime movers of beliefs, appropriators of philosophy, custodians and crystallizers of cultural practices. The teacher is represented in the film *Somewhere in Africa: The cries of humanity* (Arase, 2011) through the use of language and images by the film director.

First, the film portrays teachers as the watchdogs of society. Through knowledge acquired, a teacher documents history, preserves and transfers knowledge through a pedagogic process that is emancipatory. Though the students, led by Nivera, Mr. Christopher Archibong's daughter, are the revolutionaries, Mrs. Archibong, their teacher, and Luema, as the Reverend Father, a teacher in his own right, although in a religious setting, are the prime movers of the revolutionary process. The film begins with Mrs. Archibong in the classroom where she teaches her students. Mrs. Archibong historicizes the precedent of the situation in Kimbala before the emergence of General Mumbasa's government. She narrates the coups and countercoups engineered by the military, before sanity was finally restored by a civilian government headed by President Gabiza. However, as she describes, out of greed and the quest for power, General Yusuf Mumbasa ousted the civilian government. Her teaching illustrates the role of the teacher to incite revolution in a time when the tyrannical regime of General Yusuf Mumbasa bedevils Kimbala. It seems the General is threatened by the ideas being taught in school, so he imprisons Mrs. Archibong.

The knowledge custodian and revolution catalyst

In the film, through the use of language of signs and images, pedagogues are presented as important in knowledge creation and production to increase possibilities for instigating revolts and change. Kimbala is a metaphor for postcolonial Africa, which becomes the home of coups and countercoups. General Mumbasa's government is characterized by corruption, political assassinations, and socioeconomic recession. Within this film, the teacher metaphorically brings to the fore the subject of coups and countercoups inherent in postcolonial African societies. Through discussing the government of General Mumbasa, Mrs. Archibong reminds us of the unwholesome government of despots such as Sani Abacha of Nigeria, Idi Amin Dada of Uganda, Mobutu SeseSeko of Democratic Republic of Congo (formerly Zaire), Muammar Gadaffi of Libya, and others. In fact, she is critical of anti-democratic governments. Conversely, to General Yusuf Mumbasa, democracy is anathema and must be crushed. To him, the liberty and emancipation of the masses must be tamed.

In many societies, teachers are considered facilitators of dialogue amongst different sectors ensuring an understanding of societal issues. Sometimes, teachers put their charismatic and magnetic capacity to play, by instilling confidence in students. This is the case in the film; Mrs. Archibong is an orator who instils the aforementioned virtue in the students. Teachers and students alike immediately loathe General Yusuf Mumbasa. Mrs. Archibong informs the students that the only way to overcome oppression is to take action. The students fully comprehend her teaching. They would even resort to violence if need be, to salvage the situation. This revolutionary ideology is articulated in Udenta's (1993, p. 9) assertion that,

> revolutionary aesthetics has very specific and identifiable features as an aesthetic category and ideological weapon, some of which are service to the people and adherence to partisanship, close bonds with the working people's struggle, historical optimism, rejection of formalism and subjectivism, and of national primitivism.

Udenta's enunciation of revolutionary aesthetics in Arase's (2011) film further identifies Mrs. Archibong and Francis Luema as the prime movers and appropriators of the ideology of revolt – pedagogues as weapons of sociocultural and political reconstruction. The pragmatic action taken by the students has a productive, nay positive, effect on the present and the future of the society within the film. Thus, Francis Luema, posing as a Reverend Father, lucidly enunciates: "You have to take your future in your hands. You need to act, act now" (Arase, 2011).

When General Mombasa arrests Mrs. Archibong, Francis Luema, as the Reverend Father, takes her place. He is represented as an influence on the students. The students respect him when they see him in his collar, typically worn by church clergies. They see him as a guide and an advisor. To this end, he propels the students to take action that would facilitate the release of Mrs. Archibong. Led by Nivera Archibong, the students march to the presidential villa on a peaceful protest. They see the reason they must act: their teacher has been unjustly arrested, and as such, she must be released. Consequently, the tyrant-General Yusuf Mombasa shoots Mrs. Archibong in their presence. This action, which triggers a riot, leads to the death of many students. Mombasa's soldiers rape most of the female students, while their male counterparts are heavily assaulted. Frank Luema, who is also instrumental in the revolution, is arrested and his arm is severed.

With the information the teacher has, the teacher creates an awareness of societal issues for the students to understand the exploitative structures inherent in the social system. Thus, "education is acknowledged as an enterprise that would equip the individual with knowledge" (Ododo, 2014, p. 48). The film represents teachers as instigators of revolution and focuses viewers' attention on pedagogues' role in reconstructing social realities in society and their role as preservers and custodians of history, cultural practices, and heritage.

The sacrificial lamb

Another representation present in the film is how pedagogues are shown as highly self-sacrificing, thoughtful, resilient, and untiring revolutionaries who are strategic in their interventions. They are not only ready to teach and facilitate the revolutionary process, they are interested in being there throughout the process to support and mentor students in taking on leadership roles. Through this film, we observe that there is a shift away from negative representations of pedagogues. As can be inferred from the title, the focus of the film is on issues that concern humanity and actors who are instrumental in averting oppression meted on the people. The director used all the resources at his disposal to project the tenet of the film. For instance, the director, Arase, utilizes Close Up and Extreme Close Up shots in many situations in this film to reveal the psychological state of the characters.

The outcome of such aesthetic choices is catharsis, which leads to building empathy in the viewers.

Another significant characteristic of *Somewhere in Africa: The cries of humanity* (Arase, 2011) is the fast pace of actions and frequent cuts. The film's quality made it a success in the box office. No wonder the film had "7 nominations at the 9th Africa Movie Academy Awards for categories: Achievement in Production Design, Achievement in Costume Design, Achievement in Make-Up, Achievement in Soundtrack, Achievement in Visual effects, Best Young/Promising Actor, and Best Actor in a Leading Role" (*Somewhere in Africa*, n.d., para. 4). The lead actor, Majid Michel, received an award in the last category.

Representation or Misrepresentation of Pedagogues?

A major critique levelled against the film is the excessive killing and violence it projects. The director ran the risk of projecting teachers as freedom fighters who are not interested in non-violent means to struggle for the liberation of the people. Here arises the contradiction in trying to give us positive representations of teachers; the film perhaps pushed the representation of teachers as agents of change too far. Thus, the director's representation of pedagogues runs the risk of posing a different reading of pedagogues as reckless change agents who are ready to use any means to revolt even if it means instigating students under their care to face bullets without any means of defence.

In *Somewhere in Africa: The cries of humanity* (Arase, 2011), teachers function as narrators of the postcolonial situation. The postcolonial condition is not only characterized as the negative effects of globalization, guns, and ammunitions, but it is also marred with corruption, decadence, and laxity among leaders in society. Corruption and exploitation become the bane of the political landscape. Hence, satirical masterpieces became recurrent in the Nigerian, cum African, literary/narrative corpus. One major indigenous African filmmaker, who unravelled this tendency in his discourses, is Sembene Ousmane. His films, such as *Xala* (Ousmane, 1975), clearly satirize the profligacy of African leaders, and the political status quo in Africa. As such, novelists, poets, dramatists, and most importantly filmmakers, along with pedagogues, are vital in the call for revolution. Definitely in Russia, filmmakers played a major role in instigating the Bolshevik Revolution of 1917. Vladimir Lenin, and subsequently, Joseph Stalin, who saw that film was germane in the propagation of ideologies, adopted it as a medium for the promulgation of the dogma of socialism. Consequently, Frank Rajah Arase's (2011) film articulates revolution as a response to corruption, and the irreplaceable role of pedagogues in such revolutionary acts is immanent.

Conclusion

With the film discussed in this chapter and others, Nollywood has been able to expand the discourse on teachers' identities, people and government's perceptions, and the need for positive representations of teachers as knowledge and history preservers. Since representation is the production of meaning of concepts in our minds through language, the language and images employed to represent pedagogues is important. This chapter holds that there are limited films that show positive representations and document the unwavering contributions of pedagogues in forging revolution and desired change in Nigeria. We conclude that teachers will continue to initiate and influence the thought patterns of students and that education can be a revolutionary weapon of change and reconstruction.

REFERENCES

Ambrosetti, A. (2016). The portrayal of the teacher as mentor in popular film: Inspirational, supportive and life-changing? *M/C Journal of Media and Culture. 19*(2), 1–15.

Arase, F. R. (Director). (2011). *Somewhere in Africa: The cries of humanity* [Motion picture]. Ghana & Nigeria: Raj Films and Heroes Production.

Chidebe, M.-C. (Director). (2003). *Adams goes to school* [Motion picture]. Nigeria: Mlantex Nigeria Ltd.

Chidox, A. C. (Director). (2014). *SS3 students* [Motion picture]. Nigeria: Vin Matins Productions Ltd.

Culler, J. (1976). *Saussure.* London, UK: Fontana.

Hall, S. (Ed.) (1997). *Representation: Cultural representations and signifying practices.* Thousand Oaks, CA: Sage; Open University.

Hamilton, P. (1997). Representing the social: France and Frenchness in post-war humanist photography. In S. Hall (Ed.), *Representation: Cultural representations and signifying practices* (pp. 75–150). Thousand Oaks, CA: Sage; Open University.

Roven, C., Chang, T., Woo, J., & Segal, D. (Producers), & Hunter, P. (Director). (2003). *Bulletproof monk* [Motion picture]. USA Lakeshore Entertainment, Mosaic Media Group & Lion Rock Production.

Igwe, E. U., Enech, B., & Chidebe C. M. (Directors) (2003). *Nwa teacher* [Video file]. Nigeria: Hallmark film Ltd.

Imasuen, O. L. (Director). (2014). *Invasion 1897* [Motion picture]. Nigeria: Iceslide films & Well Entertainment.

Feitshans, B. (Producer), & Kotcheff, T. (Director). (1982). *First blood* [Motion picture]. USA: Anabasis N.V & Elcajo Productions.

Lewis, D. (Director). (1958–1988). *The village headmaster* [Television Series]. Nigeria: Nigerian Television Authority.

Ododo, S. (2014). *It's only bent, not broken: Culture, education, politics and performance art in Ebira and Ogori*. Lagos, NG: Society of Nigerian Theatre Artists.

Ogungbe, E. (2016). Media, language and democracy: A critical discourse analysis of syntactic choices in some Nigerian daily newspaper headlines. In O. Ayodabo, U. N. Butari, O. Patrick, & O. Abraham (Eds.), *Linguistics, language and literature: A festschrift for Gbenga Solomon Ibileye* (pp. 602–614). Lokoja, NG: Department of English and Literary Studies, Federal University.

Ousmane, S. (1975). *Xala* [Motion picture]. Senegal: Filmi Domireve SNC.

"Political Representation." (2005). *New dictionary of the history of ideas*. Retrieved from http://www.encyclopedia.com/history/dictionaries-thesauruses-pictures-and-press-releases/political-representation.

"*Somewhere in Africa.*" (n.d.). Wikipedia. Retrieved from https://en.wikipedia.org/wiki/Somewhere_in_Africa.

Udenta, U. (1993). *Revolutionary aesthetics & the African literary process*. Enugu, NG: Fourth Dimension Publishers.

NOTE

1. Nollywood is the film industry of Nigeria. Scholars in film studies aver that Nollywood is the second biggest film industry in the world, in terms of numbers of films being churned out annually. At least thirteen films (made in the English language) are being churned out every week; and this excludes those produced in Yoruba, Urhobo, Hausa, Igbo, and Bini languages, and so on. Films produced in indigenous languages are also very popular among the literate, semi-literate, and illiterate audience. Furthermore, Nollywood films are socio-cultural and political constructs. They explore the themes of love, rituals, politics, historical reconstruction, and so on.

An Unlikely Revolution: Portrayals of Teaching in *Strictly Ballroom*

Anita Hallewas

In Support of a Revolution

In the closing scene of the film *Strictly ballroom* (Miall & Luhrmann, 1992), Australian Dance Federation President Barry Fife dramatically unplugs the music to what is the final competition dance number. It is his strategy to stop Scott and Fran dancing their non-federation routine at the Pan-Pacific Grand Prix Amateur Championships. In the silence, Fife announces the couple are disqualified from the competition. Just as Scott and Fran begin to leave the dance floor, a single clap can be heard from within the crowd. Then there is another clap, and another, forming a strong constant rhythm. It is Doug Hastings, Scott's father, and instinctively he knows the couple need a cheerleader, a champion. He walks out onto the dance floor to demonstrate support for his son and continues to clap in time. As the watching audience appreciate the meaning of the rhythmic clap (something the film audience learned earlier on), they begin clapping too, in what becomes a community-supported protest and revolution against the dance federation's oppressing rules and regulations. This act is an overwhelming expression of the crowd's support of Scott and Fran's courage to dare to dream and break the rules doing it.

In this chapter I discuss the portrayal of teachers in the film *Strictly ballroom* that leads to this revolutionary behaviour, thereby creating a new way of thinking within a small dance studio and their wider dance community. I argue the revolution is led by the learners, not the teachers and that each have much to learn from each other. I will refer to three learning styles displayed in the film: traditional (Paolo Freire's banking concept); peer-mentoring; and collaborative/cultural sharing and how these styles link to the philosophies of educational revolutionary Paulo Freire (1996), drama-in-education pioneers Harriet Finlay Johnson, Henry Caldwell-Cook (both in Bolton, 1999), and Dorothy Heathcote (1984) as well as contemporary applied theatre theorists in support of alternate education systems.

I read *Strictly ballroom* (Miall & Luhrmann, 1992) through the lens of my roles as drama educator, applied theatre scholar and facilitator, and ardent advocate of alternative learning styles.

Art Imitating Life, or Life Imitating Art?

Strictly ballroom (Miall & Luhrmann, 1992), an iconic Australian film, was the first (and only) film I ever stood to applaud, with mutual participation from the full-house cinema audience. This ovation was not an isolated event as at the film's world premiere in Cannes it received a fifteen-minute standing ovation (Bennett, 2015). The premiere was to be held in Australia; however, the cinema chain due to release the film had dropped it, claiming it was not worthy of the big screen. Ironically, the film's themes of rejection, misjudgment, and aesthetics-over-skill were mirrored in the film's launch, although this all changed after the film's unexpected success at Cannes. *Strictly ballroom*, as with all of Baz Luhrmann's work, has a playful nature that uses film as a medium to shock the senses, taking the audience on a mercurial ride. Luhrmann's use of light and sound, unique camera angles, as well as flash-backs, flash-forwards, and narration are employed to great effect. Film reviewer Roger Ebert (1993) says of *Strictly ballroom*:

> What's best about the movie is the sense of madness and mania running just beneath its surface. In one sense, the characters care about nothing but ballroom dancing. They eat, drink and sleep it, and talk of nothing else. Their costumes alone are a tip-off that they've had no contact with the real world for years. Yet in another sense, ballroom dancing is simply the strategy they use to hold the world at bay. They are profoundly frightened of change, and have created an insular little world, with rigid rules and traditions; here they can be in control, as the larger world goes haywire.
>
> (para. 8)

Teachers as Oppressors: Freire and Education

Ebert's (1993) review taps into one of the film's most interesting themes: the absurd nature of a world in which the rules and traditions of a popular sport oppress a small community. As lead oppressor, Barry Fife controls the dancing community by setting rules and regulations that keep everyone in check, his oppression being one of "the gravest obstacles to the achievement of liberation [...] and thereby acts to submerge human beings' consciousness" (Freire, 1996, p. 33). Dancers appear unable to make decisions without consulting Fife and look to his guidance before acting even on the smallest undertaking. The idolization of Fife as the definitive authority and thereby the student's "necessary opposite" (Freire, 1996, p. 53) has meant Fife has remained president for several decades with no contention and therefore "by considering their ignorance absolute, he justifies his own existence" (Freire, 1996, p. 53). Miall and Luhrmann (1992) paint a juxtaposition of the types of teachers in *Strictly ballroom*, beginning with the traditional dance studio teachers who utilize fear, manipulation, deception, shaming, and belittling as the "necessary evil" teaching tools required to mold their students. Teachers Les Kendall's and Shirley Hastings' (Scott's mother) rigid focus on personal aesthetics, and a need to follow the stringent regulations of the sport, mean they are not afraid to use deception and guilt as strategies in discouraging Scott from following his own dream.

The "banking" education concept

In his benchmark work *Pedagogy of the oppressed*, Paulo Freire explains the education system is suffering a terrible sickness (1996, p. 52) in "which the scope of action allowed to the students extends only as far as receiving, filing, and storing of deposits" (p. 53) where students record, repeat, and memorize without realizing the true significance of what they are learning. This is Freire's "banking" concept as it is "people themselves who are filed away through the lack of creativity, transformation, and knowledge in this (at best) misguided system" (p. 53). The "banking" concept is well demonstrated in a conversation between Scott and another dancer, Wayne. When Scott enquires as to what Wayne thinks of Scott's new dance steps, a strange expression crosses Wayne's face, he is clearly struggling to formulate an answer; he eventually responds with, "You didn't win, did you?" The "banking" concept has successfully created in Wayne a passive learner incapable of creativity or transformation (Freire, 1996); he cannot see outside the mandated federation rules to make up his own mind as to whether he enjoys Scott's new "moves." Fran, as a newcomer to the school, perhaps with the benefit of a shorter indoctrination, sees something the rest of them do not and is bold enough to yell at Scott, even though he is the school's "best dancer":

> You're just like the rest of them! You think you're different, but you're not, because you're just, you're just really scared! You're really scared to give someone new a go, because you think, you know, they might just be better than you are! Well, you're just pathetic, and you're gutless. You're a gutless wonder!
> (Miall & Luhrmann, 1992)

It is Fran's boldness and honesty that gives Scott the courage for his final push into revolution.

Peer Mentoring and Problem-Posing Education

When Scott loses his dance partner to an unexpected accident, Fran, the resident ugly-duckling, offers to dance with him. Scott rejects her as "a beginner has no right to approach an open amateur" (Miall & Luhrmann, 1992), but he takes pity on her, agreeing to teach her in secret as neither his coach nor family would approve of the match. The secret training results in mutual peer mentoring, as although Fran has only been dancing for two years Scott discovers she has ideas and skills to share, too. This style of learning closely mirrors Freire's concept of problem-posing education, as "the teacher is no longer merely the-one-who-teaches, but one who is himself taught in dialogue with the students, who in turn while being taught also teach" (1996, p. 61). Early twentieth-century drama-in-education pioneer, Harriet Finlay-Johnson, saw her role as more of a coach on the side-line than teacher, stating the work "created dramatically was the children's own invention" (in Bolton, 1999, p. 15) and argued that all creative aspects should come from the learner, not the teacher. Vital to Finlay-Johnson's practice was no matter how "crude the action or dialogue from the adult's point of view" (in Bolton, 1999, p. 15), the finished product need only please the child creators and should disregard the needs or wants of observing adults or teachers. In contrast, Fife and his protégées demand high-quality and showy performances with paramount focus on audience entertainment and, of course, winning.

(Not) teaching to the exam

When Scott first meets Fran's father (Rico) and grandmother (Ya Ya), he begins to see new learning possibilities and the journey to the Pan Pacifics becomes less about winning and pleasing the judges and far more about process. Dorothy Heathcote values the benefit of process, explaining, "the difference between theatre and classroom drama is that in theatre everything is contrived so that the audience gets the kicks. In the classroom, the participants get the kicks" (1984, p. 158). Finlay-Johnson (in Bolton, 1999, p. 15) values process over product, focusing on the needs of participants not the audience and does this by allocating a role for every class member so there is no voyeur or "audience." A general consensus amongst applied theatre practitioners is that process reigns supreme over product (Preston, 2016, pp. 4, 21; Balfour, Bundy, Burton, Dunn, & Woodrow, 2015, p. 70), yet unfortunately the perfect final "product" is a powerful motive for Kendall's Dance Studio. Working towards performance or "teaching to the exam" is still a pitfall in most education systems even when overwhelming evidence states that this strategy limits student achievement and overall success (NCTE, 2014, p. 2). Throughout the film we discover Scott's father, Doug, dislikes competition and is far more interested in dance for pleasure, so does not prescribe to the regalia associated with ballroom competition. Doug instead is more interested in the little things, documenting his world with an old-fashioned camera. It is only in the final minutes of the film that the audience learns that Doug had hoped to dance his own steps at competition and missed out; it is a decision he does not want to see repeated with his own son.

(De)(il)lusions of action and free choice

It is evident that Doug felt the tight reigns of the strict dance community and so although the film appears spoof-like with over-the-top caricatures, larger-than-life personalities and absurd behaviour, Luhrmann (1992) cleverly ties in deeper themes of rejection and oppression. The dance students appear incapable of free thought and by following Fife's rules meticulously the dance community sustain an "illusion of acting through the action of the teacher" (Freire, 1996, p. 54). In contrast, Scott and Fran reject the rules set by the federation and their oppressing "bank-clerk teachers" (Freire, 1996, p. 53), revolting against their oppressor. When they liberate themselves, they liberate their oppressor too; the power that springs from the "weakness of the oppressed will be sufficiently strong enough to free both" (Freire, 1996, p. 26). To do this Scott and Fran must follow their dreams instead of what the establishment have engrained in them is "right." The journey is not easy. When Scott announces he'll dance with Fran at the championships, Fife attempts to dissuade Scott in making the "mistake of his career" (Miall & Luhrmann, 1992) by telling the tragic story of how Scott's father, Doug, ended his dance career by also attempting to dance his own "crazy, crowd pleasing steps" (Miall & Luhrmann, 1992) at the national tournament. The guilt from this lie is enough for Scott to drop Fran as his partner and take back Liz to give his father the "happiness he deserves" (Miall & Luhrmann, 1992). Fife's deception is enough for Scott to give up his dream and greatest passion.

Applied Theatre Theory

Passion, instinct, and intuition are familiar concepts within applied theatre practice and when discussing education, speak closely to me. Applied theatre scholar and facilitator Michael Balfour argues social and aesthetic instincts are fundamental to good applied theatre facilitation, "someone who can pick-up, identify and work with all the various complexities that exist within the group in a way that is respectful, flexible and structured" (2016, p. 153). Intrinsic to applied theatre is that participants are active in the creation and ownership of their work; this concept is not new, this was Finlay-Johnson's focus more than one-hundred years ago. Education revolutionary Sir Ken Robinson argues the current education system does little to "develop young people's capacities for original ideas and action" (NACCC, 1999, p. 5) and in turn is failing young learners. Yet passion in a learner (and teacher) might be more important than instinct; without passion we have no drive or excitement and no reason to move forward. Tim Prentki argues "the oyster of applied theatre can only transform the grit of human experience into the pearl of a better life by including in its processes all those elements which form part of the human being; irrational, self-destructive and passionate as they may be" (2012, p. 202). Kendall's Dance Studio fails its students by thwarting new creation and dismissing natural intuition and artistry, even if this risk-taking may involve destructive failure. Kendall's education model makes it impossible to encourage true passion or risk-taking, and in turn, removes the chance for students to experience failure.

Failure as a learning tool

Fife's strong fear of failure, both for himself and his students, pushes him into rigging national competitions, whereas Balfour argues failure and vulnerability are excellent tools in allowing for reflection and deepening attunement (2016, p. 159). In Fife's attempt to remove failure, the sport stagnates; Luhrmann cleverly demonstrates this through his representation of their world in a kind of time-warp bubble. This fear of failure means nothing changes and Freire's concept of oppressor supressing learner continues. At Scott's first meeting with Ya Ya and Rico, they bluntly tell him he is dancing the *paso doble* wrong. He takes the criticism of his own failure well, he is ready for change, and so begins a wonderful mentoring relationship. It is here that Scott realizes failure enables learning and with his ability to remove his own self-absorption he can be successful.

Liberty in the classroom

The caricature teachers are displayed as villains and bullies, incapable of truly connecting with their students due to their self-absorbed attitudes. Balfour (2016) explains that effective facilitators must completely remove themselves from self-absorption for success; instead the focus must be on the needs and abilities of the group (p. 152). Finlay-Johnson relinquished teacher power in a way that onlookers presumed she was not required and instead "spent the lesson watching from the side-lines" (in Heathcote, 1984, p. 9). Heathcote acknowledges the facilitator wears many hats: "provocateur, narrator, enthusiast, reflector dogsbody, negotiator and someone who knows when to pull back" (as cited in Balfour, 2016, p. 152), stating that the best learning occurs when "the power to influence"

(Heathcote, 1984, p. 167) is in the hands of the students. Heathcote's attempt to remove the teacher's "power to tell directly" (p. 164) is seen in her role-play and teacher-in-role[1] strategies that allow for equal respect and equal distribution of power in the classroom, removing the "one-way transmission" (p. 163); in her teacher-in-role characters, Heathcote is often "deliberately obtuse" (Preston, 2016, p. 54) to hand over that power. Henry Caldwell-Cook, encouraged "liberty" in the classroom, viewing "play" as a valuable tool as it "allowed the pupils to choose how they wanted to work" (in Bolton, 1999, p. 30). Scott and Fran find a kind of liberty in their learning with Ya Ya and Rico, and although Fran initially attempts to hide her "weird family" it is the intercultural and intergenerational aspects of this experience that lure Scott in.

Collaborative and Cultural Sharing

Much like good applied theatre practice, Scott and Fran's relationship is collaborative, each offering acceptance and support with mutual respect and with mutual gain for each dancer to follow their dreams. As the plot develops the audience learns that dancing is in Fran's blood; Rico and Ya Ya are skilled Latino dancers and suddenly Scott's learning environment widens, open to endless possibilities. This alternate learning environment, which occurs in the backyard of a run-down family home (on the other side of the railway tracks, no less), depicts collaborative mentoring through the use of instinct and passion for sharing something you love. Although Scott is ready for his revolution, seeking more learning and creative independence, Ya Ya and Rico see that Scott needs "a facilitator, a provocateur, a champion, someone to believe in them, someone to critique" (Balfour, 2016, p. 164). This mentoring appears natural and mutually respectful; the audience is given the impression this family activity might be the norm in their culture. There is a focus on hard work, listening to one another and engaging in an open dialogue. This learning style rejects education that is based on one person transferring information to another for one that is based in dialogue and acknowledges the teacher may also learn from the student. Finally, there is a strong trust of instinct, using heart and passion, something the dancers at Kendall's Studio either lack or ignore. The "banking" concept situates the learner with a kind of permanence in the learning process, there is a "finish-line," flipping this, "affirms men and women as […] unfinished, uncompleted beings in and […] that education be an on-going activity" (Freire, 1996, p. 65). Although Scott has long been considered the best dancer at Kendall's Dance Studio, through these new relationships the pretence that he knows everything is removed; Scott knows he has much to learn and that learning is very much a lifelong journey.

Portrayal of Teachers: Stereotypes

Strictly ballroom (Miall & Luhrmann, 1992) is multi-faceted with many themes, varying plotlines, and a variety of teacher portrayals. Ebert (1993) argues the film has too many storylines that risks the audience losing track, but he contends the over-exuberance still works. The film also displays stereotypes: old-fashioned teachers who see no value in innovation and change, holding onto the past, using guilt and deception as tools to maintain the status quo. The opposing binary are the dreaming revolutionaries; they are a new generation, seeing every possibility, not held back by rules or conventions, looking for teaching and learning in the unlikeliest of places, including in each other. The best examples of the portrayals of stereotypes come in the form of voices-in-the-head moments experienced by Scott throughout the film. The voices of his teachers, Les Kendall and Barry Fife, are ridden with accusation and negativity. Kendall finds fault in Scott's dancing and this plays over in his mind, whilst Fife uses guilt as a form of manipulation to get Scott to dance the regulation steps: "win the Pan Pacifics just once for your dad, he's suffered enough" (Miall & Luhrmann, 1992). In complete contrast, the whispered words he hears in his mind from new mentor, Ya Ya: "listen to the rhythm, don't be scared," (Miall & Luhrmann, 1992) are supportive and encourage Scott to take his revolutionary leap. The "banking" concept drummed into him since childhood attempts to influence his inner thoughts, yet he is ready to listen to Ya Ya for new guidance to break free from his oppression.

Conclusion: Art as a Tool for Change

Prentki (2015) argues applied theatre "is grounded in the premise that the world needs change, can be changed and that the means of making change is human agency" (p. 16). John O'Toole (2015) states that drama in education was first developed for transformational and dialogical purpose and effect (p. 94). We see this human capacity and need for change in the characters of the revolutionaries: Scott, Fran, Doug, Rico, and Ya Ya. Scott's dream to make real change is realized through kindred spirit Fran; dance is the medium in which the change and revolution will occur and becomes symbolic for revolution on a much bigger scale. The film gives the audience a tear-jerking, feel-good ending, and according to Doug, Scott's actions "break a long curse and rights a lot of wrongs" (Miall & Luhrmann, 1992). The emotional support from Doug, Ya Ya, and Rico and then finally the whole dance community is heart-warming. Even Liz Holt, one of Scott's jaded dance partners, sees the importance of supporting Scott and cleverly reconnects the music so that he and Fran can dance. Holt's act of courage shows even the most hesitant of believers – even an oppressor – can be liberated by such an event. Kendall, smiling through happy tears, finally sees why Scott so desperately wanted to dance his own steps; Kendall is another oppressor liberated. The stereotypical binary concept of teacher equals bad and student equals good is also broken. It is clear that Kendall wants what is best for Scott and is genuinely happy and proud for the courage he has taken. Possibly the most powerful message in the film is that the true "teacher" is always the learner themself. Good mentors do not spoon-feed their learners, rather they encourage learners to draw on intuition, passion, to learn through action, and to build on previous experiences. As the final dance draws to an end, President Fife falls down (no push required) knocking over an entire table of trophies and awards: tradition is crumbling in the face of revolution. Fife's empire is ruined, but perhaps in that moment, he too is liberated from the oppression (Freire, 1996). His look of resignation is perhaps realization that his ruling period has ended. I like to believe that Scott and Fran lead their community to a new world of dance, where there are no rules, where creativity is a place for innovation, genuine passion, and independent thought.

REFERENCES

Balfour, M. (2016). The art of facilitation: "Tain't what you so (it's the way that you do it)." In S. Preston (Ed.), *Applied theatre: Facilitation: Pedagogies, practices, resilience* (pp. 151–164). London: Bloomsbury Methuen Drama.

Balfour, M., Bundy, P., Burton, B., Dunn, J., & Woodrow, N. (2015). *Applied theatre: Resettlement*. London: Bloomsbury Methuen Drama.

Bennett, S. (2015, January 14). 20 things you didn't know about *Strictly ballroom*. *Herald-Sun*. Retrieved from http://www.heraldsun.com.au/entertainment/arts/20-things-you-didnt-know-about-strictly-ballroom/news-story/5dbd35c286ee03264dcdbb298bb7cce1

Bolton, G. (1999). *Acting in classroom drama: A critical analysis*. Stoke on Trent: University of Central England.

Ebert, R. (1993, February 26). *Strictly ballroom*. Retrieved from http://www.rogerebert.com/reviews/strictly-ballroom-1993

Freire, P. (1996). *Pedagogy of the oppressed*. London: Penguin.

Heathcote, D. (1984). *Dorothy Heathcote: Collected writings on education and drama* (L. Johnson, & C. O'Neill, Eds.). London: Hutchinson.

Miall, T. (Producer), & Luhrmann, B. (Director). (1992). *Strictly ballroom* [Motion picture]. Australia: M&A Productions.

National Advisory Committee on Creative and Cultural Education (NACCC). (1999). *All our futures: Creativity, culture and education*. London: DFEE.

National Council of Teachers of English (NCTE). (2014). *How standardized tests shape – and limit – student learning: A policy research brief*. Retrieved from http://www.ncte.org/library/NCTEFiles/Resources/Journals/CC/0242-nov2014/CC0242PolicyStandardized.pdf

Prentki, T. (2012). *The fool in European theatre: Stages of folly.* New York, NY: Palgrave Macmillan.

Prentki, T. (2015). *Applied theatre: Theatre for development.* New York, NY: Bloomsbury Methuen Drama.

Preston, S. (2016). *Applied theatre: Facilitation: Pedagogies, practices, resilience.* London: Bloomsbury Methuen Drama.

O'Toole, J., Yi-Ma, A., Baldwin, A., Cahill, H., & Chinyowa, K. (2015). Capacity building theatre (and vice versa). In T. Prentki (Ed.), *Applied theatre: Theatre for development* (pp. 93–134). London: Bloomsbury Methuen Drama.

NOTE

1. Dorothy Heathcote developed many drama teaching style in the 1950s and 1960s that are still in regular usage with practicing teachers today. Heathcote's "teacher-in-role" provided the teacher the opportunity to take on roles or characters within improvised play with her learners. The students, in turn, would improvise alongside her to create unscripted classroom drama. "The teacher-in-role's function is that of *dramatist*, a dramatist who not only is supplying the words but also the accompanying non-verbal signals, so that the 'reading' required of the pupils is multi-dimensional. As dramatist the teacher is dictating at both structural and thematic levels" (in Bolton, 1999, p. 184). The role-playing experience might last for several hours, or run over many weeks of meeting and allow the class to explore a world outside their own understanding.

Good Teacher/*Bad Teacher*... Is That All We Are?

Patricia Jagger

Russell: What went so wrong in your life that you ended up educating children?
Elizabeth: I don't know. Maybe I was a bad person in another life.

– *Bad teacher* (Eisenberg & Kasdan, 2011)

Introduction

Teachers have always confounded me. Perhaps what is even more confounding is that I became one myself. My memories of schooling are filled with a bizarre cast of characters who, quite honestly all seemed like exaggerated caricatures: the World Literature teacher with overly large glasses who would spend classes obsessing over Shakespeare's identity; the Math teacher who had a different cardigan for each day of the week and liked to throw chalk at students who were sleeping; the "evil" English teacher who would lock me out of her classroom for regularly arriving late to her first period class; the handsome teacher (who remembers what he taught?) who elicited nervous giggles as he walked past and was rumoured (unsubstantiated to this day) to be in a relationship with a former student – the list could go on and on. Today, through my lens of teacher and adult, I look back on these people who educated me, who I now recognize were doing their best to meet their students' needs, and whose identities are all still framed within the view of my teenage memories as either a "good teacher" or "bad teacher." They will always endure in my mind as remnants of their most quirky or outlandish personality traits. The intricacies of who they were, beyond my vision of them – details as simple as their first names or the more complex nuances of their interpersonal relationships, were of little interest or consequence to me, and are barely a glimmer in my fading memory.

Today, as a practising teacher both in a K-12 system and in a pre-service teacher education programme, my experiences have brought me to a space of what Greene (1995) refers to as "wide-awakeness," reminding me that I am always in the process of *becoming teacher*. Or, as Ng-A-Fook (2015) states, "I am forever on my way. [And that] my identity has to be perceived as multiple, [if I am to] strive towards some coherent notion of what is humane and decent and just" (p. 1), within my classroom, the world, and myself. Out of this awareness, I have come to a new understanding of the complexity of teachers' lives. I have also had moments of *deja-vu*, where the overly exaggerated teacher identities I remember from my youth have come to life in my colleagues, and if I am honest, in myself as well. Amid this new understanding lies the emergence of a recursive awareness that teaching identities, including my own, are "always worked out and performed as a manifestation" (Stillwaggon, 2008, p. 68) of the roles assigned by those we are serving – students, parents, administrators, policy-makers, often leading teachers to ignore personal needs and wants to meet the demands of the professional spaces they inhabit. Britzman (2006) reminds us that because our teaching selves "are affected by the worlds we try to affect; our sense of identity may telegraph this human condition" (p. xi). In working so closely with our students, often in the shadow of our own schooling experiences, and amid the pressures of policies and practices, educators often live in the borderlands (Alsup, 2006). This negotiation of the complex in-between space between personal and professional, between the fixed identity of student and/or of teacher, calls on teachers to be continuously reflective in their pedagogy, even when confronted with moments of discontent and unease. One must decipher a way to dwell in these borderland spaces, navigating the challenges experienced in the process of *becoming teacher*, in which the extremes of teacher identity are discovered, performed, observed, interpreted, and then re-enacted in both in life and in film and pop culture representations.

There are an endless array of films that take up the image of teachers as preternaturally gifted heroes, who possess the ability to reach out and impact the lives of the most disenfranchised and disengaged student. But I see value in examining the less flattering representations that exist, at times making us cringe, daring us to confront why these caricatured narratives exist, both on the screen and in our own stories of schooling. For this, I turn to Eisenberg and Kasdan's 2011 film, *Bad teacher*, through which audiences are introduced to a variety of corrupt, confused, and far from traditional teaching characters, in what is both "subversive and progressive film" (Gwynne, 2017, p. 130) that uses satire to explore the complex world teachers inhabit.

The Context of Bad Teacher

Bad teacher (Eisenberg & Kasdan, 2011) was filmed and set in Chicago during the early 2000s when initiatives like Teach for America, an alternative-certification programme, were at their height of popularity. Teach for America was established due to teacher shortages across the United States. As a result, it was increasingly common for American "teachers" to enter the classroom without ever having taken a class on pedagogy, curriculum, or assessment. Programs such as Teach for America placed individuals in a classroom straight out of college where they are mentored "on the job" in some of the most complex, diverse urban settings in the United States (White, 2016). Within this programme, new/emergent teachers were and still are expected to enter the classroom prepared, accountable, and able to tackle the demands of teaching, taking on all the pressures of the role. This illustrates a complex dichotomy that is found throughout discourse on teaching. Teachers are deemed by society, on the one hand, as holding one of the most important jobs as they are "significant figure[s] [...] having considerable influence; viewed as central to a student's academic achievement" (Watkins, 2008, p. 115), who ultimately contribute to the development of future generations. On the other hand, public discourse around teachers often derides them as being lazy, working short days with plentiful holiday breaks, and willing to sit on the laurels of comfy pension plans and tenured positions.

One tends to develop the "teacher face" (a mask of protection) when forced to live within this binary view of teaching, overwhelmed by the challenges and daily defeats elicited by the demand to meet the needs of every student, while at the same time sacrificing endless hours of personal time planning, assessing, and seeking new ways to improve practice under the surveillance and scrutiny of policy-makers, parents, and communities. This can result in fixed, constructed identities that Roy (2003) states "are the product of an 'arborescent model' of thought, a proud tree model of hierarchic representation that replicates the established order. I am a teacher because the statute book has laid down the model of a teacher and I am a replica of that model" (p. 196). Deleuze and Guattari challenge this formation of fixed, constructed identities, reframing by telling us that "there are no stable entities, only dynamic states – singularities – that combine and recombine and are drawn into temporary assemblages" (Roy, 2003, p. 51). However, this proves to be a challenging realization, particularly for emergent teachers who have passion for the subject that they hope to be able to impart, and are deeply invested in idealistic assumptions around the influence they will have on their students. What they have yet to realize is they are entering a profession largely impacted by what Biesta (2015) refers to as "learnification" that "encompasses the impact of the rise of a 'new language of learning in education'" (p. 76), focused around a neo-liberal model built largely around the economization of education (Spring, 2015). This language is challenging for both new teachers and seasoned teachers, who are subject to adapting to a "number of discursive shifts, such as the tendency to refer to pupils, students, children, and even adults as 'learners, to redefine teaching as 'facilitating learning,' 'creating opportunities,' or 'delivering learning experiences'" (Biesta, 2015, p. 76). As Webb (2015) points out the education system functions within the patriarchal capitalist system wherein identities are very much governed by a gender binary placing the teaching body in a feminine space and education policy in a masculine one. Binary distinctions extend even further though, as teachers are often placed in contentious, oppositional spaces through the various pressures and forces acting upon them. Smith (2014) refers to this as a "schizoid situation" situating teachers in conflicting public and professional spaces dictating that, "in public I need to be tough, self-interested, competitive, and paranoid while in my family, school, classroom I must shed all this and become sweet, gentle, accommodating, generous, and supportive of others" (p. 19). As Gwynne (2017) notes, in popular culture the ideal teacher "celebrates the power of the individual, rather than the students, in order to effect change; it is a teacher-centered model of education that positions the teacher as a saint, refusing to acknowledge students' potential for autonomy or self-directed learning" (p. 124). *Bad teacher* (Eisenberg & Kasdan, 2011) draws on these dichotomies, satirizing the role of teacher while also making subtle references to pressures they are confronted with, such as the importance of students performing well on standardized tests and pressure from parents for their children to excel.

Funny, Subversive, or Both: The Portrayal of a "Bad Teacher"

The lead character in the film is Elizabeth Halsey, a middle-school teacher who is quickly revealed to possess a variety of personality traits that stand in stark contradiction to those traditionally assigned to the image of the good and noble educator. While promoting the film, actress and comedian Cameron Diaz stated, "Elizabeth believes she doesn't belong at that school. She wants nothing to do with being a teacher [...]. She doesn't *desire* to be there and she doesn't pretend to want to be there" (ScreenJunkies, 2011). This is evident in her portrayal of Elizabeth, who, by all professional and ethical standards, is indeed a very "bad" teacher. She is self-absorbed, narcissistic, apathetic, crass, and generally disinterested in her students and colleagues. She smokes pot in the parking lot, sleeps during class, teaches exclusively through showing movies (often depicting portrayals of "good" teachers), and is openly antagonistic towards those who cross her path. When we meet Elizabeth, she is forced to continue her teaching career after her wealthy fiancé breaks up with her for being a golddigger. Intent on escaping the classroom, she sets her sights on a wealthy substitute teacher, Scott, competes with her nemesis Amy Squirrel for his attention, and rebuffs the advances of the gym teacher, Russell. Deciding that the way to win him his through getting breast implants, Elizabeth makes it her mission to raise the money, get her man, and leave the teaching profession behind.

As Beck (2012) states "the image of this bad teacher reflects the most negative stereotype of teachers in general. She displays all the most resented features of the popular imagination of what is wrong with teachers" (p. 91). *Bad teacher* (Eisenberg & Kasdan, 2011) can be interpreted as expressing hostility and suspicion towards teachers, leaving them open as targets of anger over times of uncertainty and economic hardship, scapegoating schoolteachers as "the visible agents of the official dissemination of [the] bitter pills for the true believers" (Beck, 2012, p. 92) of a more traditional society. While this depiction of a teacher can be read as trivial and disrespectful, I have lived and worked within the complex world of teaching today. Watching this film provoked a deeper analysis of my own queries around what it means to *desire* being a teacher. Additionally, as a teacher educator it brings insight to the challenges confronted by emergent teachers who are struggling to reach a personal level of self-actualization amidst the complex micropolitical environments in schools (Alsup, 2006; Uitto, Kaunisto, Syrjälä, & Estola, 2015). After repeated views, there lies a recognition that while Elizabeth's behaviour is abhorrent, it offers an opening to a conversation around increasing pressures on teachers and the subsequent impact on the desire for being/becoming a teacher during a time in which the "idealization of teaching as human profession par excellence" (Stillwaggon, 2008, p. 67) dominates educational spaces.

Bad Teacher/Good Teacher

The world of education in which Elizabeth Halsey and her counterparts live and work is unimaginable in the real teaching world. As Beck (2012) notes:

> This bad teacher's world has no dangers of job loss or down-sizing, no rescinded pay raises, no threat of physical violence, no students who do not speak English or any language known to the teacher, no mainstreamed students with special needs [...], no whimsical changes of curriculum from school boards or state legislators, no resentful students or hostile parents [...] no sexual harassment, and seems untroubled by sexual scandals with students or accusations of scandalous conduct [...]. Finally, and most startling, there is no criticism or penalty for being a bad teacher.
> (p. 91)

One does not have to watch many films about teachers to realize that "the bad teacher in the movies is generally presented as a counterpoint to the good teacher lionized on celluloid or as a potential foil for a band of teenagers" (Dalton, 2013, p. 80). Elizabeth breaks this convention as she is neither a supporting character or placed in the narrative as a "foil," rather hers is the main story of the movie and all other characters – both students and colleagues, are secondary. Additionally, she is a stark contrast to the various teaching heroes we are used to seeing "echoed in the imaginative world of pop culture," where the "teacher has been a reliable main character, whose ultimate victory is approved by the audience, with satisfaction and hope" (Beck, 2012, p. 91). Through these representations a saviour-like teacher figure is fostered, an agent of change who will provide wisdom and support for struggling students, parents, or communities. This is not the only convention of the teacher film that *Bad teacher* (Eisenberg & Kasdan, 2011) subverts: it is "unrepentantly unapologetic in foregrounding the positive sexual potency of Elizabeth's body, presented as unruly, abrasive, and chaotic, erotically charged and disruptive to the safe and nurturing pedagogical space" (Gwynne, 2017, p. 126). The film also starts at the end of a school year rather than at the beginning; the protagonist is not, as is usually the case, a new member to a disgruntled and struggling staff.

In contrast to Elizabeth, who embodies all that is assigned to the assemblage of a "bad" teacher, one must ask what, and who, defines a "good" teacher. Is it the over-eager Miss Squirrel, Elizabeth's nemesis in the film, who reports back to the principal any sign of Elizabeth not wearing her "teacher hat?" Or is it Elizabeth's suitor, Russell – the sarcastic gym teacher who is the least exaggerated of the characters, yet in many instances the only one who makes authentic connections with students within the school environment? Perhaps it is the object of Elizabeth's affection, the stereotypical "cute substitute," Scott Delacorte, who, despite coming from a wealthy and influential family, is pursuing the life of a teacher out of an inflated sense of altruism. It certainly is not Principal Wally Snur, the dolphin-obsessed, daft administrator, who, like many principals portrayed on film, is relatively clueless about both his staff and students. Realistically, none of the teachers portrayed instil great confidence and it would be easy to assume an attitude of anger at the derelict and disrespectful ways in which all the teachers in the film behave.

A Tale of Resistance

Upon closer analysis, and true to its genre of satire, the character of Elizabeth is not the only "bad" teacher in the film. A scattered array of dysfunctional characters with few portrayals depicting positive representations of teachers in this movie begs the question: how does it contribute to a meaningful and productive conversation about teacher identity? Similar to my own caricatured recollections of former teachers, the teachers in the film: Elizabeth, Scott, Wally, Amy Squirrel, and even the timid Lynn, represent negative stereotypes of the teaching profession. Building upon this acknowledgement, I would argue that while the characterizations are exaggerated and caricature-like, *Bad teacher* (Eisenberg & Kasdan, 2011) is a narrative in which portrayals of teachers move beyond the machine-like system, stand against the dominant opinions and identities imposed on teachers by policies and procedures that dictate "who they should be, what they are to do and say, and when and how they must do or say it" (Cormack & Comber, 1996 cited in Mercieca, 2012, p. 49). The satire in *Bad teacher* offers a portrayal of what happens to teachers mired in a system that denies them the opportunity to reach a place of self-actualization because "they feel overwhelmed with educational discourse that disregards their individuality and expertise" (Alsup, 2006, p. xiii). With the offer of a large bonus offered to the educator whose students achieve the highest scores on the year-end standardized exams, we watch as Elizabeth and Ms. Squirrel engage in competitive race to see who can be the *master teacher*. Driven by vastly different agendas, Elizabeth's being to fundraise for her plastic surgery and Amy's to be the best and favourite teacher, we see similar dynamics playing out between these teachers and their students.

Elizabeth Halsey and her colleagues embody the "extremes of identity available to a teacher as the 'disciplinarian' and the 'pervert' – the former concerned with the maintenance of tradition, often at the expense of relating to students" (Stillwaggon, 2008. p. 71). Elizabeth can be read as a representation of the potentialities seen when the teacher rejects the overbearing weight of accountability, in turn making students responsible for their own learning. She rejects the undefinable call to teachers to always do *what's best for students*. Through my time in the classroom, the rhetoric of building meaningful relationships was repeatedly impressed on teachers at staff meetings and through professional development. However, what is often left out of the conversation is the ways in which students have internalized the educational system and often arrive in classrooms with predetermined motivations. In the film, Elizabeth strives to reach out to a student, advising her to not let her parents predetermine her life path for her, inviting her to think about what she might want to become. The student responds with the question, "Will I get extra credit for it?" In that vital moment, a reductive question symbolizes the moments of heartbreak and disconnect that can lead to teachers giving up on their once closely held beliefs that they can be the teacher they are used to seeing in the cinema.

Elizabeth Halsey emerges (ironically) as our hero, despite contradicting the traditional school teacher narrative. This narrative is meant to include acts of heroism and sacrifice, where the protagonist is compensated for a failed social life through the glory of service to students and community, ultimately defining teachers as "agents of rationality, scholarship, and inclusiveness in addressing social issues" (Beck, 2012, p. 89). At the beginning of the film, "teaching is not a passion, but rather a consequence of circumstance" (Gwynne, 2017, p. 125) from which Elizabeth is determined to escape. Through her interactions with her students and colleagues, Elizabeth demonstrates that there is more than one way to effectively teach, reflecting that teacher identities can and should be multiple, made up of many layers and having numerous connections, and where endless 'and, and, and' allows for various possibilities" (Mercieca, 2012, p. 43). This is demonstrated through her relationship with Garrett, the geeky young man who she aids in getting the attention of popular girl in class, and Sasha, the overzealous student who learns that there is more to life than getting straight As.

Conclusion

Through examining the portrayals of teachers in *Bad teacher* (Eisenberg & Kasdan, 2011), and the ways in which the characters behave, particularly in the rivalry between Elizabeth and Amy, there emerges a recognition of the lack of interconnections within a system that places teachers in competitive, prescribed spaces of accountability. The idea of a "master teacher" thrives in contexts where personal desires have been stripped away, or at the very least lost within the "abstract machine that captures the multidimensional and polyvocal flows of possibility forc[ing] them into one dimensionality and univocity" (Thompson & Cook, 2012, p. 381). *Bad teacher* (Eisenberg & Kasdan, 2011) subverts this, offering a counter-narrative of possibility for teachers to explore multiple identities, many of which result in more meaningful relationships with their students and a recognition of their own identities as emotional beings.

Through "exploring education as a process deeply rooted in the whole human experience – emotion, thought, knowledge, body and intra-actions with the rest of the world" (Kidd, 2015, p. 33) there lies the possibility of moving beyond the pressures of policy, procedures, prescribed programs, and standardized tests. This move relocates teaching and learning into a space where teachers are empowered to acknowledge their own existence as complex, multilayered beings who are able to find agency within the rigid system in which they are expected to survive. Whether the vacuous Elizabeth Halsey ever reaches this level of self-actualization is perhaps too much of a moral lesson to seek from this Hollywood satire. We leave Elizabeth having abandoned her plastic surgery plan, happily dating the gym teacher (who accepts her for who she is) and taking a new role in the school, as the school guidance counsellor. Most importantly, she has re/discovered her desire to teach, having discovered a place of belonging in the school on her own terms. At the end of a long school day that is something to make all teachers smile.

REFERENCES

Alsup, J. (2006). *Teacher identity discourses: Negotiating personal and professional spaces.* Mahwah, NJ: Lawrence Erlbaum.

Beck, B. (2012). The teacher for the black lagoon: Revenge of the bad teacher. *Multicultural Perspectives, 14*(2), 89–92.

Biesta, G. (2015). What is education for? On good education, teacher judgment, and educational professionalism. *European Journal of Education, 50*(1), 76–87.

Britzman, D. P. (2006). Foreword. In J. Alsup (Ed.), *Teacher identity discourses: Negotiating personal and professional spaces* (pp. ix–xii). Mahwah, NJ: Lawrence Erlbaum.

Cormack, P., & Comber, B. (1996). Writing the teacher: The South Australian junior primary English teacher, 1962–1995. In B. Green, & C. Beavis (Eds.), *Teaching the English subjects: Essays on English curriculum history and Australian schooling* (pp. 118–144). Geelong, VIC: Deakin University Press.

Dalton, M. M. (2013). *Bad teacher* is bad for teachers. *Journal of Popular Film & Television, 41*(2), 78–87.

Eisenberg, L. (Producer), & Kasdan, J. (Director). (2011). *Bad teacher* [Motion picture]. USA: Columbia Pictures.

Friesen, G., Meyer. A. (Producers), & Hughes, J. (Director). (1985). *The breakfast club* [Motion picture]. USA: Universal Pictures.

Greene, M. (1995). *Releasing the imagination: Essays on education, the arts and social change.* San Francisco, CA: Jossey-Bass.

Gwynne, J. (2017). Good teachers, bad teachers, and transgressive comedic performance in popular American cinema. In J. A. Chappell, & M. Young (Eds.), *Bad girls and transgressive women in popular television, fiction, and film* (pp. 121–134). Basingstoke, UK: Palgrave Macmillan.

Kidd, D. (2015). *Becoming Mobius: The complex matter of education.* Carmarthen, Wales: Independent Thinking Press.

Mercieca, D. (2012). Becoming-teachers: Desiring students. *Educational Philosophy and Theory, 44*(Supplement 1), 43–56.

Roy, K. (2003). *Teachers in nomadic spaces: Deleuze and curriculum.* New York: Peter Lang.

ScreenJunkies (2011, June 10). Cameron Diaz *Bad teacher* interview [Video file]. Retrieved from https://www.youtube.com/watch?v=dDGCCJSS2eQ

Smith, D. G. (2014). *Teaching as the practice of wisdom.* London: Bloomsbury.

Spring, J. (2015). *The globalization of education: An introduction.* New York, NY: Routledge.

Stillwaggon, J. (2008). Performing for the students: Teaching identity and the pedagogical relationship. *Journal of Philosophy of Education 42*(1), 67–83.

Thompson, G., & Cook, I. (2013). Mapping teacher-faces. *Studies in Philosophy and Education, 32*(4), 379–395.

Uitto, M., Kaunisto, S. L., Syrjälä, L., & Estola, E. (2015). Silenced truths: Relational and emotional dimensions of a beginning teacher's identity as part of the micropolitical context of school. *Scandinavian Journal of Educational Research, 59*(2), 162–176.

Watkins, M. (2008). Teaching bodies/learning desire: Rethinking the role of desire in the pedagogic process. *Pedagogy, Culture, & Society, 16*(2), 113–124.

Webb, P. T. (2015). Fucking teachers. *Deleuze Studies 9*(3), 437–451.

White, T. (2016). Teach For America's paradoxical diversity initiative: Race, policy, and Black teacher displacement in urban schools. *Education Policy Analysis Archives, 24*(16).

PART III

Pedagogies/Pedagogical Moments

O Brave New World? The Role of Arts Education as Presented in *Hunky Dory*

Claire Coleman & Jane Luton

Introduction

Hunky dory (Finn & Evans, 2012) is a light-hearted film set in a comprehensive school in Swansea, Wales during the infamous "heat-wave" of 1976. It focuses upon Vivienne May and her attempts to rehearse and stage an ambitious Bowie infused 1970s rock opera of Shakespeare's *The tempest* (1611/2014) despite hostile teachers, teen angst, and the destruction of the school hall. Its UK release in 2011 coincided with the introduction of the UK government's austerity measures, which made significant cuts to Arts programmes (Higgins, 2011). Recently acknowledged as detrimental, these cuts led to greater educational and cultural impoverishment particularly for the most disadvantaged (Neelands et al., 2015).

This chapter discusses how *Hunky dory* both maintains and subverts the dominant discourses around arts in education. A fable for our times, this film highlights the value, challenges, and complexities of arts education and reflects upon their position within a wider educational context.

Education in Time

Existing simultaneously within the dual time periods of the film (mid-1970s) and its audience (2010s), it provides a rich understanding of the impact of political power upon educational movements. The introduction of comprehensive schools in the United Kingdom heralded a period of experimentation with progressive philosophies, which continued into the late 1970s (Newsom, 1963; Plowden, 1967; Pring, 2014). As 1980 approached, however, the conservatives began preparations for a National curriculum, which would "specify only the basics of English, maths and science" (Wilby, 2013). The subsequent Education Reform Act of 1988 divided schooling into four "key stages" for each core subject and reinserted high levels of testing and accountability (Kipling & Hickey-Moody, 2016). This return to formal standardized learning was solidified in 1992 when the ideals of progressivism were rejected in favour of assessment outcomes (Alexander, Rose, & Woodhead, 1992). Through the early 2000s to 2013 this focus on accountability narrowed the curriculum in the United Kingdom, lessened children's creative confidence and led to a significant decrease in students taking arts subjects in the General Certificate of Secondary Education (GCSE) (Neelands et al., 2015).

Prior to this conservative shift, drama was valued as a space in which to express and experience (Bolton, 2007). Brian Way applied drama as a cross-curricular tool for developing creativity (Taylor, 2000) while Slade focused on drama as pedagogy to foster personal development (Bolton, 1986, 2007; Way, 1967). Dorothy Heathcote gained significant traction for employing drama as mode of inquiry, and despite some detractors, her work remains foundational to educational drama (Dunn, 2016; Heathcote & O'Neill, 2014; Hornbrook, 1991). The reassertion of the conservative party cast a new shadow over arts in the curriculum and the policies of the late 1980s and 1990s eroded much of the earlier progressive work. Drama in the United Kingdom was until recently kept safe within the English curriculum as the discrete study of plays, but still struggles for legitimacy as a stand-alone subject.

Portrayal of a Drama Teacher

Teachers are often considered embodiments of the subjects they teach; portrayals of drama teachers on screen are often less than flattering but hint at shades of truth. Flamboyant drama teacher Mr. G in the fictional Australian parody *Summer heights high* is "the emphatically showbiz drama teacher" (Raeside, 2017). Believing himself at the cutting edge of education, his self-reflections are often misjudged, yet his desire to engage differently with students is instantly recognizable.

As the central character in *Hunky dory*, we are given numerous opportunities to see Viv socializing, organizing, rehearsing, and encouraging her working-class students. Young, beautiful, and carefree, her existence seems idyllic, though her role as the drama teacher is never confirmed. This ambiguity around her professional position corresponds to the ambitious production and its uneasy presence within the school environment. Does she belong in the school or outside of it? This ambiguity enables both her and the production to operate within a shifted physical and pedagogical space. In an early scene she invites the class to tell their own stories "from the heart" and when pressed tells her own – a fairy-tale narrative in which the Princess' dreams came true and "then she woke up one day and realized she wasn't very happy so she went home to teach" . Viv's decision to return to Wales to teach is motivated by genuine passion. However, the implication that she left a successful but unhappy acting career reinforces the mythology of drama teachers as failed actors and teaching as a second option career choice.

Elevating the emotional connection by asking students to name "artists that we love," Viv treats the arts seriously. An outlook, echoed by the film through additional scenes of the students engaging with and being affected by contemporary music, art, drama, and dance. Her ability to fulfill multiple roles as director, choreographer, performer, counsellor, musician, and conductor is both absurd and familiar. This upholds the expectations of the super teacher who produces outstanding productions alone and without support – endorsing either an impossible goal or implying that the arts can and should survive on the strength of one person. Either interpretation reaffirms the arts' lowly status and weakens their position as a powerful media for critical thought and student efficacy (Greene, 1995).

Challenging the didactic expectations of schooling, Viv connects personally with students. She demonstrates the relational behaviour necessary for an arts teacher and creates the trusting and productive relationship essential to effective drama teaching (Cody, 2013). Based on the principles of a democratic learning process, the teacher facilitates rather than imposes learning – remaining open, flexible, and approachable while ensuring a safe working environment (Taylor, 2000; Winston, 1998).

Viv, however, traverses the boundaries of a teacher as we see her getting drunk at the school leavers' dinner, denigrating other teachers, allowing a student into her home, and kissing him. While the ideal relationship between drama teacher and student operates outside the normal school dynamic (Bolton, 1998), Viv's behaviour transgresses – signalling a very real tension, one that exists between the closeness achieved through collaboration and a teacher's professional responsibilities (Cody, 2013).

Teacher stereotypes are also exemplified in Viv's colleagues; Tim the heavy drinking Art teacher and Sylvie the lascivious French teacher further relegate the arts teachers to a position of fictional absurdity. These two-dimensional characters satisfy audiences' expectations of arts teachers as bohemian hipsters, a stigma that plagues the arts today (Ross, 1975). Viv is not the hero of the film, nor is she trying to be a hero; she is, thankfully, neither the obsessed do-gooder nor the desperate spinster.

Having detailed how the drama and arts teachers reflect or contradict dominant views, we will now speak to the representation and treatment of the arts within the film more broadly. Arts in Education has long been maligned and viewed by dominant populations as nice to have, but not academically vital (Ross, 1975). As discussed above, it had greater efficacy in the 1970s, but its positive effects have been eroded since the introduction of National Standards and a return to core subjects. The publications *Culture white paper* (Department for Culture, Media and Sport, 2016) and the Warwick commission report *Enriching Britain: Culture, creativity and growth* (Neelands et al., 2015), both call for greater public support of art and culture and advocate for increased opportunities for young people to engage with the arts.

Presenting the Arts in Education

In our reading, there is dramatic irony in the title *Hunky dory*, a term that suggests that everything is fine in arts education, while the film warns of the precarious location of arts within schooling and curriculum. The film maintains many of the mythologies that keep the arts at the margins of schooling, while hinting at the wider implications of arts practices. As an artwork, the film remains ambiguous in its final position and invites the audience into a space of uncertainty and possibility.

Toeing the line

There are several ways in which *Hunky dory* colludes with the dominant view of the arts as academically unimportant in terms of its status, value, and position. The predictable selection of the PE teachers as adversaries for the arts replicates a common stereotype that pits teachers against one another and draws unhelpful boundaries around subjects. As sexist bullies, PE teacher Cafferty and his "off-sider" or assistant uphold the stereotype of "hard man" masculinity. Established as working class, they show little empathy for students, relishing instead in the power that teaching affords them (Giroux, 1988), though they appear foolish henchmen rather than evil masterminds of a neo-liberal takeover. Despite a similar respect for embodied and active learning, the Drama and PE teachers pitted against one another maintain stereotypical divisions, reducing them to isolated cogs within the institution of the educational machinery.

Noticeably evocative of the future prime minister Margaret Thatcher, Miss Valentine, the social studies teacher, offers a more formidable opponent. She openly opposes Viv, labels the production a waste of time, demonstrates contempt for her students, and is assured in her superiority. Miss Valentine's openly hostile stance towards Viv supports the recent attacks of the New Right to destabilize education, and vilify and deprofessionalize teachers (Giroux, 2013).

Hunky dory unsurprisingly centres on the school production, epitomizing the school drama as the chief responsibility of the drama teacher (O'Connor, 2010). Despite a wealth of literature endorsing the significance of process in drama education, the privileging of performance remains (Greenwood, 2009). As the publicity machine, school productions are prized, whilst classroom drama remains marginalized as a non-academic subject. The film does not portray any drama instruction outside of this production and all the focus is upon creating a successful production. This privileges dominant hegemonic cultural capital as students are charged with meeting the expectations of a white, middle-class theatre audience.

Electing to perform Shakespeare conforms to a historical, culturally determined concept of drama and yet incorporating rock music subverts this. Featuring the music and influences of Bowie and his contemporaries offers a glimpse of hope at how, through playful experimentation, even the cultural capital of the dominant class may be destabilized (Bourdieu, 1993; Doyle, 1982). In the film, magic seems to be sprinkled over the entire production. While rehearsals for *The tempest* (Shakespeare, 1611/2014) are often disrupted, they still happen, almost miraculously. The orchestra is tuneful and self-governing; microphones are not required and everyone can sing. Rehearsals all appear to be held outside of normal school hours and participation is subject to student behaviour and parental approval. Excluded from dedicated curriculum time, students ditch rehearsals for rugby, dates, and swimming, reinforcing drama's lowly status within society. The attitude that the arts are considered by many to be ornamental is further reinforced as Viv pleads and battles for time, students, and financial resources; a battle that continues in schools today (Luton, 2015).

Bucking the trend

Despite familiar stereotypes throughout the film, subtle hints are given at the greater potential of the arts to covertly question dominant ideologies; as Viv declares, "In this hall normal rules don't apply, everything out there forget about it/ explore what you like, ideas, emotion" . In this initial monologue, Viv offers an alternative to the participants' normal world – a creative space. Viv seizes the opportunity to extend her students' learning experiences beyond the classroom and give them a range of new spaces in which to operate (Neelands, 2011). These are ambiguous, unknown worlds in which the students cast in new roles, in new physical, fictional, and relational spaces, play outside the reach of social divisions (Heathcote, Johnson, & O'Neill, 1984; Pammenter, 2013). Her passion and belief in the value of dealing in "human emotions" gains validity as we recognize how viscerally relevant dealing with emotions is to the turbulent lives of her students. Contrasted with the social studies lesson in which they are told scornfully, "You are working class", the arts offer an alternative/third space in which participants may reinvent and explore questions of identity (Heathcote et al., 1984). The arts are presented hopefully, as a location in which students can realize their identities and potentialities beyond the dominant social structures.

As a meta-text the film presents a world based in historical fact but reimagined. As Brecht or Shakespeare might have done, this film shines light on contemporary education and politics through the lens of the 1970s (Willett, 1964). Elements of fact and fiction blend to challenge and unsettle the "history" we remember. This historical and nostalgic tale signals the precarious position of the arts in education today and the curtailing of arts education by a dominant class loyal to maintaining the status quo.

One of the central questions the film raises is: Should the arts be brought into the establishment or left to the fringes? Forced outside by the destruction of the school hall, in the final moments of the film, students sing, dance, play, and recite Shakespeare beneath the stars and amongst the trees. This enhances its aesthetic, endorsing the location of the arts outside the physical and perhaps metaphorical bounds of institutionalized education. As O'Connor (2009) suggests, perhaps remaining on the periphery of schooling is best – ensuring the arts may navigate new spaces liberated from the tyranny of national standards. Entrenched in the trappings of the institution, the headmaster embodies this tension. His internal struggle between the mandate of his officially sanctioned position and his personal ideals is epitomized as he shrugs off his academic regalia and changes into civilian clothes to join rehearsals, revealing his other self.

Political Resonances

"Is she the future?" asks Viv of Miss Valentine, foreshadowing the rise of a prescriptive education system fixated on testing. Miss Valentine is an emissary of the Conservatives' views of education and of its then recently appointed leader, Margaret Thatcher: that education should be utilitarian. The mandate of the Education Reform Act of 1988 that education should prepare pupils for the opportunities, responsibilities, and experiences of adult life reinforced an attitude that situated education in the marketplace as "consumer-oriented" (Benn & Chitty, 1996; Giroux, 2013). Reconceptualizing education as a public good altered the aim of education away from the nurturing of citizens and towards the development of human capital and consumers (Biesta, 2009). Competencies fostered through arts practices; critical thinking, reimagining the world, and developing a strong sense of personal agency were unwelcome within this new world order (McLaren, 2005).

As a nostalgic nod to the past, this film idealizes elements of the 1970s, while hinting at the dark times ahead. The seemingly endless and "idyllic summer" (Newton, 2015) of 1976 is romantically remembered through languid hazy tones, while accurately capturing the era through its wardrobe, fixtures, settings, and pastimes. The skinheads, racism, homophobia, sexism, and palpable class divide are all present though not highlighted. As the credits roll, we are given short biographies of the characters future lives. These fictional "histories" offer a sense of hopeful imaginings. No one goes down the mine, as might be expected, and there is a sense that each individual walked their own path. In this film, Viv and drama made a real difference to these students, spurring them onward to individual choices of their own making. The arts offer hope.

As a cautionary tale for the future, the film warns its characters of the days of the future to come and for the viewer, signals the days of future present. Ironically, depicting Davey's dad, a working-class, single father, in his underpants watching footage of Thatcher wielding her dustpan to "sweep Britain clean of socialism" (Iconic, 2010) foreshadows the ravaging effects of Thatcher's government upon the working-class population (Wilby, 2013).

Burning down the school hall acts as a tangible warning to arts educators operating to challenge the status quo. This act of violence perhaps symbolizing the cuts made to the arts through the austerity measures – removing resources, spaces, and artists from educational spaces (Higgins, 2011; Luton, 2012). Forcing the arts to the margins ensures that only those wealthy enough to indulge have access and opportunity, restricting cultural capital and sustaining class division.

It Feels Like Magic

As exemplified by Davy (Aneurin Barnard), the students of *Hunky dory* possess a remarkable amount of talent. At rehearsals, the self-conducting orchestra is tuneful, and everyone can perform. While the high levels of talent and minimal rehearsals depicted here discount the hard work involved in staging a production, they allow for a satisfying final performance. This is a film, not a documentary. Drama is a condensation of time, it "isn't real life, and it isn't a copy of real life. It's just a point of access" (Catton, 2008, p. 40). As viewers we are willing to suspend our disbelief to imagine what might be possible through the arts. Portraying the arts through the arts invites the audience to imagine "what if" and sustains an upbeat ending to the film. Concerns about realism would seem petty in comparison with the joy of hearing Bowie sung so exquisitely beneath the trees. Unapologetic in its politics, this film offers hope. Hope that acknowledges its context, flaws and unanswered questions. Its protagonists are not defined by their participation in the arts, but perhaps ever so slightly changed by it.

Conclusion

When asked if Miss Valentine is the future of education the headmaster's response: "O brave new world that has such people in it" evokes both *The tempest* (Shakespeare, 1611/2014) and the dystopian science-fiction novel *A brave new world* (Huxley, 1932). Aligned by themes of power, control, and social justice, both texts recognize the potential of the arts to capture and engage with human emotions. *Hunky dory*, though flawed, raises questions about the place of the arts, arts teachers, and the narratives that surround them. Itself an artistic response to austerity, it challenges the inevitability of history repeating itself and invites discourse. Its ending is uncertain. Viv does not bask in the glow of an exalted triumphant ending, but walks away, leaving the students to enjoy their own moment. The arts do not solve everything, nor are they suddenly beloved by all. It is not that straightforward and so, questions remain. Gloriously ambiguous in places, *Hunky dory* is both a reminder and representation of the tenuous, but vital position of arts education.

REFERENCES

Alexander, R., Rose, J., & Woodhead, C. (1992). *Curriculum organisation and classroom practice in primary schools: A discussion paper*. London, UK: Department of Education and Science. Retrieved from http://dera.ioe.ac.uk/id/eprint/4373

Benn, C., & Chitty, C. (1996). *Thirty years on: Is comprehensive education alive and well or struggling to survive?* Michigan, IL: David Fulton Publishers.

Biesta, G. (2009). Good education in an age of measurement: On the need to reconnect with the question of purpose in education. *Educational Assessment, Evaluation and Accountability, 21*(1), 33–46.

Bourdieu, P. (1993). *The field of cultural production: Essays on art and literature*. New York, NY: Columbia University Press.

Bolton, G. (1986). *Selected writings on drama in education*. London, UK: Longman.

Bolton, G. (2007). A history of drama education: A search for substance. In L. Bresler (Ed.), *International handbook of research in arts education* (pp. 45–62). Dordrecht, NL: Springer.

Cody, T-L. (2013). *Drama education in New Zealand schools: The practice of six experienced drama teachers* [Unpublished doctoral dissertation]. University of Canterbury, Christchurch, NZ.

Department for Culture, Media and Sport. (2016). *Culture white paper*. Retrieved From https://www.gov.uk/government/uploads/system/uploads/attachment_data/file/510798/DCMS_The_Culture_White_Paper__3_.pdf

Doyle, C. (1982). *Drama as a critical form of pedagogy* [Unpublished doctoral dissertation]. University of Boston, Boston, MA.

Dunn, J. (2016). Demystifying process drama: Exploring the why, what and how. *NJ, 40*(2), 127–140.

Finn, J. (Producer), & Evans, M. (Director). (2012). *Hunky dory* [Motion picture]. UK: Film Agency for Wales.

Giroux, H. (1988). *Teachers as intellectuals: Toward a critical pedagogy of learning*. Granby, MA: Bergin & Garvey.

Giroux, H. (2013). Neoliberalism's war against teachers in dark times. *Cultural Studies: Cultural Methodologies, 13*(6), 458–468.

Greenwood, J. (2009). Drama education in New Zealand: A coming of age? A conceptualisation of the development and practice of drama in the curriculum as structural improvisation with New Zealand's experience as a case study. *Research in Drama Education: The Journal of Applied Theatre and Performance, 14*(2), 245–260.

Heathcote, D., Johnson, L., & O'Neill, C. (1984). *Dorothy Heathcote: Collected writings on education and drama*. Evanston, IL: Northwestern University Press.

Heathcote, D., & O'Neill, C. (2014). *Dorothy Heathcote on education and drama: Essential writings*. New York, NY: Routledge.

Higgins, C. (2011, March 30). Arts council England funding cuts: The great axe falls. *The Guardian*. Retrieved from https://www.theguardian.com/culture/2011/mar/30/arts-council-england-funding-cuts

Hornbrook, D. (1991). *Education in drama: Casting the dramatic curriculum*. London, UK: Falmer.

Huxley, A. (1932). *Brave new world: A novel*. London, UK: Chatto & Windus.

Iconic. (2010, November 8). Margaret Thatcher giving her speech on brushing socialism from Britain [Video file]. Retrieved from https://www.youtube.com/watch?v=o1W1hAho4mQ

Kipling, A., & Hickey-Moody, A. (2016). The practice of Dorothy Heathcote as a pedagogy of resistance. In A. Hickey-Moody, & T. Page (Eds.), *Arts, pedagogy and cultural resistance: New materialisms* (pp. 59–78). London, UK: Rowman & Littlefield.

Luton, J. (2015). *Playing on the barricades: Embodied reflections on passion and melancholia in drama education by key practitioners* [Unpublished doctoral dissertation]. University of Auckland, Auckland, NZ.

McLaren, P. (2005). *Capitalists and conquerors: A critical pedagogy against the empire*. Lanham, MD: Rowman & Littlefield Publishers.

Neelands, J. (2011). Drama as creative learning. In J. Sefton-Green, P. Thomson, L. Bresler, & K. Jones (Eds.), *Routledge international handbook of creative learning* (pp. 168–176). London, UK: Routledge.

Neelands, J., Belfiore, E., Firth, C., Hart, N., Perrin, L., Brock, S., Holdaway, D., & Woddis, J. (2015). *Enriching Britain: Culture, creativity and growth* (Report by the Warwick Commission on the Future of Cultural Value). Retrieved from http://www2.warwick.ac.uk/research/warwickcommission/futureculture/finalreport/warwick_commission_final_report.pdf

Newsom, J. (1963). *Half our future: A report of the Central Advisory Council for Education*. London, UK: H.M.S.O.

Newton, G. (2015). *Hunky dory: Teaching resource*. Cardiff, UK: Ffilm Cymru Wales. Retrieved from http://learnaboutfilm.com/pdf/HUNKYDORY-ENG.pdf

O'Connor, P. (2009). Remembering horses drawn in the sand: Reflections on drama education on the edge. *NJ: Drama Australia, 33*(1), 19–30.

O'Connor, P. (Ed.). (2010). *Creating democratic citizenship through drama education: The writings of Jonathan Neelands*. Stoke on Trent, UK: Trentham Books.

Pammenter, D. (2013). Theatre as education and a resource of hope: Reflections on the devising of participatory theatre. In A. Jackson, & C. Vine (Eds.), *Learning through theatre: The changing face of theatre in education* (3rd ed., pp. 83–101). New York, NY: Routledge.

Plowden, B. (1967). *Children and their primary schools: A report of the Central Advisory Council of Education*. London, UK: H.M.S.O.

Pring, R. (2014). *John Dewey*. London, UK: Bloomsbury Publishing.

Raeside, J. (2017, April 18). *Summer heights high*: The 10 most Ja'mie-zing moments. *The Guardian*. Retrieved from https://www.theguardian.com/tv-and-radio/2017/apr/18/summer-heights-high-chris-lilley-mr-g-comedy

Ross, M. (1975). *Arts and the adolescent: A curriculum study*. London, UK: Evans Brothers, Methuen Educational.

Shakespeare, W. (2014). *The tempest* (A. T. Vaughan, & V. M. Vaughan, Eds.). London, UK: Bloomsbury. (Original work published 1611)

Taylor, P. (2000). *The drama classroom: Action, reflection, transformation*. London, UK: Routledge Falmer.

Way, B. (1967). *Development through drama*. London, UK: Longmans.

Wilby, P. (2013, April 15). Margaret Thatcher's education legacy is still with us: Driven on by Gove. *The Guardian*. Retrieved from https://www.theguardian.com/education/2013/apr/15/margaret-thatcher-education-legacy-gove

Willett, J. (Ed.) (1964). *Brecht on theatre: The development of an aesthetic*. London, UK: Methuen.

Winston, J. (1998). *Drama, narrative and moral education: Exploring traditional tales in the primary years*. London, UK: Falmer Press.

"You're Not Hardcore (Unless You Live Hardcore)": Exploring Pedagogical Encounters in *School of Rock*

Mitchell McLarnon

Introduction

The purpose of this chapter is to explore and interpret the pedagogical encounters (including the music) in the film *School of rock* (Rudin & Linklater, 2004). I have selected *School of rock* because the protagonist (Dewey) employs a creative and artful approach to teaching while positioning himself as a co-learner and content creator, implicitly demonstrating how teacher and student work can hold educational, social, cultural, and economic value. Dewey's pedagogy and investment in his students offers a portrayal of what twenty-first-century teaching and learning might look like in the context of teacher professional development and pre-service teacher training. The analysis offered in this chapter is not seeking truths or absolutes. I base my inquiry on several observations that I have made as an educator and researcher, combined with conceptual reactions and reflections from watching *School of rock*. My interpretations invite readers to consider how films might influence public discourse on education, and how identity plays a role in pedagogy.

The Plot: School of Rock

In the film *School of rock*, musician Dewey Finn, known for his ten-minute-long guitar solos, has just been kicked out of the band he formed. Upon returning home, Dewey is informed by his friend, roommate, and former bandmate, Ned Schneebly, that he owes several thousand dollars in overdue rent. Ned (and his girlfriend Patti) tells Dewey that unless he can pay what is owed, he will soon be kicked out of his apartment as well. One morning the phone rings and Dewey answers. The principal of Horace Green Elementary, a prestigious local school, is looking for a substitute teacher. Posing as Ned, Dewey accepts the job.

Once arriving at the school, Dewey (acting as Ned) asks the students to call him "Mr. S" and informs them that he is hung over. He then harasses the students for food and goes on a tirade, criticizing the current educational and assessment structures before dismissing the students for recess. The following day, he observes the students in music class and, recognizing their talents, decides to drop the formal curriculum in place of starting a rock band to compete at an upcoming Battle of the Bands. In preparation for the Battle of the Bands, Dewey assigns each student a role within the rock band ranging from band member, to band manager, to lighting specialist, to security guard.

Despite his bizarre and unconventional teaching approach, Dewey slowly gains the trust of his principal, Ms. Mullins. On the eve prior to the Battle of the Bands, there is a parent-teacher meeting at Horace Green Elementary. Many suspicious parents ask Dewey why their children are only talking about rock and roll and not academics. Suddenly, the meeting is interrupted by Ned, Patti, and a police officer who informs everyone (students and parents) that Dewey is not a teacher as Dewey flees the scene. The following day, amongst themselves, the students decide that they want to play the show. They arrive at Dewey's apartment with a bus and head to the competition to play a song that one of the students has written. While Dewey's class does not win the competition, the students understand that their work holds educational, social, cultural, and economic value. There are no criminal charges laid for Dewey's deception, and in the closing credits Dewey and Ned are seen rocking out with the students in what looks like a music class. Throughout the film, Dewey embraces his identity as an artist and his pedagogy shows signs of creativity and co-learning/collaboration.

Current Academic Context

Before analyzing specific scenes from the film, I want to situate the discussion within twenty-first-century teaching and learning. Commenting on current approaches to schooling, Brown, Lauder, and Ashton's (2008) significant literature review recognizes the need for new approaches to K-12 education. While much of popular culture, media, and research speak to the need for reinventing the school, equal attention is given to exploring the role of the teacher (Schrag, 2008). The scholarly trope of the teacher's role is that it is historically, conventionally, and narrowly conceived as information delivery

(Freire, 1970). Many educational theorists have attempted to complicate this (for a short list, see Dewey, 1938; Freire, 1970; Gramsci, 1995; Greene, 1995). While not a novel idea, being perceived as a co-learner is an integral part of shifting the teacher's positioning from a transmitter of information to a public intellectual. Palmer (2009) suggests that a teacher's role also needs to be united with how they identify themselves (e.g., artist, athlete, scientist, or many identities in combination).

This chapter will explore pedagogical and educational impressions in the film *School of rock*. I position Dewey's (Jack Black's character) identity and pedagogy as integral to the analysis, but also examine Dewey's *way of being* a teacher as significant in twenty-first-century learning environments. Contextualized within twenty-first-century teaching and learning and the growth of the digital and creative economies (United Nations, 2010), curricula and educational policies have shifted towards competency-based learning, and terms such as innovation and creativity are ever-present in pre-service teacher training and teacher professional development. Without a fulsome understanding of how to embed innovation and creativity in teaching and learning processes, these concepts risk being devoid of meaning. As such, major curriculum renewals are not likely to meet their broad goals of greater communication, thinking, and personal and social development, unless significant attention is given to reconceptualizing the role of the teacher.

Film Analysis

For the purpose of this chapter, I watched and analyzed the film using a qualitative content (film) analysis approach (Denzin, 2004; Neuendorf, 2002). According to Denzin (2004) qualitative film analysis can be employed to study an assortment of transcripts and social interactions from within a film. Specific to this inquiry, I included musical renderings co-created through student-teacher collaborations in the film in my analysis. Denzin (1989) states that by using films in the research process, further insight can be obtained about "how cultural representations form lived experiences" (p. 37). Examining Dewey's pedagogical approaches through content analysis offers a strong framework for incorporating the musical renderings from the film. I analyzed transcripts from within film from the following perspectives: (a) a "realistic" (Denzin, 2004, pp. 238–240) perspective where the analysis is based on a realistic reading, providing a truthful representation of the film; and (b) a "subversive" (p. 240) perspective, where I disrupt the realistic reading and position my own subjectivities and interpretations within the analysis.

In other words, I will present a transcript from the script of the film, then I will analyze the transcript using applicable concepts. Combining both realistic and subversive modes of construction within qualitative film analysis provides a more holistic representation. Below, I present my interpretation compiled and analyzed both traditionally and poetically.

Realistic Perspective: The Man

The following excerpt takes place early in the film as Dewey, pretending to be Ned, and modelling a bad substitute teacher, is refusing to teach and instead is trying to nap while attempting to dismiss the students for an early recess. In this scene, two students (Summer and Freddy) interact with Dewey as he is still reeling from getting kicked out of his band. Summer continues to press him and says, "My parents don't spend $15,000 a year for recess." Dewey reacts to the provocation and informs the students that there is no point in trying in school or in life because the world is run by "The Man." The students, not understanding his reference to "The Man," ask Dewey for clarification. He begins to rant:

> Oh, you don't know The Man? Well, he's everywhere. In the White House, down the hall. Miss Mullins, she's The Man. And The Man ruined the ozone, and he's burning down the Amazon, and he kidnapped Shamu and put her in a chlorine tank. There used to be a way to stick it to The Man. It was called rock'n roll. But guess what? Oh, no. The Man ruined that too with a little thing called MTV! So don't waste your time trying to make anything cool or pure or awesome. The Man's just gonna call you a fat, washed-up loser and crush your soul. So do yourselves a favor and just give up!

The door opens. Ms. Mullins, the school principal, enters the room as Dewey concludes his tirade on "The Man." She informs Dewey that the students should be on their way to music class. Moments later, Dewey sees the students in music class. Impressed with their abilities, his attitude about teaching appears to change as he decides to start a rock band with the students.

Subversive Conceptions

Teaching and learning are messy processes. Deleuzian theory can offer insight on the messy mundaneness that educators experience daily.

For my analysis of the following scene from *School of rock*, I fuse the Deleuzian encounter (O'Sullivan, 2006) with what Deleuze (1994) writes about pedagogy in *Difference and repetition*. O'Sullivan (2006) explores an array of Deleuze's (1994) and Deleuze and Guattari's (1987) writings and describes the Deleuzian encounter as the breaking of habit, or breaking of a usual *way of being* in the world, or simply responding differently to the world around us. Therefore, the encounter can occur when faced with something that we are unfamiliar with, or, in other words, when faced with what we do not already know. Perhaps such an encounter could be defined as a conflict of identity. O'Sullivan (2006) states that there could be two moments to the encounter: the rupture and the acceptance. While I subscribe to O'Sullivan's (2006) understanding of the encounter, I contend that there are three moments to the encounter, as prior to the rupture, there is often a refusal, or an increase in pressure, that leads to the rupture. Thus, with the Deleuzian encounter, there is a refusal of the unknown. Then there is a rupture, which I argue occurs when one can relate or compare an experience to what is new and unfamiliar. And finally, after the rupture there is the potential for a moment of affirmation: a moment of acceptance. There is the possibility that in some cases there is a non-acceptance. However, to truly encounter something is to say yes to new understandings and possibilities (Deleuze, 1994). While this is one interpretation of the encounter, it can be critiqued for embracing a compartmentalized way of thinking as refusal, rupture, and acceptance (or non-acceptance) indicate specific defined states that are each vastly different. As Deleuze and Guattari (1987) reject binary ways of thinking, I acknowledge that there is space for something more fluid within the processes of refusal, rupture, acceptance, and non-acceptance.

In relation to the scene above, we witness the first moment in Dewey's pedagogical encounter. Before entering the classroom, Dewey's life revolved around music. Music and being an artist were most familiar to him. Teaching was not. Reeling from getting kicked out of his band, Dewey refuses to teach. He also offers a critique of power relations in his rant about "The Man," showing signs that he does not approve of authoritative structures, something with which Deleuze and Guattari would agree. Before he is interrupted by Ms. Mullins entering the room, it appears that Dewey is offering bits of himself to the students. Here, Dewey is subscribing to a form of transmission-based pedagogy, or information delivery; however, the information Dewey is transmitting is not related to the curriculum, but to his own experience and identity, which is familiar to him and much different from the traditional structure of schooling. Soon after, while wandering the school hallways, the pressure builds prior to Dewey's rupture as he watches the students in music class, as teaching and interacting with youth was unknown to him, though music was not. This creates for him an interconnection between what he knows and a new experience.

The following day, Dewey arrives at school with instruments and what appears to be a completely different attitude towards teaching, and towards the students. Still self-serving, his attitude here reflects his interest in using the students to form a band for his own personal benefit and profit. Considering the Deleuzian encounter, here the pressure is increasing before the rupture (O'Sullivan, 2006). Dewey's rupture happens several scenes later as Dewey observes an encounter between a student and his father. During this short interaction, the student (Zach) is being reprimanded by his father. Zach's father is telling Zach that he cannot play music until all his homework is completed. As Dewey watches, perhaps Zach's dad, and his authoritarian tone, embody aspects of "The Man." When class begins several minutes later, Dewey facilitates a discussion on the purpose of rock and roll and encourages the students to "stick it to The Man." After Dewey's rupture is the acceptance and affirmation in *becoming* pedagogical as Dewey embraces his role as a teacher while maintaining his identity as an artist. As the film progresses, Dewey's pedagogy shifts as he begins to work collaboratively and alongside his students to prepare for the upcoming Battle of the Bands.

According to Deleuze (1994), teaching is about enabling a *moving with* (Davies & Gannon, 2001). "We learn nothing from those who say do as I do;" we learn from those who say, "do with me" (Deleuze, 1994, p. 23). Learning, teaching, and working with students are movements in relation. Within these movements, the diverse and dissimilar develop in the interaction between sign and response, creating the potential for intimacy and intensity in the encounter. This is a process of becoming. In a Deleuzian pedagogical model, it is paramount to find ways for teachers to expand their capacity for moving with learners: for shifting roles or moving fluidly between being a teacher and being a learner, and vice versa. What forces teachers to think creatively and move beyond the boundaries of education and our current habitual thought is a "fundamental encounter" (p. 134). At the centre of the encounter is an openness to the prospective influence of the "degrees of power which combine, to […] correspond [with] a power to affect and be affected, active or passive effects, [and] intensities" (Deleuze & Parnet, 2002, p. 92).

During the film, as the students take on roles within the band, Dewey (embracing his identity as an artist while appointing himself as band leader) is forced to relinquish power and to negotiate the power structures of the classroom and creative control of the band. For example, in the early formation of the class rock and roll band, Dewey proposes that the class sing a song he has composed for the upcoming Battle of the

Bands. As he performs his song for his students, he outlines his disagreements with his former band. In this song, he sings to the students about his own identity as an artist, and states that "You're not hardcore, unless you live hardcore," a message that the students seem to take seriously. Closer to the competition, the lead guitarist from the class, Zach, tells Dewey that he has written a song. As Dewey listens to Zach's lyrics, he moves with Zach, acting as co-learner. Here, in these movements in relation, both Dewey and Zach are in a state of becoming. In the intimacy of this encounter, Dewey realizes that Zach's work is equally valuable. Rather than stick to the original song, Dewey encourages the class to embrace the work of their fellow student. As Deleuze (1994) states, moving with and fluidly through the encounter, new theoretical spaces open for "discovering [and] opening new possibilities of life" (p. 101). The lyrics of Zach's song discuss the structure and approach to traditional education and demonstrate the possibilities of the encounter through co-learning. Both verses begin with a response and a critique to the traditional and compliant approach to school that leaves students "in a dumb daze [...and] hypnotized" and "rais[ing] my hand before I could speak my mind." Referring to Dewey as the magic man, Zach tells us that since Dewey arrived, he has been more awake and engaged in school. Furthermore, before the end of the second verse, Zach comments on Dewey's approach to co-learning: "And then that magic man said to obey... do what magic man do, not what magic man say."

To extend Zach's song, and considering Deleuze (1994), I also represent my analysis poetically:

---

do we need an education?
hegemony, testing, socialization. we want innovation and co-creation, aesthetically addressing thought domination.
education is more than the economy. there's hate, inequity, and no autonomy.
it's time to move beyond Reading, wRiting and aRithmetic: discrete competencies make us sick.
let's focus on our hand, head and heart, or what's the point of being smart?
we need stand up to capitalism, racism, sexism and neo-liberalism and require creative, solution oriented people who understand pluralism.
or why learn the rules to the game?... because these rules often change.

So What?

It is important to note that much of Deleuze's (1994; Deleuze & Guattari, 1987) work does not seek conclusions and as such, neither will I. Instead, my analysis recognizes that "theory is no longer an abstract but rather an embodied living inquiry, an interstitial relational space for creating teaching and learning" (Irwin et al., 2006, p. 72). It is my hope that this film analysis helps to interrupt and challenge traditionally understood approaches to teaching and learning, while emphasizing interconnections and the importance of expanding the teacher's role using creativity and embracing one's own identity. In Dewey's case, his identity as a musician strengthened his pedagogy.

Using films as part of the inquiry process could help pre-service and in-service teachers understand how popular culture can influence lived experience and how films can represent societal expectations. Seeing Dewey's transformation on screen can help teachers re-consider their *ways of being* in the classroom. The exploration of the teacher's role using scenes and music from *School of rock* might allow teachers to: 1) understand how popular culture can form lived experience; 2) integrate co-learning and co-creation alongside their students, demonstrating that school work can hold educational, cultural, social, and economic value; 3) use research to inform pedagogy, which can draw greater links between teachers who are creators of content in their respective areas of expertise (e.g., music, photography, dance, etc.) and their teaching approaches; and 4) familiarize themselves with processes of knowledge creation enabling teachers to implement emerging pedagogical theories into their practice.

Increasingly, educational trends in western nations create teachers, schools, and curricula that attempt to treat all students *equally*. The form of equality employed in today's schooling compounded with the need for preparing students for the job market has promoted approaches like standardized testing, which require more memorization and less creativity. Educational philosopher and advocate for the arts Maxine Greene (1995) states that, "we are all the same, that is, human, in such a way that nobody is ever the same as anyone else who ever lives, lived, or will live" (p. 156). By treating everyone the same and expecting standardized results, educational stakeholders are making a judgment on what is best for students, which appears to be based on society's understanding of *what is right* (Beames & Brown, 2016). Yet, the major challenges of our era (such as climate change, conflict, public health, poverty, and so on) demand creative solutions that will not come from students who have simply learned how to memorize content for a test. Society needs people who have been educated to address sociocultural and sociopolitical issues, which will involve engaging with complex interpersonal relationships within diverse groups of people. The way Dewey employs pedagogy in the film permits the types of interactions suggested above. With increasing global issues to resolve, and in working alongside students, we need a rupture from memorization, while affirming more critical and creative thinking. In other words, it is not productive to learn the rules of the game when the game keeps changing. Teachers and learners need to be autonomous and creative thinkers, not information deliverers and test-takers.

REFERENCES

Beames, S., & Brown, M. (2016). *Adventurous learning: A pedagogy for a changing world.* New York, NY: Routledge.

Brown, P., Lauder, H., & Ashton, D. (2008). Education, globalisation and the future of the knowledge economy. *European Educational Research Journal, 7*(2), 131–156.

Davies, B., & Gannon, S. (Eds.). (2009). *Pedagogical encounters* (Vol. 33). New York, NY: Peter Lang.

Deleuze, G. (1994). *Difference and repetition* (P. Patton, Trans.). New York, NY: Columbia University Press.

Deleuze, G., & Guattari, F. (1987). *A thousand plateaus: Capitalism and schizophrenia* (B. Massumi, Trans.). Minnesota, MN: University of Minnesota Press.

Deleuze, G., & Parnet, C. (2002). *Dialogues II* (H. Tomlinson, & B. Habberjam, Trans.). London, UK: Continuum.

Denzin, N. K. (1989). Reading the tender mercies: Two interpretations. *Sociology Quarterly, 30*(1), 1–19.

Denzin, N. K. (2004). Reading film: Using films and videos as empirical social science material. In U. Flick, E. von Kardorff, & I. Steinke (Eds.), *A companion to qualitative research* (pp. 237–242). London: Sage.

Dewey, J. (1938). *Experience and education.* New York, NY: Kappa Delta Pi.

Dimitriados, G., & Kamberlin, G. (2006). *Theory for education.* New York, NY: Taylor & Francis.

Freire, P. (1970). *Pedagogy of the oppressed.* New York: Continuum.

Gramsci, A. (1995). *Further selections from the prison notebooks.* Minneapolis, MN: University of Minnesota Press.

Greene, M. (1995). *Releasing the imagination: Essays on education, the arts, and social change.* San Francisco, CA: Jossey-Bass.

Irwin, R. L., Beer, R., Springgay, S., Grauer, K., Xioung, G., & Bickel, B. (2006). The rhizomatic relations of a/r/tography. *Studies in Art Education, 48*(1), 70–88.

Neuendorf, K. A. (2002). *The content analysis guidebook.* New York, NY: Sage.

O'Sullivan, S. (2006). *Art encounters Deleuze and Guattari: Thought beyond representation.* New York, NY: Springer.

Palmer, P. J. (2009). *The courage to teach: Exploring the inner landscape of a teacher's life*. San Francisco, CA: John Wiley & Sons.

Rudin, S. (Producer), & Linklater, R. (Director). (2004). *School of rock* (Motion picture). USA: Paramount Pictures.

Schrag, F. (2008). The school is the problem, not the solution. *Theory and Research in Education, 6*(3), 283–307.

United Nations. (2010). *Creative economy report 2010: Creative economy – A feasible development option*. Retrieved from http://unctad.org/en/Docs/ditctab20103_en.pdfh

Harry Potter and the Order of the Phoenix: A Pedagogy of Misdirection

Matthew Krehl Edward Thomas & Bernadette Walker-Gibbs

Introduction

This chapter interrogates the role of government intervention in schooling as it manifests in educational performativity and as a disconnect between policy and the routines, rituals, and realities of those who experience education as a dystopic pedagogy of misdirection. Under such misdirection, the realities of schooling are constructed by those in authority and imposed on those with little or no power. In educational contexts, teachers become impelled to raise standards, but their work practices only serve to reify neo-liberal established practices of performativity and surveillance, leaving the students subservient to the whims of changing policy agendas.

The fifth instalment of the Harry Potter heptology, *The Order of the Phoenix* (Barron, Heyman, & Yates, 2007), frames a "Potterian world" (Levy & Snir, 2017, p. 3) in which a surly Harry Potter returns to his school, Hogwarts, at a time when the governmental regulatory body – the Ministry of Magic – exerts significant influence. This marks a departure for the young witches and wizards whose educative place in a larger schemata is yet to be fully realized, whilst previously their curricula had been divergent (Helfenbein & Brown, 2008).

Throughout the film, the viewer witnesses the encroaching Ministry of Magic, and the interplay of performativity in education (Rasmussen, Gustafsson, & Jeffrey, 2014) belies a cumulative effect on the identities of teachers and students. Perplexingly, the iterative influence of the Ministry is rarely addressed. Instead, through a sloth-like dislocation of "research, policy and practice" (Mason, 2013, p. 228), the Ministry enforces a version of social order mirroring our own world (Gabbard, 2010). Set as a backdrop to when rhetoric punctures a place between belief and acceptance by interrogating mass-mediated understandings of dominant discourses and cast in a time when emotion trumps reason (Nichols, 2017), the school is a marketplace (Campbell, Proctor, & Sherington, 2009) and students' choice is a misnomer (Gaztambide-Fernández & Parekh, 2017); this is troubling indeed.

In the following sections, we create assemblages of simulacra, simulation, and hyperreality (Baudrillard, 1994b) to examine the complex social conditions that comprise the wizarding world in *The Order of the Phoenix* (Barron et al., 2007). We deploy Baudrillard to illustrate possibilities for the ways in which meanings forge a "plastic surgery of the social" (Baudrillard, 2008, p. 38) that serve to break apart both the complex and oppressive qualities of schools to understand the inter-imbricated nature of Hogwarts as both positioned and positioning in turbulent times.

Simulacrum and Simulation

At the dawn of the film, the viewer is orientated to the notion that change is afoot at Hogwarts. This occurs through the replicating effect of a series of simulacrums "never exchanged for the real, but exchanged for [real] itself, in an uninterrupted circuit without reference or circumference"(Baudrillard, 1994b, p. 6). From the earliest student welcome, we are introduced to the puppet headmaster, the Ministry's saccharine Delores Umbridge, who by directly addressing the student body signals a break with tradition; as Hermione notes "the Ministry is interfering at Hogwarts." Whilst we may take umbrage with Umbridge's assertion of the righteousness of the Ministry's role as the arbiter of social order in the wizarding community, we are nevertheless propelled to pay attention to a new, harsher reality of bureaucratic overreach within the schooling community of Hogwarts. Under such a guise, "rules are paramount, questions are ignored and theory is more age-appropriate than practice" (Flaherty, 2004, p. 95); the grim parallels with our own educational institutions are pervasive. We can see similar control and accountability regimes borne out through the establishment of the Australian Curriculum (Brennan, 2011), Common Core (Schneider, 2015) in the United states, and the National Curriculum in the United Kingdom (Barber & Graham, 2012; Maylor, 2016). Through a centralization of power, the Ministry and other such top-down interventionist approaches are corrupted by a simulacrum that clouds the maintenance of a common social fabric. The Ministry, through Umbridge, creates a pedagogy of misdirection, a deliberate and subversive process of appropriating the new commonsensical in education, by fostering illusions of "increased prescription and centralisation" (Cohen, Manion, Morrison, & Wyse, 2010, p. 8) to achieve a unified common core curriculum.

Under the auspices of creating greater transparency and unification, subversion and alternate voices are quashed, made suspect and side-lined. Whilst we may deduce that we "teach who we are" (Palmer, 2012, p. xi), who we are is a conglomerate of pedagogical practices that over the past decade, in tandem with educational policy initiatives, have positioned how teachers teach. This governmental overreach is exemplified in educational institutions like Hogwarts through the increasing presence of the Ministry as an arbiter of normalization (Tomlinson, 2004). *The Order of the Phoenix* playfully invokes this arbitration through the installation of Umbridge at Hogwarts, initially in the post of the Defence Against the Dark Arts teacher, whereby she insists on the complete removal of practicality in favour of pure theory, establishing a futile conflict between "accountability and authenticity" (Dickinson, 2006, p. 508). Her Ministry-approved approach follows a careful syllabus in which rote learning, and vacuous regurgitation is rewarded through high stakes testing. In Australia these same outcomes-driven values are foregrounded when initial teacher education is reduced to the testing of literacy and numeracy skills, pivoted on producing teachers who are in the top 30% of the country for literacy and numeracy (Australian Council for Educational Research, 2017). Meanwhile, the complexities of what it means to become a teacher, the need to grapple with the impact of context and engagement with relationships are pushed aside so that quantifiable measures are privileged.

As Umbridge's hegemonic grasp escapes the dungeon classroom and spreads across the Hogwarts campus, her educational decrees line the great hall. Ominously portrayed through an iconography that alludes to a plague-like iconism of the dark ages (Eco, 1976), these publically posted decrees threaten tangible punishment(s), whilst their gradual accumulation effectively shifts students towards a "more brutal reality" (Woodford, 2004, p. 72). One such example is Education Decree 31 which stipulates that "Boys and Girls are not permitted to be within 8 inches of each other" – masking through policy, values-based government intervention. The signification is one of increased power, which is typically centered on the disruption of student voice (disbanding organizations), identity (uniformity and dress-code violations) and ever-increasing compliance measures in the form of staff appraisal, echoing the United Kingdom's Office for Standards in Education, Children's Services and Skills (OFSTED, 2008), and teaching inspectors. The Ministry's many Machiavellian manoeuvres belie the seemingly insignificant revolutions of governmentalized intervention enacted in classrooms today, such as the banning of non-educational items (Jones, MacLure, Holmes, & MacRae, 2012) ranging from yo-yo's and trading cards to fidget spinners.

The dissonance between government bureaucracy and school governance, in our world and in the "Potterian world" (Levy & Snir, 2017, p. 3), draws credibility from the undermining of relationships, which is "corrupt, yet it has public support"

(Levy & Snir, 2017, p. 32), presenting a "mutually inconsistent and contradictory" (Levy & Snir, 2017, p. 32) model, as exemplified globally in everyday classroom practices through the streaming of classrooms and gender stereotypes in curriculum. Baudrillard's notion of simulation that "threatens the difference between the 'true' and the 'false,' the 'real' and the 'imaginary'" (Baudrillard, 1994b, p. 3) would liken the "Potterian world" (Levy & Snir, 2017, p. 3) to a simulation, further problematizing what it means to grasp the multiplicity of what it is that teachers are pushing back against.

Hyperreality

Critical to the misdirection of teachers and students in *The Order of the Phoenix* is the overt and deliberate overreach of the Ministry, which occurs when teaching becomes more performative than it is foundational. For when "[t]here is no distinction between the real and the false of teaching, there is only the hyperreal" (Page, 2017, p. 10). The hyperreal is a "real without origin or reality" (Baudrillard, 1994b, p. 1), which at once both destabilizes and nullifies.

Umbridge, for example, reflects back to the viewer a manifestation of the strict school marm; we are then able to identify and loathe her almost instantaneously. Her sickening representation, an idyll simulacrum of tenderness, bellies her veracity. Therein, the simulation of what a teacher is, turns into the hyperreal, where the subtleties and nuances of what a teacher might be in reality are emphasized and distorted above and beyond. Hogwarts becomes important from an analytical viewpoint, in that it is a "representation of, or counterpart to, the real" (Baudrillard, 1986, p. 16), so much so that it "appropriates reality for its own ends" (Baudrillard, 1986, p. 16) such that there is "no real and no fabrication: there is only the hyperreality" (Page, 2017, p. 11). Indeed, whilst Harry and Hogwarts are unaware of the symbolic exchange they enact, as viewers, our role is to bear witness, and indeed to see our own experiences of schooling for what they are, a parody of education and an amalgamation of over-the-top stereotypes of what it means to be a teacher.

At the root of the Ministry, integration and deliberate destabilization of accepted practice within Hogwarts is a profound distrust of teachers and teaching by the regulatory authority. This is perhaps most evident in our everyday context in the teach to the test (Lingard, Thompson, & Sellar, 2015) mentality that comes to the fore in today's school systems across the globe. The educational bent, built on distrust, is clearly pronounced with Ministry-approved textbooks, geared towards a "massification" (Sharma, 2008, p. 43) of education where the iconology in the film heralds a "back to basics" (Mockler, 2013, p. 287) focus that is also reflected in schools. This can be seen in National programs such as in Australia, the Language and Numeracy Test for Initial Teacher Education (Australian Council for Educational Research, 2017), and the Programme for International Student Assessment (PISA) results (Prenzel, Kobarg, Schöps, & Rönnebeck, 2012), where there is an attempted progressive alteration of the curriculum towards a preference for policy-flavoured, results-orientated classrooms globally.

Teachers and their schools revel in hyperreality if they fully embrace the performative nature of what education has become: open days, presentations, big data and glossy billboards, representing more the teachers we watch on our screens, instead of the teachers we are, or know. When the two blend, a hyperreal status is assured and teaching becomes an inauthentic hyperreal performance that is unable or undesired to be replicated in actual practice. An example of this can be seen in the disconnect between Hogwarts students, Fred and George Weasley, who are portrayed as the rebellious and mischievous prankster twins spiralling towards expulsion, and those who submit to the rules of the Ministry. This cannot be understood as a simplistic binary, rather, it is yet another misdirection in which we only notice or misrecognize the triumph of the pair, whilst the many submissive students remain. As viewers, we might be inclined to reach with confidence and celebrate these gestures of rebellion as emancipatory and as representative of possibilities to change the system; however, according to Baudrillard "[w]e are wrong. They only seem to resemble things, to resemble reality, events, faces. Or rather, they really do conform, their conformity itself is diabolical" (Baudrillard, 1986, p. 14). Amidst the contagion of possibility, the viewer and the students for a time forget the larger threats for which Umbridge and the Ministry are mere simulacrum, the rise of *He Who Must Not Be Named*.

Conclusion

Perhaps the most pervasive lesson, which may be gleaned from the Potterverse, is the illusory nature of progress in contemporary educational practices. Whilst reformations promise school improvement (Ainscow, Dyson, Goldrick, & West, 2012), student possibilities (Winzer & Mazurek, 2005) and efficiencies (Mockler, 2013), instead "teaching has become a simulation – not in the general sense of being a rehearsal – but in the sense that the simulation has replaced what the profession once considered real with its notions of autonomy and individual judgement" (Page, 2017, p. 11). An illusory disconnect forces teachers to comply amidst the simulacra, with their operational responsibilities preventing them from seeing the fractures or articulating the ways in which the minutiae they promulgate serve a broader and perhaps, more suspect ideological purpose. This occurs explicitly, implicitly, and fictively, but from hyperreal and simulated perspectives, the Potterverse (and our parallel realities) "is no longer a question of imitation, nor of duplication, nor even of parody. It is a question of substituting the signs of the real for the real" (Baudrillard, 1994b, p. 2).

Whilst the hyperreal encourages a disconnect between policy and practice, such illusions are fictively realized at Hogwarts through pedagogical practices that teachers employ, such as archaic and sadistic punishments to cajole the student body towards submission and an effective misrecognition – towards "the deviation of all truths, an exaltation of the malicious use of signs" (Baudrillard, 1990, p. 2). This manifests in the cruel torture of Harry in which Umbridge's beliefs surface.

As Umbridge's is a world in which the Ministry is resolute and infallible, Harry disrupts such a worldview. Framed by the strictures of a Ministry-approved sensibility, in which policy represents reality, the cyclical and futile nature of Umbridge's reign is unrealized within the community. Her cruelties are bounded by a perspective in which there exists a right and a wrong – a correct and an incorrect. For Umbridge, quashing rebellion is necessary as the students are operating outside the bounds of acceptability. However, within the logic of her character and imbued by a worldview that is underwritten by unpalatable policy, her wiles are given dark life. Similar to any unthinking bureaucrat, she is a manifestation of certainty endowed by corporate interests.

Harry Potter and the Order of the Phoenix illustrates a world that mimics our own with alarming parallels in its global push towards performativity and submission to the dictates of an authority. The lives of teachers are forged within a space that encourages both a desire for social order and also a need to resist that is ultimately futile and fatally flawed.

Our argument has been that the film *Harry Potter and the Order of the Phoenix* reflects and is reflective of today's schools. The ever narrowing of choice means that teachers' abilities to make decisions about teaching and learning is limited. The centralization of policy, curriculum, and the everyday, with clearly delineated sets of outcomes, paints a nice fairy-tale, but also engenders a distortion between what a teacher is and what a teacher can be in this new regime. Ultimately, we must begin by embracing the paradox and complexities of a pedagogy of misdirection. By watching schooling unfold on film we are bearing witness to "artificial montage and non-meaning" (Baudrillard, 1994a, p. 15) dressed up as meaning. We must appreciate that whilst Hogwarts may suggest possibilities to the viewer, and our schools may indeed reflect such a reality, there ultimately is no magic utopia capable of dispelling a hyperreal world.

REFERENCES

Ainscow, M., Dyson, A., Goldrick, S., & West, M. (2012). Making schools effective for all: Rethinking the task. *School Leadership & Management, 32*(3), 197–213.

Australian Council for Educational Research. (2017). LANTITE: Literacy and numeracy test for initial teacher education students. Retrieved from https://teacheredtest.acer.edu.au/

Barber, M., & Graham, D. (2012). *Sense and nonsense and the national curriculum*. London, UK: Routledge.

Barron, D. P., Heyman, D. P. (Producers), & Yates, D. D. (Director). (2007). *Harry Potter and the Order of the Phoenix* [Motion picture]. USA: Warner Brothers.

Baudrillard, J. (1986). *The evil demon of images* (P. Patton, & P. Foss, Trans.). Sydney, Australia: Power Institute of Fine Arts.

Baudrillard, J. (1990). *Seduction* (B. Singer, Trans.). New York, NY: St. Martin's Press.

Baudrillard, J. (1994a). *The illusion of the end* (C. Turner, Trans.). Stanford, CA: Stanford University Press.

Baudrillard, J. (1994b). *Simulacra and simulation* (S. F. Glaser, Trans.). Ann Arbor, MI: University of Michigan Press.

Baudrillard, J. (2008). The violence of images, violence against the image. *ArtUS*, (23), 38–45.

Brennan, M. (2011). National curriculum: A political-educational tangle. *Australian Journal of Education, 55*, 259–280.

Campbell, C., Proctor, H., & Sherington, G. (2009). *School choice: How parents negotiate the new school market in Australia*. Crows Nest, Australia: Allen & Unwin.

Cohen, L., Manion, L., Morrison, K., & Wyse, D. (2010). *A guide to teaching practice* (5th ed.). New York, NY: Routledge.

Dickinson, R. (2006). Harry Potter pedagogy: What we learn about teaching and learning from J. K. Rowling. *The Clearing House: A Journal of Educational Strategies, Issues and Ideas, 79*(6), 240–244.

Eco, U. (1976). *A theory of semiotics*. Bloomington, IN: Indiana University Press.

Flaherty, J. (2004). Harry Potter and the freedom of information: Knowledge and control in *Harry Potter and the Order of the Phoenix*. *Washington & Jefferson College Review, 54*, 93–102.

Gabbard, D. A. (2010). Education is enforcement! The centrality of compulsory schooling in market societies. In K. J. Saltman, & D. A. Gabbard (Eds.), *Education as enforcement: The militarization and corporatization of schools* (2nd ed.) (pp. 57–72). New York, NY: Routledge.

Gaztambide-Fernández, R., & Parekh, G. (2017). Market "choices" or structured pathways? How specialized arts education contributes to the reproduction of inequality. *Education Policy Analysis Archives, 25*(41).

Helfenbein, R. J., & Brown, S. K. (2008). Conjuring curriculum, conjuring control: A Reading of resistance in *Harry Potter and the Order of the Phoenix*. *Curriculum Inquiry, 38*(4), 499–513.

Jones, L., MacLure, M., Holmes, R., & MacRae, C. (2012). Children and objects: Affection and infection. *Early Years: An International Research Journal, 32*(1), 49–60.

Levy, D., & Snir, A. (2017). Potterian economics. Social Science Research Network. Retrieved from https://ssrn.com/abstract=2902914

Lingard, B., Thompson, G., & Sellar, S. (2015). *National testing in schools: An Australian assessment.* New York, NY: Routledge.

Mason, S. A. (2013). The federal challenge to university-based education research in the United States: Turning research into policy and practice. In B. Levin, J. Qi, H. Edelstein, & J. Sohn (Eds.), *The impact of research in education: An international perspective.* Bristol, UK: Policy Press.

Maylor, U. (2016). "I'd worry about how to teach it": British values in English classrooms. *Journal of Education for Teaching, 42*(3), 314–328.

Mockler, N. (2013). The slippery slope to efficiency? An Australian perspective on school/university partnerships for teacher professional learning. *Cambridge Journal of Education, 43*(3), 273–289.

Nichols, T. (2017, January 15). Our graduates are rubes. *The Chronicle of Higher Education.* Retrieved from http://www.chronicle.com/article/Our-Graduates-Are-Rubes/238865

OFSTED. (2008). *The annual report of Her Majesty's Chief Inspector of Education, Children's Services and Skills 2007/08.* London, UK: Stationery Office.

Page, D. (2017). The surveillance of teachers and the simulation of teaching. *Journal of Education Policy, 32*(1), 1–13.

Palmer, P. J. (2012). *The courage to teach: Exploring the inner landscape of a teacher's life.* New York, NY: Wiley.

Prenzel, M., Kobarg, M., Schöps, K., & Rönnebeck, S. (Eds.) (2012). *Research on PISA: Research outcomes of the PISA Research Conference 2009.* Dordrecht, NL: Springer.

Rasmussen, A., Gustafsson, J., & Jeffrey, B. (Eds.) (2014). *Performativity in education: An international collection of ethnographic research on learners' experiences.* Stroud, UK: E&E Publishing.

Schneider, M. K. (2015). *Common core dilemma: Who owns our schools?* New York, NY: Teachers College Press.

Sharma, R. (2008). The Australian perspective: Access, equity, quality, and accountability in higher education. *New Directions for Institutional Research, 2,* 43–53.

Tomlinson, H. (2004). *Educational management.* London, UK: Routledge Falmer.

Winzer, M., & Mazurek, K. (2005). Current reforms in special education: Delusion or solution. In J. I. Zajda (Ed.), *International handbook on globalisation, education and policy research: Global pedagogies and Policies* (pp. 643–658). Dordrecht, NL: Springer.

Woodford, D. C. (2004). Disillusionment in *Harry Potter and the Order of the Phoenix. Washington & Jefferson College Review, 54,* 63–72.

Playfulness, Relationships, and Worldviews: Indigenous Pedagogy and *Conrack*

Matthew "Gus" Gusul

Introduction

A young Jon Voight's performance of Pat Conroy in *Conrack* (Ritt & Frank, 1974) is a dramatic portrayal of a teacher from which I draw inspiration. The film *Conrack* captures my imagination because of the adventurous spirit shown by Conroy both in how he leads his life and for how he educates. The film is based upon an autobiographical book titled *The water is wide* by Pat Conroy (Conroy, 1972). Conroy is a white male, a fresh university graduate tasked with teaching black children on a remote island off USA's South Carolina coast. Using an unconventional, playful pedagogical approach to teaching literacy and numeracy while focusing on relationship building, Conroy achieves positive results with the children. His efforts push against the administration's disciplinarian approach, which results in his firing. This film represents a fictional portrayal of an educator utilizing the pedagogical approaches of relationship building and playfulness that resonates with my experiences of working with rural Indigenous communities in Alberta, Canada. Voight's portrayal of Conroy shows a humane and dynamically complex representation of a teacher with the central plot of the film hinging upon a dispute over his pedagogical approach. My purpose in writing this chapter is to highlight the strength in Conroy's pedagogy in three different areas: his use of playfulness in his teaching approach, his focus on creating relationships with community members allowing them to support his lessons, and his work to understand the worldviews of his students through insight into community members' moral and ethical compasses; and, to show other educators how these three pedagogical approaches have helped me in rural Indigenous Albertan communities.

Plot Synopsis and Conroy's Pedagogy

The film *Conrack* (Ritt & Frank, 1974) depicts Pat Conroy as an effective educator because of the pedagogical approaches he uses in a remote community setting. Conroy, fresh from graduating with his teaching degree, begins his first job on Yamacraw Island. Conroy's first impression of his new job is painted by a meeting with Principal Scott in which she tells him to discipline his students. This is not Conroy's style; rather, he adopts a playful approach. He employs games, singing, and makes the students laugh. With this approach, there are moments when the students are almost tricked into learning. His aim was to share his thirst for learning and to cultivate the students' passion. As he further questions them, he finds that the children do not know the alphabet, some cannot count to ten, and that they know little of American culture or current events. Fuelled by his passion for knowledge, Conroy exposes the children to a well-rounded liberal arts education. He shows them the world through reading Shakespeare, playing classical music records of Beethoven and Korsakov, singing songs, teaching botany and geography, and watching films. Conroy focuses on developing personal relationships with each student so that he can better understand their barriers to learning. He also develops relationships with the different stakeholders in the community in which he is teaching. He becomes friends with community members and works to understand the mindset of the local population to help his communication with the students. He experiences immediate results as the students recall facts they have learned and show pride in themselves. However, when Superintendent Skeffington makes a visit to watch Conroy with the class, his authoritarian influence results in the students misbehaving. Mr. Skeffington uses physical violence to calm the classroom.

As the end of October draws near, Conroy starts asking the children about Hallowe'en and is shocked to discover that they have never heard of the holiday. He becomes dedicated to taking the children off the island to the nearby town of Beaufort to dress-up and trick-or-treat for candy. First, he approaches people in Beaufort to find a place for the children to stay overnight. In the predominantly white community, he is initially confronted by racist attitudes, but eventually finds Mrs. Sellers who boards the children for the night. He then approaches the Superintendent, who disagrees that the children should visit Beaufort. He forbids Conroy from taking the students off island. Conroy says in response, "Those children are gonna celebrate Hallowe'en just like every child in America. If you wanna raise hell about it, go ahead." This was not Conroy's only hurdle. The children's guardians and parents did not like the idea of them leaving the island with a white man. Conroy approaches one of the most respected community members who is called Queen Bee. She does not want the children to leave the island because she is afraid of the water. Conroy convinces her it will be safe and the other parents allow the children to travel off island to Beaufort. The children are afraid to leave on the boat, but quickly adapt. They are wowed by the huge roads and library in Beaufort. The children dress up at Mrs. Sellers' house and leave on foot to go trick-or-treating, thoroughly enjoying their outing. Upon returning to Yamacraw Island, Conroy has a letter waiting for him telling him he is fired. After a battle mounted by both the local community and by Conroy against the authority of the Superintendent, the decision remains final and Conroy is forced to leave. The unfortunate ending to film does not over shadow the strong pedagogical success demonstrated by Conroy throughout the film.

Before discussing the relevance of Conroy's pedagogical approaches to Indigenous pedagogy, I must address a major shortcoming of his approach. Conroy's choice of content material used to educate these young children is Eurocentric and purely focused on Americana. This is explicable in the historical context of the film. In 1974, educators in North America were less savvy in terms of intercultural education. Since that time, much has been learned in terms of the need for diverse cultural inclusion; the Eurocentric canon has been challenged. His choice of music and literature for his lessons is likely because this is what he had been taught and was passionate about. Nevertheless, like many well-intentioned educators, Conroy's heart was in the right place. He was trying to light a fire in the children, so they would gain a love of learning.

Indigenous Pedagogy

My introduction to Indigenous pedagogy began when I accepted a position working with Frontier College[1] to administer a programme aimed at the creation of culturally appropriate summer literacy camps in rural Indigenous communities throughout Alberta, Canada in the spring of 2016. I had experience working with Indigenous Canadians but I had never studied Indigenous philosophy or pedagogy. I was introduced to Sandy Grande's (2004) *Red pedagogy: Native American social and political thought.* She introduces the reader to Indigenous pedagogy by first detailing the history of education for Indigenous people of North America through three stages: education delivered by missionaries from the sixteenth century to the nineteenth century, education controlled by the federal government from the late-nineteenth to the mid-twentieth century, and finally, a "period of self-determination" from the mid-twentieth century to the present. The first two stages were periods in which the colonial powers were using the education as a way of wiping out Indigenous peoples' cultures.

Measures were taken to eradicate Indigenous languages and spiritualties and replace them, with the language, culture, and religion of the colonial power (Grande, 2004). It is during the mid-twentieth century into the present that an Indigenous pedagogy emerges.

Indigenous Pedagogy has emerged from the efforts of self-determination by Indigenous communities. Grande (2004) reviews studies proving that the efforts of past education systems to assimilate Indigenous students resulted in a population that suffered from poverty, illiteracy, and other social injustices. The push for self-determination during the late twentieth century has resulted in a system thirsty for Indigenous pedagogy. The emerging pedagogy resembles revolutionary models based on the desire for Indigenous peoples to gain access to greater social justice and equity. These models value the teaching of Indigenous traditional knowledge, and hold hope for the future (Grande, 2004). Grande writes about the idea of hope within Indigenous pedagogy: "a hope that lives in contingency with the past – one that trusts the beliefs and understandings of our ancestors as well as the power of traditional knowledge" (p. 28). Indigenous pedagogy leans on traditional teachings and upon Elders' involvement with the hope of breathing new life into Indigenous cultures.

Another important Indigenous scholar to whom I look is Leanne Simpson (2011) who writes about the emerging Indigenous presence in North America in her book *Dancing on our Turtle's back: Stories of Nishnaabeg re-creation, resurgence and a new emergence*. In it, Simpson details an event that occurred on June 21, 2009, in Ontario, when a group of Indigenous artists, dancers, and others took to the streets of their community and took over space. The purpose was not protest or influencing non-Indigenous peoples. The Indigenous people were seeking to be Indigenous within a space that was less influenced by colonization. I see this action as being hugely significant to the emerging Indigenous pedagogy. Simpson describes the event as an "opportunity to celebrate our survival, our continuance, our resurgence: all of the best parts of us" (Simpson, 2011, p. 12). She writes, "for an hour that day, we created a space where the impacts of colonialism were lessened, where we could feel what it feels like to be part of a united, healthy community, where our children could glimpse our beautiful visions for the future" (Simpson, 2011, p. 12). In what she writes there is hope – the same hope as in Sandy Grande's (2004) *Red pedagogy*. The hope in Simpson's case is in a brighter future for her people.

Over the past decade, the Canadian government has taken steps in establishing better relations between Indigenous and non-Indigenous Canadians. Central to these efforts was the Truth and Reconciliation Commission of Canada (TRCC), which wrote a final report (2015) that summarized the findings of the commission. The commission held public events in which Indigenous and non-Indigenous Canadians spoke about their experiences of Canada's residential school system that segregated Indigenous Canadians into boarding schools. They were taken away from their home communities with the purpose of stripping the Indigenous children of their culture, language, and spirituality, and replacing that identity with an education rooted in European culture, the English language, and Christianity. In the summary, the commission proposed 94 "Calls to Action" for the Canadian government and all Canadians. I am drawn to the tenth "Call to Action." In this "Call to Action," the TRCC recommends " [d]eveloping culturally appropriate curricula" and "[p]rotecting the right to Aboriginal languages, including the teaching [of] Aboriginal languages" (TRCC, 2015, p. 151). These specific recommendations are extremely important for educators currently working with Indigenous people. The highlighting of Indigenous language and culture will be important in current programming for Indigenous students because it will help the establishment of the identity lost in the residential schools.

My introduction to Indigenous pedagogy has been invaluable in my work with Indigenous people. I see a relationship between what I have learned from using Indigenous pedagogy in rural communities and in what the teacher Conroy experiences in *Conrack* (Ritt & Frank, 1974).

My Programming in Rural Indigenous Alberta Communities

I administer camps throughout Alberta's rural Indigenous communities primarily to assist with the management and training of the staff. I do not directly teach at any of the literacy camps; rather, I train the local educators, who facilitate the camps. My approach to instructing facilitators for the remote communities relates to the pedagogical approaches depicted in *Conrack* (Ritt & Frank, 1974). The focus on playfulness and building relationships is prevalent within staff training and in my practice of collaborating with communities. I also work to understand the worldviews of the Indigenous peoples with whom I collaborate.

Every community I work with is different in terms of their Indigenous identities and cultures. Each community must take ownership over their camp. The communities range from being immersed in their Indigenous languages and spiritualties with multiple knowledge holders present in the community, to communities that have few direct ties to their Indigenous traditions and are striving to find their identities. Therefore, as the needs of each are different, local educators have sovereignty to decide the content for their summer camps. The local educators link with important community members and create culturally appropriate environments for learning. This aspect of my approach allows me to avoid the limitations (Eurocentricism) I mentioned with Conroy's approach.

Playful pedagogy

Many of the individuals hired to facilitate the camps are Educational Assistants and Teaching Assistants at the elementary schools in the communities. Also, many of the camps take place in schools because they are the only facilities in the communities with adequate kitchens for preparing healthy lunches for the children. An important part of our training process is a focus on planning fun-filled playful activities to ensure the children do not associate the camps with summer school. Literacy is embedded in games and other activities. The camps are meant to offer a distinct educational atmosphere with no grades – with enjoyment of learning through fun activities as the focus. This play-based approach is adhered to by Conroy in the film (Ritt & Frank, 1974) and works well with young children as it employs energy and enthusiasm. We take care to ensure that the principle of playfulness infuses the camps and I work to include it in the centralized training programme for the local educators.

A section titled "Sport and culture: 'It was a Relief'" appears in the *Final Report of the Truth and Reconciliation Commission of Canada* (TRCC, 2015, p. 110). Survivors of Canada's residential school system reminiscence that their only positive experience in this system was when the lessons included art or sports. Educators in the summer camps utilize the playfulness within sports-related and artistic activities to teach literacy in their camps. Paul Andrew, an Indigenous man who survived residential school, said, "There were times when I felt dumb and stupid. But put me in a gym, there was not too many better than I am" (TRCC, 2015, p. 111). The playfulness within sports is an area in which children find comfort. The TRCC included many examples of teams from Indigenous communities competing well against teams from non-Indigenous communities. They had pride in these accomplishments. Within artistic activities, Indigenous Canadians also found space to excel. Indigenous Canadians are well known globally for their artistic accomplishments (TRCC, 2015). Within our camps, the local educators play sports with the children and offer playful approaches that lead the children to be creative in their writing and critical thinking skills. Approaches to this can look simple. For sports-related games, some camps have running race spelling games, or baseball where the player has to spell a word at each base. Arts-based activities include reading a story aloud and asking the children to draw their favourite part or to have the children write another story about one of the characters in the original story. Camps utilize the playfulness within sports and arts-based activities to help children develop literacy skills, which are close to how Conroy used his playful pedagogy in *Conrack*.

Relationship building

As Conroy did, camp facilitators are encouraged to nurture relationships with local community members to help in the education of the children. Many camps include Elders and knowledge holders, as well as local fire departments, yoga instructors, athletes, artists, songwriters, and politicians. This is helpful in ensuring that multiple generations are working to assist in the education of the children and agrees with the "Call to Action" proposed by the TRCC, which recommends involvement of parents, knowledge-holders, elders, and community members (TRCC, 2015). Also of importance are my relationships with community members. As a programme administrator, I need to be aware of the diverse people in the community. The best camps are influenced by a diverse group of community members, allowing the children to be exposed to multiple perspectives. The more community members I know, the easier it is for staff to include them in the camps. This focus on relationships is of utmost importance when developing ties with Elders and knowledge holders and essential to the diversity of the camps. Indigenous children need to have exposure to Elders and knowledge holders to ensure culture is passed to the next generation.

Understanding community worldviews

In the film *Conrack* (Ritt & Frank, 1974), Conroy develops a friendship with a local man. While the friendship between Billy and Conroy is developing, one scene displays how Conroy works to try to understand the worldview of the people on Yamacraw Island. The scene takes place on the beach while the sun is setting and Billy is engaged in a reading lesson with Conroy. Mad Billy asks Conroy why he lives on the island as the only white man. Conroy proclaims that he was once racist, but realized the error of his ways and made a dedicated life change. The scene continues:

> Conroy: You ever been off this island.
> Billy: No.
> Conroy: Ever want to get off this island?
> Billy: No.
> Conroy: Want to see the rest of the world... ?
> Billy: No, I get my shoelaces here... tobacco and coals... linen and cheap candy... And now I can read.

This scene reveals the back-story for Conroy's passion for teaching the black children. In this brief conversation, he shows his desire to understand Billy's mindset. Conroy desires travel and to experience the world, whereas Billy is content to stay on his island. This resonates with my experiences in Indigenous communities. In conversations I have had with Elders, knowledge holders, and educators, they have communicated their dedication to staying with their people, on their land. As Conroy struggles to understand Billy's dedication to stay, many non-Indigenous people in Alberta do not understand Indigenous peoples' commitment to their land. In this regard and others, educators who work interculturally should work to understand the worldviews of the community members to which their students belong.

Hopper (2016) articulates a component of the gap in thinking between Indigenous and non-Indigenous people in Alberta in relation to the land. Hopper writes:

> We non-indigenous love to move. We don't just see it as good economic policy but as a virtue [...]. While the rest of the world has poems and songs about sacred soil and the footsteps of generations past, our songs are about the exact opposite. "Four Strong Winds," the tear-jerking unofficial Alberta anthem, is an ode to leaving town when the money runs out. [...] The bones of my ancestors aren't buried beneath my feet. My culture and language weren't shaped by the land and climate around me. I've never had to fight to defend this soil – and I've never even considered that it could be taken away. I, like many non-indigenous Canadians, will never fully appreciate why someone would be reluctant to desert their family, friends, and homeland in order to seek prosperity.
>
> (2016, para. 10-12 & 30-32)

From my experience working and living in Alberta, Hopper well describes the feeling of non-Indigenous peoples. Many non-Indigenous Albertans or their families before them migrated to Alberta for economic opportunity. This is story of the ancestry on both my mother's and father's sides. On my father's side, my grandmother immigrated to rural Manitoba in the 1930s from Ukraine to be a nurse, and my father left Manitoba for better work opportunities in Calgary; on my mother's side, my great grandmother and grandfather immigrated from Poland to Round Hill, Alberta in 1905 as they were offered land to farm, and my mother has never lived further than 50 km away from that farm. Stories like mine are common across the prairies. I left the prairies for my Ph.D. studies and to live abroad, and I suspect if work was ever to dry up here, I would proudly move along to find another opportunity, as "Four Strong Winds" has taught me. Understanding that Indigenous people in Alberta do not feel this way, and that the non-Indigenous Albertan spirit to move along is not unusual, has helped me understand the difference of worldview between Indigenous and non-Indigenous peoples.

Glen Sean Coulthard (2014), a professor of Political Sciences and First Nations Studies and a Yellowknives Dene First Nations member, writes of the differences between Indigenous and non-Indigenous worldviews in his book *Red skin, white masks: Rejecting the colonial politics of recognition*. He writes about how Indigenous peoples in Western Canada view history as cyclical while non-Indigenous people have a more linear view of history. He describes the values of Indigenous peoples as being rooted in "place-based ethics" (Coulthard, 2014). His analysis of place leads him to the Marxist concept of dispossession, in which the people who possess the means of production are also the owners of their livelihoods as workers (Coulthard, 2014). In the case of Indigenous peoples of Western Canada, according to Coulthard, the land can be thought of as the means of production for their traditional lifestyles and for their spiritual practices. They have a "reciprocal relationship" with the land in which the land provides for their lifestyles. Coulthard writes, "it is a profound misunderstanding to think of land or place as simply some material object [...] instead, it ought to be understood as a field of 'relationships of things to each other'" (2014, pp. 60–61). For non-Indigenous people in Western Canada, their relationship in the Marxist paradigm is more time-based than place-based, meaning the lower classes sell their time to work (Coulthard, 2014). Marxist oppression then exists differently for Indigenous and non-Indigenous people. For Indigenous people, the struggle is spatial in the fight against their dispossession of their traditional lands; for non-Indigenous people, the struggle is over the exploitation of time (Coulthard, 2014). This differentiation offered by Coulthard helps my understanding of Indigenous worldviews echoing much the same spirit of Hopper's (2016) *moniyâw mind*. For a non-Indigenous person, the sale of their time and the courage to move on for economic gain are celebrated. For Indigenous persons, place-based ethics and modes of traditional spirituality relating to the land are worthy of celebration. The difference between these two worldviews reverberate in much the same tone as the conversation between Conroy and Billy: "Conroy: Ever want to get off this island? Billy: No."

Conclusion

In returning to *Conrack* (Ritt & Frank, 1974), I have rediscovered a film, which can offer pedagogical support to educators working in remote communities and especially to educators working interculturally. The approach Conroy uses, focusing on playfulness, fostering relationships with, and understanding the worldviews of community members helped the quality of education he could provide for the children. I am glad this 1974 film advances the perception of an educator as a dynamic person, who extends beyond a stereotype of teacher as disciplinarian, which would have been common at the time. In the end, the film hinges on a debate about pedagogical styles. I have been able to find relevance to today's world in this film and the teacher portrayal of Pat Conroy, and I would suggest that other educators could as well.

REFERENCES

Conroy, P. (1972). *The water is wide*. New York, NY: Penguin Random House.

Coulthard, G. S. (2014). *Red skin, white masks: Rejecting the colonial politics of recognition*. Minneapolis, MN: University of Minnesota Press.

Grande, S. (2004). *Red pedagogy: Native American social and political thought*. Oxford, UK: Rowman & Littlefield Publishers.

Hopper, T. (2016, April 27). Why Canadian white people have so much trouble understanding why somebody wouldn't want to leave Attawapiskat. *National Post*. Retrieved from https://nationalpost.com/opinion/tristin-hopper-why-canadian-white-people-have-so-much-trouble-understanding-why-somebody-wouldnt-want-to-leave-attawapiskat

Ritt, M., & Frank, H. (Producer), & Ritt, M. (Director). (1974). *Conrack* [Motion picture]. USA: Twentieth Century Fox.

Simpson, L. (2011). *Dancing on our turtle's back: Stories of Nishnaabeg re-creation, resurgence and a new emergence*. Winnipeg, MB: ARP Books.

Truth and Reconciliation Commission of Canada. (2015). *Final report of the Truth and Reconciliation Commission of Canada volume one: summary: honouring the truth, reconciling for the future*. Winnipeg, MB: Truth and Reconciliation Commission of Canada.

NOTE

1. Frontier College is a literacy education organization, with a rich and storied history of delivering poverty-reducing literacy education in remote and rural communities in Canada since 1899. www.frontiercollege.ca

Bill & Ted's Assessable Adventure: A Frame Analysis of Assessment Representations in Popular Culture Through *Bill & Ted's Excellent Adventure*

Rachael Jacobs

Introduction

Strange things are afoot at the Circle K
– Bill & Ted's Excellent Adventure (Kroopf, Murphey, Soisson, & Herek, 1989)

Assessment is an integral component of formal schooling around the world and is often portrayed in film, television, and popular culture with several cultural constructions and mythologies attached. Notions of "pop quizzes," cramming strategies for exams, or "cheat sheets" pepper the terminology illustrating the assessment landscape in schools. Assessment is often represented as being high-stakes, summative, stress and anxiety-inducing, exhausting, and, at times, the entire focus of students' academic efforts at schools. Such essentialist or positivist portrayals prize knowledge as a truth, which can be acquired and possessed, and assessment tasks as linear attempts to make students reproduce those truths (Delandshere & Petrosky, 1994).

The reality of schools today might mirror aspects of this assessment paradigm; however, assessment regimes are often continuous, using formative or highly engaging instruments, allowing students to capitalize on their strengths. Schooling today frequently uses tasks that are influenced by post-structuralist thinking about knowledge (Britzman, 1986, 1992; Foucault, 1972). For these tasks students produce understandings from what exists within the possibilities of their language or discourse, rather than pursue discrete instances of truths. Further to this, McMillan (2000) asserts that "good" assessment is fair and ethical, uses multiple methods, is valid and feasible, and enhances instruction. But how often is assessment popularly portrayed with these attributes in cultural settings such as film? It seems theatrically heightened to present assessment as inherently unfair, often with few ethical boundaries, unfeasible under the given conditions and something that protagonists must contend with, rather than something that enhances their learning. This is the case in the 1989 science-fiction comedy film, *Bill & Ted's excellent adventure* (Kroopf et al., 1989). The two central protagonists are challenged to present an oral history report for which they must achieve an A+ grade, or face dire consequences. The film documents their journey to achieving their A+ grade, but also presents several assessment myths that are pervasive in popular depictions of classrooms.

This chapter engages in a frame analysis (Edmiston & McKibben, 2011; Goffman, 1974; Gray & Williams, 2012), in conjunction with a textual analysis of the representations of assessment in *Bill & Ted's excellent adventure*. The frames that emerged from the analysis are: the task, the learners, and the audience. These frames combine to provide an example of the way assessment tasks can be popularly characterized on film. These popular characterizations give rise to mythologies, which are often inconsistent with current practice in schools and research on "good" assessment practice. This chapter uses these three frames to discuss the ways in which assessment is portrayed, and the reasons these myths are pervasive in popular culture.

Frame Analysis

Understandings of assessment representations emerging from this essay have been derived from the theory of frame analysis, based on Goffman's (1974) work on framing, later adapted by Edmiston and McKibben (2011), Gray and Williams (2012), and Rainio and Marjanovic-Shane (2013). Frame analysis is used here to interrogate the ways in which assessment is defined and problematized in the film, and the subsequent effect that this has on broader perceptions of assessment. Despite being a light-hearted comedy, there are culturally constructed understandings of education at play in *Bill & Ted's excellent adventure*. The protagonists' quest is primarily concerned with an assessment task, which can be viewed through numerous frames. Goffman described frames as "schemata of interpretation" through which individuals or groups "locate, perceive, identify, and label" events and phenomena (1974, p. 21). In other words, frame analysis attempts to explain how and why people behave, interact, or organize themselves in particular ways.

Through frames, we are able to develop deeper understandings of an issue, from multiple perspectives. One of the benefits of using frame analysis is that it allows an exploration of the dynamics between different points-of-view and the potential for transformation (Virkki et al., 2014). Goffman (1974) also stresses the malleability of frames: shifts can occur from one frame to another, frames can be combined, and in this way they are actively modified. This chapter identifies three frames for discussion; however, the frames interact and have bearing on one another. When layered over each other, they provide a fuller picture of popular portrayals of assessment.

The concept of frames also has a natural synergy with the cinematic world. Although frame analysis in this context does not refer to a visual analysis of shots or cinematography, there is a certain likeness between Goffman's (1974) shifting frames that capture deeper understandings from multiple perspectives, and the practice of viewing artistic mediums, such as film, from multiple perspectives. Additionally, the medium of film uses frames to convey different perspectives to tell a story, often helping us understand the human experience from multiple perspectives.

In order to arrive at the frames for this analysis, I gathered "data" through extensive journaling over multiple viewings of the film. The scripted language used to discuss and reference the assessment task was captured as data, then analyzed, as were environmental factors pertaining to the task, perceptions of schooling and schoolwork, and dispositions of the learner. During the first stage of the analysis, I classified and grouped into themes key elements of the assessment task. During the second stage of the analysis, I broadened the themes to examine the causes that give rise to the assessment landscape and the protagonists' response to their quest. Through iterative categorization of the data, frames were inductively constructed and layered over each other, with my intention of providing a picture of assessment as portrayed in the film.

Frame 1: The Task

With only a few days before their high-school graduation, budding rock-stars Bill S. Preston, Esquire and Ted "Theodore" Logan would rather rock out than study. Their band, "Wyld Stallyns," is yet to be discovered. In fact, they can only barely play their instruments. Bill and Ted attend their history class, only to find that they are in grave danger of failing, which will result in their expulsion from school. Their history teacher gives them a final opportunity to pass; they must achieve an A+ on their final history report the next day. In the teacher's own words, they need to deliver *something very special*.

The task is an oral presentation in which they must describe how a historical figure would view their hometown of San Dimas, California. The assignment is a classic historical analysis task. Students are required to blend content knowledge about historical figures, their main achievements, and philosophies with a sociological analysis of the present-day world, applying the values of the historical figure to parallel ideas in the modern world. Students additionally have to demonstrate oral competence, proficient communication skills, and understanding of audience engagement. Bill and Ted are initially stumped as to how to approach this task. They begin in the positivist mind-frame, reiterating facts and dates. This goes particularly badly, as they have not previously engaged with any of the material, and are barely able to demonstrate any surface understanding of historical knowledge as the following exchange illustrates:

> Mr Ryan: Who was Joan of Arc?
> Ted: Noah's wife.
>
> (Kroopf et al., 1989)

The pair moves to the local convenience store car park to pursue this reductive mode of learning, asking passers-by the answers to factual historical questions. They have assumed the task requires them to reproduce pre-determined knowledge (Ross, 1991), as they have understood the task to be part of a "testing" regime.

Eisner (1998) critiqued testing as it aspires a set of common correct responses, focuses on pieces or segments of information, and emphasizes the acquisition of products produced by others. However, the assessment task featured in the movie requires much more than recall. The task requires the learners to engage what Simon (1973) termed "ill-structured" learning processes whereby multiple approaches and a range of possible solutions are acceptable. These style of tasks can accommodate contextual variations and differences in individuals' solutions, which are highly suitable to Bill and Ted, who eventually choose to present a response consistent with their worldview and lived experience (albeit with the assistance of time travel). Ill-structured tasks such as this one reflect post-structuralist thinking about knowledge (Britzman, 1986, 1992; Foucault, 1972; Said, 1985) whereby understandings are produced by individuals from what exists within the possibilities of their language or discourse.

Bill and Ted's understandings of the task and the possibilities for their response evolve over the course of the film. To the audience's knowledge, they have been given few boundaries or guidelines, except that they are expected to produce *something very special*. The film reveals no assessment criteria, yet Bill and Ted have an understanding of the assessment "game" (Orrell, 2005). Orrell has written widely about students' understandings of what he refers to as the "rules of the game." While his research is located in a higher education context, it has relevance to the school context depicted here, as knowing the rules-of-the-game equates to anticipating the teacher's criteria or agenda. This metaphor can sit somewhat uncomfortably in a school context where a teacher is acting supportively, but it seems appropriately magnified in the context of this film. Likening the assessment process to game playing implies that students must use underhanded methods to discover a secret code shielded by the teacher until found out. Hidden agendas or secrecy are often portrayed in popular culture as being rife in schools. The final frame, the audience, discussed at a later stage in this chapter, explores some of the reasons why this might be the case. Within this frame it is noted that no specific assessment criteria are discussed. Still, Bill and Ted are able to respond meaningfully and insightfully to the historical question posed, as well as create a highly engaging response for their audience. Their intrinsic understanding of implied assessment criteria leads them to create a highly performative response, which eventually wows their audience.

Bill and Ted construct their own understandings about how to respond to assessment tasks, independent of supplementary information, if it is provided. This is an example of students' personal curriculum at play. This personal curriculum, as defined by Jackson (2011), is also referred to as a "lifewide" curriculum (p. 109) in which students develop their own understandings, personal knowledge, priorities, confidence, agency, and identity through engagement inside and outside formal education. As part of this frame, Bill and Ted's personal curriculum has been evidently formed by their previous experiences of school learning, which takes place within and outside of formal classes. Students more broadly are able to take leadership when they craft their assessment responses, applying their own priorities and personal curriculum to their understanding of a task.

Frame 2: The Learners

Those who have seen *Bill & Ted's excellent adventure* may balk at the protagonists being described as "learners." The film's comedy centres on their "stupidity," supported by slapstick devices, *lazzi,* and crude humour. Bill and Ted are not regular attendees at school. They rarely make meaningful contributions to lessons. In a previous History assessment, they describe Caesar as a "salad-dressing dude" (Kroopf et al., 1989). The film frames them as learners who are somewhat at a disadvantage. They have been given the seemingly impossible task of achieving an A+ on their final history report, with one evening to prepare.

Bill and Ted approach the assessment task with entirely extrinsic motivations. The pair is initially motivated by fear and threats. In addition to the threat of school expulsion, Ted's father has threatened to send him to military school if he fails, thus breaking up the band and any chance of future musical success. Later, they discover, from time traveller Rufus, that their music will one day change the course of human existence, putting an end to war and poverty, aligning the planets, and allowing meaningful contact with all forms of life. The intervention of Rufus provides further extrinsic motivation for their academic success. As it has been long established, intrinsic motivation is deeper and longer lasting than extrinsic motivation (Maslow, 1970), although in literature on assessment there is some acknowledgement that an achievement orientation can lead to deep learning (Biggs, 1993, 1999; Biggs & Tang, 2011).

Throughout the film Bill and Ted are almost entirely lacking in intrinsic motivation and the factors that create it, including enjoyment of learning (Inyengar & Lepper, 1999, 2000), deep understandings of content, and the ability to make connections (Malmeer & Zoghi, 2014). Nonetheless, they arrive at deep connections with the material, through the aid of meaningful engagements with historical figures. Although they lack motivation to learn about history, their final presentation demonstrates mastery of some key elements of historical engagement, such as empathy, critical thinking, and appropriation. Additionally, the learners are changed by the authentic learning experience that time travel provides. They are no longer idiots and class clowns. Bill and Ted philosophize with Socrates, escape a medieval execution, repair a time machine, and manipulate time travel in order to avoid detainment from their presentation. The authentic learning environment has allowed genuine engagement with transferable skills. While they did not approach the assessment task with intrinsic motivation, engagement in the task allowed them to achieve meaningful understanding of historical concepts and to develop valuable life skills.

Frame 3: The Audience

Bill and Ted are "most triumphant" at the end of the film. They are able to harness the opportunities of assessment to genuinely engage with the task's implied learning outcomes and collaboratively present a product that can be successfully rewarded by the teacher and appreciated by their audience. Their final presentation is truly spectacular, with lighting, sound, historical characters in role, re-enactments, and visual aids supporting their factual information and analysis. Working with the implied criteria, they are able to achieve the required A+ grade, avoiding separation, the military academy, and expulsion from school. The protagonists' success creates a mood of jubilation, aiming to incite a sense of satisfaction from the film's audience, as if order has been restored and justice has prevailed. The third frame emerging from the analysis is that of the movie's audience – the consumers of the film, for whom it was created. The audience is fed familiar narratives about schooling and assessment, many of them mythologies, around which the tension of the story is based.

Mythologies in this context can be understood as uninterrogated understandings, or largely unquestioned or uninformed bodies of knowledge (Finneran, 2009), rather than untrue stories or fables. Barthes, as analyzed by Moriarty (1991) adds that myths are not characterized by truth, rather by the way in which they utter a message. There are several utterances about schooling and assessment in *Bill & Ted's excellent adventure*. However, this chapter does not seek to establish alternative truths or engage in myth-busting. Rather, mythologies are explored with the intention of interrogating perceptions of assessment that are perpetuated in popular culture.

The film's writers have chosen to characterize the assessment regime as unfair and cruel, requiring the protagonists to triumph over insurmountable odds. While their history teacher, Mr. Ryan, is not unjust (indeed, he allows them a final opportunity for redemption), the situation seems hopeless. The tension-inducing storyline coerces the audience to sympathize with the loveable rogues. Here, schooling and assessment are mythologized in a number of ways. The teacher and school have devalued sustained engagement in the learning environment, as a superior performance in one task, crafted in just one night, is assumed able to compensate for a year of academic deficiency. As discussed previously, no criteria for performance was given and teacher gave the students no guidance on the task, nor had he seen the ideas in development. While this level of distance may be commonplace for some tasks, work of a performative nature is often done under guidance, or even in collaboration (Bird, 2006) between teachers and students.

The portrayal of secrecy surrounding assessment is pervasive in popular representations of assessment, as if students must crack a secret code shielded by the teacher until found out. When students ultimately do succeed, they are shown to have beaten the system through their own perseverance, cleverness, or street-smarts, as opposed to the system having facilitated a meaningful learning experience. The protagonists are portrayed as unique, displaying out-of-the-box thinking that is uncorrupted by the academy and its oppressive, highly theoretical ways. This representation of the protagonists has echoes of the "noble savage," a mythological construction that posits that humanity is happier and morally superior in its original utopian state, free of absolutist rules (Greer, 1993), able to demonstrate unstifled creativity.

The popular appeal of the noble savage and assessment myths is significant, in that it perpetuates a worldview that schools are overly theoretical, unconcerned with students' dispositions, while devaluing real-world skills. The pervasiveness of these myths in film suggests that audiences, at least in part, identify schools as oppressive, or at best an obstacle to be negotiated. Within this, it is largely accepted that assessment is a challenging, even painful, but necessary engagement that must be endured. Popular culture rarely presents schooling devoid of stressful endeavours and rich with formative tasks crafted in the students' interest. To do so would compromise the tension of the performative space and the appeal of the film. It is understood that movies are made within an industry characterized by mass-marketing and large-scale appeal. However, many of the mythologies perpetuated for large-scale audiences have a disconnect with assessment practices in modern schooling. Assessment is inherently complex and multi-faceted. These complexities are largely uninteresting for a film-going audience; therefore, the perceptions discussed in this chapter are allowed to endure.

Assessment Representations: A Bogus Journey?

This chapter has presented three frames through which we can view representations of assessment in *Bill & Ted's excellent adventure*. These three are not a definitive list of frames. Other frames that emerged included the teachers' attitude to assessment, the performative response, and defiance as a pathway to success in assessment. This film operates in an American context, and their schooling system and accompanying assessment culture is also a frame for further examination. Brevity and the defined focus of this chapter prevent further discussion of other frames here. However, an interesting inquiry would be the portrayals of assessment in film, literature, and performed texts, in order to determine if the representations are generally shrouded in negativity, and to identify spaces for alternative portrayals that are more aspirational.

Frames have separate and discrete qualities, yet unfold further meanings when layered over each other. The frames explored in this chapter create a fuller picture of the assessment environment as represented in a popular film. When exploring the way the task and the learner are presented to the audience of film consumers, we find some conclusions that can be drawn about the popular characterization of schooling and assessment. As is shown throughout this book, schools are heightened spaces for dramatic action. The presence of eclectic and diverse crowds, cultural norms, children, and adolescents in their raw and formative states and rituals and hierarchies creates an environment ripe for great viewing. Schools are also spaces that are familiar to most audiences. While we may not have all been in hospital, on a tour of duty, or in space, most of us have been to school. Most people have negotiated school's social structures, been taught by teachers of varying degrees of comfort and competence, and engaged in assessment. Despite the use of time travel as a plot device, audiences of *Bill & Ted's excellent adventure* are dealing with a known entity. It is understandable that screen-writers fall back on stereotypes and myths. These myths on screen perpetuate themselves, as in this case, casting assessment as an enemy to be conquered. At the same time, we rejoice when the protagonists are triumphant, as we have all been tested at some time. We are all too familiar with the "bogus journey," but we also know that success feels "most excellent."

REFERENCES

Biggs, J. (1993). From theory to practice: A cognitive systems approach. *Higher Education Research and Development, 12*(1), 73–85.

Biggs, J. (1999). *Teaching for quality at university*. New York, NY: SRHE; Open University Press.

Biggs, J. B., & Tang, C. S. (2011). *Teaching for quality learning at university: What the student does* (4th ed.). Maidenhead, UK: McGraw-Hill; Society for Research into Higher Education; Open University Press.

Bird, J. (2006). One-on-one: What is the role of the drama teacher in the process of teaching the solo performance? *NJ (Drama Australia Journal), 30*(1), 79–89.

Britzman, D. (1986). Cultural myths in the making of a teacher: Biography and social structure in teacher education. *Harvard Educational Review, 56*(4), 442–456.

Britzman, D. P. (1992). The terrible problem of knowing thyself: Toward a poststructural account of teacher identity. *Journal of curriculum theorizing, 9*(3), 23-46.

Delandshere, G., & Petrosky, A. R. (1994). Capturing teachers' knowledge: Performance assessment a) And post-structuralist epistemology, b) From a post-structuralist perspective, c) And post-structuralism, d) None of the above. *Educational Researcher, 23*(5), 11–18.

Edmiston, B., & McKibben, A. (2011). Shakespeare, rehearsal approaches, and dramatic inquiry: Literacy education for life. *English in Education, 45*(1), 86–101.

Eisner, E. (1998). *The kind of schools we need: Personal essays*. Portsmouth, NH: Heinemann.

Finneran, M. (2009). *Critical myths in drama as education* [Unpublished doctoral dissertation]. University of Warwick, Coventry, UK.

Foucault, M. (1972). *The archaeology of knowledge & the discourse on language*. New York, NY: Pantheon.

Goffman, E. (1974). *Frame analysis: An essay on the organization of experience*. New York, NY: Harper & Row.

Gray, D., & Williams, S. (2012). Facilitating educational leadership: Using frames to increase action. *Leadership & Organization Development Journal, 33*(6), 583–593.

Greer, S. (1993). The noble savage. *Winds of Change, 8*(2), 89–92.

Hounsell, D. (1997). Contrasting conceptions of essay-writing. In F. Marton, D. Hounsell, & N. Entwistle (Eds.), *The experience of learning* (2nd ed.) (pp. 106–125). Edinburgh, UK: Scottish Academic Press.

Inyengar, S., & Lepper, M. (1999). Rethinking the value of choice: A cultural perspective on intrinsic motivation. *Journal of Personality and Social Psychology* 76(3), 349–366.

Inyengar, S., & Lepper, M. (2000). When choice is demotivating: Can one desire too much of a good thing?. *Journal of Personality and Social Psychology, 79*(6), 995–1006.

Jackson, N. (2011). *Learning for a complex world: A lifewide concept of learning, education and personal development.* Bloomington, IN: Authorhouse.

Jacobs, R. (2015). *Drama performance assessment in senior secondary years: A study of six Australian schools* [Unpublished doctoral dissertation]. University of Western Sydney, Penrith, Australia.

Kroopf, S., Murphey, M. S., Soisson, J. (Producers), & Herek, S. (Director). (1989). *Bill & Ted's excellent adventure* [Motion picture]. USA: Orion Pictures Corporation.

Malmeer, E., & Zoghi, M. (2014). Dynamic assessment of grammar with different age groups. *Theory and Practice in Language Studies, 4*(8), 1707–1713.

Maslow, A. H. (1970). Motivation and personality. New York, NY: Harper & Row.

McMillan, J. H. (2000). Fundamental assessment principles for teachers and school administrators. *Practical Assessment, Research & Evaluation, 7*(8). Retrieved from http://PARE-online.net/getvn.asp?v=7&n=8

Moriarty, M. (1991). *Roland Barthes.* Oxford: Polity Press.

Norton, L. S. (1990). Essay writing: What really counts? *Higher Education, 20*(4), 411–442.

Orrell, J. (2005, Nov). *Assessment literacy: A precursor to improving the quality of assessment.* Paper presented at the Evaluation and Assessment Conference. University of Technology, Sydney, Australia.

Pain, R., & Mowl, G. (1996). Improving geography essay writing using innovative assessment. *Journal of Geography in Higher Education, 20*(1), 19–31.

Rainio, A. P., & Marjanovic-Shane, A. (2013). From ambivalence to agency: Becoming an author, an actor and a hero in a drama workshop. *Learning, Culture and Social Interaction, 2*(2), 111–125.

Ross, M. (1991). The hidden order of arts education. *British Journal of Aesthetics, 31*(2), 111–121.

Said, E. (1985). *Beginnings: Intention and methods.* New York, NY: Columbia University Press.

Simon, H. S. (1973). The structure of ill-structured problems. *Artificial Intelligence, 4*(1), 181–201.

Virkki, T., Husso, M., Notko, M., Holma, J., Laitila, A., & Mäntysaari, M. (2014). Possibilities for intervention in domestic violence: Frame analysis of health care professionals' attitudes. *Journal of Social Service Research, 41*(1), 6–24.

PART IV

Ethics and Desire
in Teaching

Teaching as a Moral Act: Reflections on Five Plays Featuring Teachers and Students (Shaw's *Pygmalion*, Kanin's *Born Yesterday*, Riml's *RAGE*, Mamet's *Oleanna*, and Russell's *Educating Rita*)

Monica Prendergast

Introduction

Drawing on ethnographer and performance theorist Dwight Conquergood's (1985) seminal essay "Performing as a moral act," this chapter reflects on five plays with a teacher–student relationship at their heart. Four plays are placed onto quadrants of Conquergood's model of moral mapping that considers ethical tensions between identity/difference and detachment/commitment in ethnographic performance. One play is placed into the middle, what Conquergood calls the space of *dialogical performance*. Conquergood's moral map was intended to critique ethnographers' performative representations of the "other," including his own, as ethically laden. I use his insights here to explore the portrayals of characters and teacher–student relationships in the plays as a way to better see how these playwrights' artful and deliberate portrayals of teacher–student relationships may be viewed through an ethnographic lens that allows an audience insight into the cultural practices of education.

The chapter raises class difference, commonly inherent in the relationship between teacher and student, as a key feature that cuts across these plays. When underprivileged, lower class students engage with more privileged, higher class teachers, moral questions around how these encounters are portrayed on stage become pressing. Avoiding the risks of selfishness, superficiality, sensationalism, or cynicism – that are arguably seen in four of the five plays discussed herein – allows for a more critical understanding of class difference in both plays and films featuring educational settings and characters. The fifth play offers a more humane and complex portrayal across the spectrums of identity and difference, detachment and commitment, which can be considered an example of dialogical performance.

The five plays addressed in this chapter are *Pygmalion* by George Bernard Shaw (1916/2005), *Born yesterday* by Garson Kanin (1946), *RAGE* by Michele Riml (2014), *Oleanna* by David Mamet (1992), and *Educating Rita* by Willy Russell (1981). I note that four out of five plays are written by men, adding another potential layer of critique (that of patriarchy, with professional theatre remaining a male-dominated art form to this day [Burton, 2006; MacArthur, 2015]) to my consideration of class difference.

I will begin by summarizing Conquergood's key points and sketching out his moral mapping model. Then I will place each play onto the ethical pitfall areas of Conquergood's model with reflections on my reasons. Finally, I will consider the one play that invites a more equitable encounter across class difference as a model of dialogical performance.

Conquergood's Moral Map

Conquergood spent a number of years living with and conducting ethnographic research with the Lao and Hmong refugee communities in Chicago in the early 1980s. The trust and relationship he built with his participant groups led to Conquergood telling traditional tales from these cultural groups as ethnographic performances at conferences and in community presentations. In the first part of his essay, Conquergood describes how audiences reacted to this early ethnographic performance work: "I have been attacked, not just in the sessions of discussion and response immediately following these performances" (1985, p. 3). He was able to negotiate and mediate the negative responses from academics, social workers, and others concerned with his use of oral storytelling as legitimate research. That said, many in his audiences were deeply moved by the authenticity and respect shown in his representation of the "other."

This experience led Conquergood (1985) to consider the ethical implications of performing these stories: "I can be grateful to my detractors for forcing into my awareness the complex ethical tensions, tacit political commitments, and moral ambiguities inextricably caught up in the act of performing ethnographic materials" (p. 4).

In order to address these moral and ethical concerns, Conquergood (1985) outlines four "ethical pitfalls" (p. 4) of performative stances towards a culture under investigation. He considers any ethnographic performance that corresponds to these quadrants of the map morally problematic. The key to authentically conveying a culture is through "dialogical performance […] the moral center that transcends and reconciles" (p. 5).

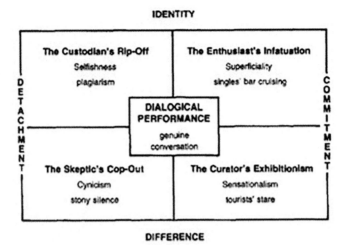

FIGURE 1: "Moral mapping of performative stances toward the Other"(Conquergood, 1985, p. 5). Reproduced with permission from Taylor & Francis Group.

Conquergood's four problematic stances are: The Custodian's Rip-Off, or a stance of "strong attraction toward the other coupled with extreme detachment" (p. 5); The Enthusiast's Infatuation, or the realm of the "quick-fix, pick-up artist" that is unethical because it "trivializes the other" (p. 6); The Curator's Exhibitionism, or the practice of astonishing the audience rather than promoting understanding in which the manifest sin is sensationalism (p. 7); and The Skeptic's Cop-Out, or the refuge of "cowards and cynics" who refuse to face up and struggle with the ethical tensions of performing culturally sensitive materials (p. 8).

The five plays featuring a central relationship between a teacher and a student that I wish to survey here can be effectively placed onto Conquergood's model. In this way, we can consider a body of plays with a shared topic as falling into ethical pitfalls around the ethnographic representation of teachers and teaching on stage. The fifth play, for me, functions as a model of dialogical performance: "The aim of dialogical performance is to bring self and other together so that they can question, debate and challenge one another" (p. 9).

The custodian's rip-off: *Pygmalion*

George Bernard Shaw's popular 1913 play *Pygmalion* (1916/2005) has become even better known in its musical adaptation *My fair lady* (Loewe & Lerner, 1956). In the original play, Professor Henry Higgins, a well-known phonetician, makes a bet with a friend that he can pass off a Cockney flower girl as a duchess. This young girl, Eliza Doolittle, gives Higgins a run for his money in her spiritedness and independence. Their class difference is a central feature of the play. Shaw's plays often feature social critique and in this case the teacher figure of Higgins is shown to be brilliant yet blindly arrogant and socially inappropriate in upper-class contexts. The student Eliza comes from an impoverished background, but has ambitions to rise up in the world. Her dream is to become socially acceptable enough in her speech and manners to work in a flower shop rather than sell flowers on the street.

This class disparity between teacher and student is more marked in *Pygmalion* (1916/2005) than any of the other four plays discussed in this chapter. Much of the humour in the play comes from the clashes between Higgins and Doolittle as he tries to teach her to speak in a higher class way.

> Liza: Garn!
> Higgins: There! As the girl very properly say, Garn! Married indeed! Don't you know that a woman of that class looks a worn out drudge of fifty the year after she's married?
> Liza: Whood marry me?
> Higgins: *[suddenly resorting to the most thrillingly beautiful low tones in his best elocutionary style]* By George, Eliza, the streets will be strewn with the bodies of men shooting themselves for your sake before I've done with you. [...]
> Liza: *[rising and squaring herself determinedly]* I'm going away. He's off his chump, he is. I don't want no balmies teaching me.
> Higgins: *[wounded at his tenderest point by her insensibility to his elocution]* Oh, indeed! I'm mad, am I? Very well, Mrs. Pearce: you needn't order the new clothes for her. Throw her out.
>
> (Shaw, 1916/2005, p. 32)

By the play's end the bet has been won, but Eliza has decided to leave Higgins and marry a young suitor whilst also becoming a flower shop clerk as she had dreamed. There is a romantic tension between Higgins and Doolittle that is made overt in the musical version. Shaw himself was very resistant to this romanticization; he was more realistic in believing that the class gap between these two characters could never be bridged ("*Pygmalion,*" n.d.).

In terms of Conquergood's (1985) moral map, I see that Shaw (1916/2005) portrays the character of Higgins in his relationship to Doolittle as guilty of the sin of selfishness which is central to the ethical pitfall of the custodian's rip-off. "A strong attachment to the other coupled with extreme detachment results in acquisitiveness instead of genuine inquiry, plunder more than performance" (p. 5). Higgins' ill treatment of Eliza is a theme that runs throughout the play. He is repeatedly castigated by his mother, Colonel Pickering, and his housekeeper for how thoughtlessly he treats his student. Shaw is making a satirical point about the poor behaviour of the so-called upper classes. Yet we can also see Higgins' portrayal by Shaw as a good model of Conquergood's concerns. In this dramatic setting, it is about an upper-class teacher's extreme detachment leading to acquisitiveness and plunder of a working-class student for his own ends.

The enthusiast's infatuation: *Born yesterday*

Garson Kanin's (1946) comedy *Born yesterday* opened on Broadway in 1946 and ran for two years starring Judy Holliday in the role of gangster moll and former showgirl Billie Dawn. In the play, Billie's long-time boyfriend Harry Brock has arrived in Washington D.C. to buy off a congressman in support of his "junk" business. Billie's lack of knowledge embarrasses Brock enough to hire journalist Paul Verrall as her tutor. Billie and Paul fall in love as he teaches her about American politics and history. They come to realize Harry's corruption, intervene to prevent it happening, and make plans to run off together. The 1950 film version was directed by George Cukor and features Holliday in her stage role as Billie, William Holden as Paul, and Broderick Crawford as the uncouth and abusive Harry.

Kanin's (1946) play places a stereotypical "dumb blonde" at its centre; not an easy thing for a twenty-first-century audience to witness. However, the twist in the play is that, as Billie gains an education, her intuition tells her that Harry has been up to no good. She decides, with her tutor and new romantic partner, to set things right. That said, the first act of the play gives the audience a portrayal of an empty-headed and ignorant lower-class young woman who knows very little of the world. Her boyfriend is repeatedly verbally abusive to her and later in the play Brock hits Billie. She also tells Paul about being beaten by her father.

Mapped onto Conquergood's model, we see a good fit in Kanin's (1946) portrayals of the characters, in particular Billie, with the issue of superficiality. "Too facile identification with the other coupled with enthusiastic commitment produces naïve and glib performances marked by superficiality" (p. 6). For an urbane and educated theatre audience, watching *Born yesterday* puts spectators into a position of class superiority, laughing at Billie's unknowingness and bristling at the boorish Brock. The relationship between teacher and student, Paul and Billie, is an example of facile identification; Paul's enthusasm for the job is clearly connected to his sexual attraction to Billie. The twist in the plot is that Billie turns out to have an innate intelligence that no one has expected to see, least of all Billie herself. "Billie: Because when ya steal from the government, you're stealing from yourself, ya dumb ox" (Kanin, 1946, p. 87). The infatuation both Paul and the audience feel for Billie is one in which "[t]he distinctiveness of the other is glossed over by a glaze of generalities" (Conquergood, 1985, p. 6). In this case it is the stage portrayal of a clichéd, attractive but uneducated young woman whose ignorance earns laughs. While the character grows into knowledge, the audience is left with their stereotypes and class prejudices intact.

The curator's exhibitionism: *RAGE*

This play will be the least familiar to an international reader. *RAGE* is a Canadian Theatre for Young Audiences (TYA) play by playwright Michele Riml (2014). It was produced by Vancouver's Green Thumb Theatre, one of Canada's top TYA companies, in 2004–2005 and 2006–2007. The play has two characters with high-school student Raymond (who goes by the name Rage) confronting his guidance counsellor Laura in 70 minutes of real-time onstage. The encounter begins as a debate about non-violence, with the student clearly trying to provoke a response from the pacifist teacher, whose views he disrespects. Then things get heightened when nihilist (and suicidal) Rage tells idealist Laura he has a gun in his backpack and that if she will not kill him with it then he will kill her. The play ends with the characters in a physical struggle over the gun. It goes off and Rage collapses.

Vancouver theatre critic Colin Thomas (2004) echoes the concerns I had when I saw the play in 2007:

> It's too much about the thrill of the gun and not enough about the issues the gun represents By depending so much on the narrative force of the weapon, Riml runs the risk of contributing to our desensitized, voyeuristic relationship to violence.
>
> (2004, para. 6–7)

The play fails its young audiences because it falls into Conquergood's (1985) ethical trap of exhibitionism and sensationalism "that wants to astonish rather than understand" (p. 7). As I wrote in an online review (Prendergast, 2007):

> For me, the literalness of the play, played out in real time, is its downfall. The theatre is built on metaphor. When you pull out a gun, it's just a gun, a killing machine that shuts down debate, empathy, hope. I long for a theatre that engages me (and, more crucially, young people) through metaphors that lift and transcend to become glimpses of the solution, not a theatre trapped in the hopelessness of the problem, as this play is.
>
> (para. 3)

The play's representation of the teacher–student relationship also falls victim to sensationalism that Conquergood (1985) condemns as "an immoral stance because it dehumanizes the other" (p. 7). The class difference between teacher and student is less stark than the other plays discussed, but the shock tactic of the gun creates a dehumanization of Rage's character when it appears out of his backpack halfway through the play. Until that point we do not know if he is just testing his teacher's beliefs. When the gun appears, Rage is suddenly reduced to his violent potentiality. Thus, a teacher–student encounter across difference is also reduced to voyeuristic melodrama.

The skeptic's cop-out: *Oleanna*

David Mamet's 1992 play about a professor meeting with an unhappy college student is well known for the controversy surrounding it. Mamet has always been a provocative playwright, unafraid to push his audience's buttons, to destabilize and unsettle their expectations. The two characters in *Oleanna* are equally unlikeable, making it very difficult for an audience to find where their sympathies lie. Professor John comes across early in the play as distracted and condescending towards Carol, who is meeting with him due to her anxiety that she is failing his class. He offers her platitudes while at the same time answering many phone calls about his upcoming house purchase; the reward he is anticipating after being granted tenure. Near the end of the first scene he puts his arm around Carol to comfort her.

In the next scene we hear that she has launched a complaint against John. The tables begin to turn in their power relationship as she charges him with sexism and elitism. John's tenure is threatened and he desperately tries to figure out how to placate Carol. She reveals that she has been meeting with a feminist group. Her language becomes more and more politically correct as she gains status. At the end of the second scene, he physically prevents her from leaving his office and she cries out for help.

In the third and final scene, they meet once again (a highly unlikely scenario, given what has happened, but granting dramatic licence). John has lost his job and his new home. Carol has charged him with attempted rape. The scene becomes a brutal attack on each other that culminates in John physically assaulting Carol after she demands that a number of books (including his own) be banned from campus and she tells him not to call his wife "Baby" over the phone. The last line of the play is Carol's: cowering on the floor she says, "Yes. That's right… yes. That's right" (Mamet, 1992, p. 80). All her beliefs about patriarchy and male violence have been confirmed. But has she been culpable in creating this situation?

I saw this play in Toronto in the early 1990s. It was a very discomfiting play to witness and certainly sparked a lot of intense debate. Ultimately, though, I do consider that the teacher and student characters Mamet portrays in the play fall into Conquergood's (1985) moral map under the heading of skepticism and cynicism.

"There is no null hypothesis in the moral universe. Refusal to take a moral stand is itself a powerful statement of one's moral position" (p. 8). Conquergood considers this the most reprehensible ethical stance of all "because it forecloses dialogue" (p. 8). What we see in *Oleanna* is the impossibility of dialogue, due to entrenched positions on both sides. Mamet's depiction of deep cynicism about education and political correctness comes across in Conquergood's description: "The skeptic, detached and estranged, with no sense of the other, sits alone in an echo-chamber of his own making" (p. 9).

Dialogical performance: *Educating Rita*

In contrast with the four plays discussed above, Willy Russell's 1981 play *Educating Rita* offers a dramatic portrayal of a teacher–student relationship that Conquergood would call a "genuine conversation" (p. 5). In the play, Northern English hairdresser Rita takes an Open University course in English literature with lecturer Frank. Frank is openly cynical and alcoholic, burned out and embittered. Rita blasts into his office for tutoring like a spring wind. From the first scene, we realize the equality between these two. Despite their class differences and roles as teacher and student, it is clear that Frank has more than met his match in the remarkable Rita. She calls him on his drinking, his negativity, his sense of failure. She challenges him to rise to the job of teaching her, and her hunger for learning pushes him to do so. They discuss literature and theatre, but also issues around working-class versus middle-class culture, their personal relationships with their partners, and Rita's hopes for a better future:

> Rita: I don't want pity, Frank. Was it rubbish?
> Frank: No, no. It's not rubbish. It's a totally honest, passionate account of your reaction to a play. It's an unashamedly emotional statement about a certain experience.
> Rita: Sentimental?
> Frank: No. It's too honest for that. It's almost – erm – moving. But in terms of what you're asking me to teach you of passing exams… Oh, God, you see, I don't…
> Rita: Say it, go on, say it!
> Frank: In those terms it's worthless. It shouldn't be but it is; in its own terms it's – it's wonderful.
>
> (Russell, 1981, p. 33)

By the end of the play, Rita has left her husband and has succeeded in passing her exams. Frank has been sent on an extended leave, due to his inappropriate drinking, and is headed for a new life in Australia. There is a spark of romantic longing between Frank and Rita to which she does not submit; Rita is the stronger character and the final moment of the play shows this as she grabs a pair of scissors to cut Frank's unkempt hair.

As quoted earlier, "[t]he aim of dialogical performance is to bring self and other together so that they can question, debate and challenge one another" (Conquergood, 1985, p. 9). *Educating Rita* provides the best example in this chapter's survey of five plays featuring a central teacher–student relationship of a cross-class encounter that is an "intimate conversation" (p. 10). Both are changed by their encounter, they become close friends who can tell each other the truth, even when it hurts. Their relationship becomes a gift they both treasure: "one cannot begin a friendship without beginning a conversation" (p. 10).

Conclusion

Dwight Conquergood's influential essay has provided a useful model in my interdisciplinary inquiry that has surveyed five plays with educational themes as ethnographies of cross-class encounters between teachers and their students. The ethical pitfalls Conquergood warns against are seen in the plays in which selfishness (*Pygmalion*), superficiality (*Born yesterday*), sensationalism (*RAGE*), and cynicism (*Oleanna*) prevent the teacher and student characters from engaging in a genuine encounter across difference. Only in *Educating Rita* do we see the possibility of a dramatization of a teacher–student relationship that is dialogical, intimate yet appropriate, and within which each character is changed for the better by the experience.

From a feminist perspective, only one of the five plays features a woman teacher figure, in the only play written by a woman. This speaks to the ongoing issue of a lack of women in leadership roles in theatre; women playwrights, directors, and artistic directors make up only a third of the profession in Canada (see Burton, 2006; MacArthur, 2015). What would shift in what we see on stage in a theatre world that had achieved gender equity? That is a broader and deeper question than can be addressed here, but one that was raised as a result of my investigation.

My intention here has been to invite readers who are educators or facilitators to consider their own class and gender biases when working in classrooms or other educational settings (such as community-based ones in applied theatre). How often and how much do we fail to "see" a student/participant across the chasm of difference? These differences may be rooted in culture, gender, sexuality, class, or even in areas less defined such as "personality." Nevertheless, the job of a teacher/facilitator is to teach in the most ethically responsible way possible. What have these five plays, and my analyses of them here, taught me? That I must never teach without making the wholehearted effort to enter into a dialogical relationship with my students. Learning who my students are, and sharing with them who I am, is foundational to my pedagogy as a drama educator. We cannot create together without that basis of knowledge and trust. That is how an effective performance ensemble (from the French "together") is formed; through a process of authentic engagement with each other and with ourselves.

Conquergood concludes his essay by calling on performance ethnographers to find the energy, imagination, and courage to enter into authentic engagement with the "other." "The ethnographic movement in performance studies will die if it does not reach out to share the human dignity of the other, the other-wise, with audiences…" (p. 11). I have examined five plays featuring a teacher–student relationship and found that the portrayal too often slips into moral morasses that limit the "human dignity of the other." Fortunately, one play offers an alternative in its humorous yet sincere portrait of a flawed teacher and a motivated student who are deeply and positively changed through their encounter across difference.

REFERENCES

Burton, R. (2006). *Adding it up: The status of women in Canadian theatre* [Report]. Toronto, ON: Playwrights Guild of Canada. Retrieved from www.playwrightsguild.ca/sites/default/files/AddingItUp.pdf

Conquergood, D. (1985). Performing as a moral act: Ethical dimensions of the ethnography of performance. *Literature in Performance, 5*(2), 1–13.

Kanin, G. (1946). *Born yesterday*. New York, NY: Dramatists Play Service.

Loewe, F. (Composer), & Lerner, A. J. (Lyrics and book). (1956). *My fair lady* [Musical]. New York, NY: Herman Levin.

Mamet, D. (1992). *Oleanna*. New York, NY: Vintage.

MacArthur, M. (2015). *Achieving equity in Canadian theatre: A report with best practice recommendations*. Toronto, ON: Playwrights Guild of Canada. Retrieved from https://equityintheatre.com/achieving-equity-canadian-theatre

Prendergast, M. (2007, February 12). *RAGE* at Green Thumb Theatre. [Web log review]. *Victoria Theatre Reviews*. Retrieved from http://vicreviews.blogspot.ca/2007/02/rage-at-green-thumb-theatre.html

Riml, M. (2014). *RAGE*. In E. Hurley (Ed.), *Once more with feeling: Five affecting plays*. Toronto, ON: Playwrights Canada Press.

Russell, W. (1981). *Educating Rita*. New York, NY: Samuel French.

Shaw, G. B. (2005). *Pygmalion*. Clayton, DE: Prestwick House. (Original work published in 1916)

Thomas, C. (2004, December 2). RAGE [Web log review]. The Georgia Straight. Retrieved from http://www.straight.com/article/rage

Granting "the Wherewithal to Resist": The Erotic as Pedagogical Supplement in Alan Bennett's *The History Boys*

Ian Tan Xing Long

Introduction

Having enjoyed a successful run at the UK's National Theatre in 2004 and an equally impressive stint in the United States on Broadway in 2006, Alan Bennett's (2004a) play *The history boys* has always managed, in the words of reviewer Michael Billington (2004), to "[capture] the public imagination" (p. 2) with its vibrant and trenchant evocation of the dynamics of the interactions between teachers and students, and the shaping influence educators have over their impressionable charges. Beyond the aspects of its appeal and how Bennett seizes upon the dramatic potential of the presentation of the play's three teachers and their attitudes towards education and pedagogical methods, I argue that the play invites complex responses to the relationships between education and truth, the classroom and the forces of the wider world, and the professional role of teachers and their humanity. I will start by examining Bennett's portrayal of teachers Hector, Irwin, and Mrs. Lintott as representatives in a debate. The play opens up about "two sorts of teaching" (Bennett, 2004b). If Vineberg (2006) is right to see a "dialectic" (p. 20) between Hector and Irwin, this contrast does not merely pertain to their teaching styles and personalities, but also to their conceptualizations of the ultimate aims and ends of education.

Using the philosopher Jacques Derrida's (1967) notion of the *supplement* as that which is peripheral to a main body of discourse, but which also becomes constitutive and therefore ends up undermining it, I argue that in contrast to Irwin's disingenuous presentation of historical fact, which turns truth into a matter of self-serving "presentation" (Bennett, 2004a, p. 9), the appeal of Hector's pedagogical method lies in *both* its absolute periphery to the education system as laid out by the headmaster and in its centrality: "it is the only education worth having" (p. 109). More troublingly, however, Hector's transgressive sexual actions with respect to his students provide another instance of the operation of the supplement that challenges our understanding of the humanity of teachers, as Hector's deviant behaviour can be read as both a sign of his flawed humanity and as being central to his identity as a teacher. Our response to Hector is thus complicated when we have to negotiate our admiration for his integrity in the classroom with recognition of the illicit impulses behind it. Rather than offering stereotypical portrayals of teachers, Bennett's (2004a) play destabilizes our conventional ideas about teachers and teaching to open up imaginative and intellectual space through which deeper questions can be asked about the nature of the profession itself, and the place of education in society.

Two Models of Teaching: Irwin and Hector

Bennett (2004b) notes in his Introduction to *The history boys* that his play seems to be about "two teachers [...] who were teaching more or less in the present" (p. xix) and their impacts on their students. It will therefore be instructive to examine Bennett's portrayal of Irwin and Hector and how their distinctive pedagogical styles seek to establish Bennett's self-conscious treatment of "presentation" (p. xxv) through the dramatic medium of theatre. While having immediacy as characters in themselves, Bennett employs the figures of Irwin and Hector to probe deeper questions about the relationship of education to society, which particularly hinges on the question of how classroom knowledge and its transmission establishes truth.

In his interaction with his students, the supply history teacher Irwin seeks not to emphasize "competence," but "singularity" (Bennett, 2004a, p. 18). His teaching method involves the foregrounding of an obscure but original approach to the subject matter. In a comment about student essays on the Reformation, he highlights how "some silly nonsense on the foreskins of Christ will come in handy so that [the] essays [on the topic] will not be dull" (p. 19). For Kelleher (2005), Irwin's teaching method "seems to sit somewhere between the excitements of a certain sort of flashy critical theory and the no less 'postmodern' imperatives of accumulation and self-advancement" (p. 51). Kelleher's emphasis on Irwin's flashiness in seeking and flaunting a counterintuitive way to frame historical material highlights Bennett's ironic look at the relativism inherent in historical inquiry; indeed, as Irwin notes,

> Our perspective on the past alters. Looking back, immediately in front of us is dead ground. We don't see it and because we don't see it this means that there

is no period so remote as the recent past and one of the historian's jobs is to anticipate what our perspective of that period will be.

(Bennett, 2004a, p. 74)

If our perspectives of the past turn out to be contested ground, then historical truth cannot be accessed apart from the way it is represented and *taught*. In contrast to the liberating potentialities associated with the opening up of alternative versions of history, Bennett interrogates the politics of teaching through Irwin by suggesting a certain degree of disingenuousness behind his avowed penchant to shock. By framing his contrarian approach to history with the aim of standing out for "oddity, extremity and flair" (Bennett, 2004b, p. xxiii) *solely* for the purposes of entry into Oxford and Cambridge, Irwin packages knowledge as "cultural capital, how to have it but also *profit* by it" (Kelleher, 2005, p. 51, emphasis added). The cynicism inherent in the student, Dakin's, profession that history is "turning facts on their head [...] like a game" (p. 80) presents Bennett's criticism of how knowledge can be turned into a commodity to serve baser, more utilitarian ends. It is little wonder that in his later role as a presenter of history on popular television, Irwin chooses to emphasize the materialism that is, he claims, at the basis of monastic asceticism.

As if in direct contrast to Irwin, Bennett portrays Hector, the school's English teacher, as someone who directly resists "the commodification of education" (Jacobi, 2006, p. 77) as represented both by Irwin and the headmaster. If Billington (2004) is right to see one of the central conflicts of the play as "between bustling pragmatism and beleaguered humanism" (p. 3), Hector's determined resistance to the dictates of the educational system involves giving his students "literary insulation, proof against the primacy of fact" (Bennett, 2004a, p. 75), which equates to the coarsening of sensibility and deadening of spirit. Jacobi summarizes Hector's pedagogical approach as such:

> Hector's alternative to commodification could be called an "erotics of education," in which clearly articulated curricula, lesson plans, and daily class content are secondary to the ability of the teacher to inspire his students and to engage their desire to learn for its own sake.
>
> (2006, p. 78)

Hector thus ironically calls his lessons "a waste of time" (Bennett, 2004a, p. 5); the grammar lessons he gives magnificently descend into "calculated silliness" (p. 94) and comic farce when the original scene of a Parisian brothel changes into a military battlefield after the unexpected intrusion of the headmaster, who becomes the butt of the collective joke through his unwitting participation in the preposterous nature of the scene. Elsewhere, the students' farcical role-playing from melodramatic films for Hector's benefit serves not for intertextual dialogue with the original as much as sheer delight in the self-conscious performance and parody of the original. Hector's polemical stance that his teaching gives his students "the wherewithal to resist" (p. 23) the systemic nature of education sets him in contrast to Irwin and his manipulation of historical facts to appear "clever, dramatic, and eye-catching rather than 'true' both to itself and its practitioners" (Stansky, 2009, p. 685). Indeed, Hector insists that the quotations he makes his students memorize are "learned *by heart* [...] where they belong and like other components of the heart not to be defiled by being trotted out to order" (p. 48, emphasis original). Whereas Irwin devalues knowledge by making it fit some predetermined agenda, Hector stresses the engraving of literature in the minds and hearts of his charges and an appreciation of its capacity to mean something to them in the future and outside of the classroom.

Bennett's (2004a) use of irony, however, allows his audience to understand the larger complexities surrounding the relationship between education and society, and how much of an impact teachers can really have on their students. Despite Bennett's (2016) observation in his autobiography *Keeping on keeping on* that the allure of school and examinations (upon which his play draws) is the bestowal of "a breathing space" in which "life can be put off" (p. 419), *The history boys* (Bennett, 2004a) ironically gestures towards the disappointing outcomes of its students despite their triumphant entries into Oxford: Timms succumbs to substance abuse; Dakin has internalized Irwin's disregard for truth in his profession as a tax lawyer by "telling highly paid fibs" (p. 107); and Posner, who among all the students took "the words of Hector" (p. 108) to heart, ends up disenfranchised and broken. Surveying what the students have become after leaving school and university, it is hard to ignore Mrs. Lintott's observation about Hector that he teaches the way he does "as some sort of insurance against the boys' ultimate failure" (p. 69). More dispiritingly, Bennett's play demonstrates how other educational institutions and societal structures share affinities with Irwin's rhetoric: Posner passes his interview because he plays down the question of the Holocaust to suggest his detachment; Lintott describes Oxford to be like "everybody else" (p. 93) in its cynical materialism; and Irwin himself ends up as a politician, who tries to advance a morally questionable bill by the same "presentational" strategies he has taught his students. How then would we read this against the play's more optimistic regard of Hector's teaching, which despite its futility is seen ultimately as "the only education worth having" (p. 109)? Perhaps Jacques Derrida's (1967) notion of the supplement can provide an interesting philosophical perspective through which to consider Hector's pedagogy in relation to the education system *as system*.

The Function of the Supplement and Its Relationship to the System

Most commonly associated with the critical method of deconstruction, the French philosopher Jacques Derrida (1967) outlines his notion of the *supplement* in his book *On grammatology*. In it, he describes the paradoxical function of the supplement as something that both *adds to* and *replaces* a main body of discourse. In its first sense, the supplement "adds itself, it is a surplus, a plenitude enriching another plenitude, the *fullest measure* of presence. It cumulates and accumulates presence" (1967, p. 144, emphasis original). The supplement is exterior to the thing it supplements; it is therefore marked with deficiency, belatedness, and inadequacy compared to the thing. However, playing on the semantic ambiguity of the word, Derrida insists on another contradictorily coherent signification of the supplement. In this second reading, "the supplement supplements. It adds only to replace. It intervenes or insinuates itself *in-the-place-of*; if it fills, it is as if one fills a void [...] the supplement is an adjunct, a subaltern instance which *takes-(the)-place*" (1967, p. 145, emphasis original). If the supplement adds, it also replaces, for what is revealed is the absence of the thing and its lack of a solid foundation.

For Derrida (1967), the supplement deconstructs the classic metaphysical oppositions of inside/outside, interiority/exteriority, and proper/improper, for the supplement is *both* peripheral and central to ideological concepts, which it surrounds and replaces. The purity and stability of the concept is questioned, as the supplement "institutes and deconstitutes" (Derrida, 1967, p. 141) its intelligibility and coherence. Once we discover the lack of foundation at the heart of a dominant body of discourse through the functioning of the supplement, what analysis uncovers is a "sequence of supplements [...] an infinite chain, ineluctably multiplying the supplementary mediations that produce the sense of the thing they defer: the mirage of the thing itself, of immediate presence, of originary perception" (Derrida, 1967, p. 157). Meaning is not to be sought in the concept, but is instead produced in the chain of supplements that endlessly defer final signification. What can be discerned in *The history boys* (Bennett, 2004a) is an analogous functioning of the supplement that ultimately destabilizes its audience's understanding of what the aims of education and the role of teachers should be. Utilizing a Derridean analysis of the play might allow us to probe our complicated responses to who Hector is and what he stands for, and appreciate how "radical" (Billington, 2004, p. 2) a play like Bennett's is.

Hector as Supplement

Hector's teaching can be defined as supplementary in relation to the educational "curriculum" as defined by the headmaster. Despite the resentment that the headmaster is "the chief enemy of culture" (Bennett, 2004a, p. 50) of the school, his dictates that lessons should be geared towards pushing the school up "league tables" (p. 8) go unquestioned and unchallenged. Hector's own insistence that "education [is] the enemy of education" (p. 48) aptly demonstrates a self-negating impetus to his lessons – this puts his teaching methods at odds with the presumed "larger goals" of the headmaster. In a pointed commentary about Hector, the headmaster states that his way of teaching is "unpredictable and unquantifiable and in the current educational climate that is no use" (p. 67). In a system structured according to demonstrating quantifiable and calculable results, Hector's lessons remain wilfully, almost obstinately, peripheral in their structures and outcomes. Indeed, Hector's idiosyncratic use of literary quotations in his lessons dramatically enacts the Derridean chain of supplements, which do not so much point to their own self-enclosed sufficiency of meaning as gesture towards other quotations. Posner senses an aspect of the insufficiency of this way of teaching when he opines that the reason why Hector does not serve as a good mentor is his propensity to dispense decontextualized literary quotations to his students in the place of useful and straightforward advice. There is perhaps some reasonable justification behind the headmaster's words that "it's not how much literature that they know. What matters is how much they know *about* literature" (Bennett, 2004a, p. 49, emphasis original). In short, Hector's lessons seem to be about and to achieve nothing; his students abuse the quotations he teaches them by mindlessly parroting them, showing little more than a superficial absorption of their content.

In true supplementary fashion, however, what is peripheral to the discourse of "education" in the play ultimately becomes that which is central to it. If Loveridge (2004) is right to note that one aspect of *The history boys* (Bennett, 2004a) is about "the widening gulf between the politics of educational measurement and teaching as a vocation" (p. 4), the ending of the play demonstrates a counter-logic, one that points towards a redefinition of education on Hector's terms. In his eulogy of Hector after his tragic accident, the headmaster notes that Hector succeeded in "open[ing] a deposit account in the bank of literature and [making his students] all shareholders in that wonderful world of words" (p. 106). The overt metaphors of acquisition and accumulation not only provide an interesting juxtaposition to Hector's own aversion towards functionality, but also uncannily repeat the headmaster's dull utilitarian impulses. Bennett's radical implication here might be that education, modelled after Hector's teaching, has the greatest use precisely when it has no use – indeed, it is "the only education worth having" (p. 109). The supplement has thus come to redefine and destabilize the dominant discourse on its own terms. If Bennett's play has a "political" element to it, it can be found in this reevaluation of the social function of education.

An examination of the character of Hector will also bring into focus the most controversial aspect of the play, which is what Loveridge (2004) describes as "the relationship between pedagogy and pederasty" (p. 3). Interestingly enough, in its 2006 run on Broadway, reviewer Steve Vineberg (2006) claims that "the attitude of the history boys toward the sexual desires of [Hector and Irwin] for their senior male students is conspicuously – and refreshingly – non-judgmental" (p. 20). Vineberg goes on to further state that Bennett (2004a) "refuse[s] to build in any sort of dramatic platform for our possible disapproval" (2006, p. 20) of Hector's sexual transgression. To claim, as Vineberg does, that Bennett refuses to treat Hector's action as morally questionable is surely an inaccurate judgment, not least in the words of Lintott, who exposes Hector's disingenuous rhetoric on why he touches his students inappropriately: "A grope is a grope. It is not the Annunciation" (p. 95). I argue instead that Bennett encourages a complicated response towards Hector by depicting his pederastic inclinations as another instance of the supplement in relation to his teaching.

Although Hector and Irwin espouse fundamentally antagonistic methods of teaching, both are similar in their homosexual leanings towards the students under their charge. While Irwin successfully represses his illicit desires, Hector unfortunately uses his position as beloved teacher to act them out, with disastrous consequences. Vineberg (2006) is right to note that Hector's students "don't think of [his] vehicular attentions as sex; they treat it as a joke, an eccentricity" (p. 20); however, I argue that this attitude stems from them (as well as the audience) treating this flaw of his as supplementary to (and therefore extrinsic to) his way of using literature to "connect" with his students. A closer examination of the play reveals the uneasy link between connection and sexual desire. In one of the play's most memorable scenes, Hector ends a discussion of a poem with these words and gesture:

> The best moments in reading are when you come across something – a thought, a feeling, a way of looking at things – which you had thought special and particular to you. Now here it is, set down by someone else, a person you have never met, someone even who is long dead. And it is as if a hand has come out and taken yours.
> *He puts out his hand, and it seems for a moment as if Posner will take it, or even that Hector may put it on Posner's knee. But the moment passes.*
> (Bennett, 2004a, p. 56, emphasis original)

As the stage directions make clear, the language of connection and "touching" is the language of sexuality. That this moment arrives after the headmaster's angry berating of Hector for his "hand on a boy's genitals" (p. 53) serves to punctuate the uneasy point that the mode of Hector's teaching is sexual in nature. What reviewers and critics of the play like Vineberg (2006) fail to see is how Bennett refuses to separate Hector's sexual desires and transgressions from his way of teaching; indeed, as Hector quips: "The transmission of knowledge is in itself an erotic act" (Bennett, 2004a, p. 53). In a sense, critics' reactions are symptomatic of how the supplement tends to be treated as external and supplementary to our ideological assumptions of how a teacher should behave and what values he should have, apart from his humanity as a person. Mrs. Lintott gives voice to the complicated logic within the play as such: "One of the hardest things for boys to learn is that a teacher is human. One of the hardest things for a teacher to learn is not to try and tell them" (p. 42).

There is no clear separation between Hector the teacher and Hector the flawed human being; his inspirational moments are inextricably linked with the darkest sides of his personality. Derrida's (1967) analysis of the supplement enables us to understand how the official ideology of "teaching" is contaminated by abuse of power. To teach, and to teach well, is to transgress. Looking at Hector in this light complicates our understanding of Hector and what he stands for, and attunes us better to Bennett's complex portrayal of a memorable and inspirational teacher. Indeed, if the play at the end is ultimately optimistic in its envisioning of "a *different sort* of economy to that promoted by the Headmaster [...] an economy in which things are explored, recognized, given over, held in trust, shared out" (Kelleher, 2005, p. 53, emphasis original), the dominant metaphor to recognize here is unmistakably erotic in nature:

> Pass the parcel.
> That's sometimes all you can do.
> Take it, feel it and pass it on.
> Not for me, not for you, but for someone, somewhere, one day.
> Pass it on, boys.
> That's the game I wanted you to learn.
> Pass it on.
>
> (Bennett, 2004a, p. 109)

Conclusion

The history boys (Bennett, 2004a) offers an entertaining and intellectually engaging perspective on the realities of relationships between teachers and students, teachers and school administrators, and the education profession and societal forces. Bennett's wry portrayal of two different methods and philosophies of teaching embodied in Hector and Irwin touches on larger issues such as the relevance of truth to the question of its representationality, and the way knowledge is taught and transmitted. However, the play's dramatic power ultimately draws from Bennett's critical and destabilizing look at our notions of education and teaching, opening up important questions about the aims and purposes of teaching, and the function of education in an increasingly disenchanted and bureaucratic world.

REFERENCES

Bennett, A. (2004a). *The history boys*. London, UK: Faber & Faber.

Bennett, A. (2004b). Introduction. *The history boys* (pp. vi–xxvii). London, UK: Faber & Faber.

Bennett, A. (2016). *Keeping on keeping on*. London, UK: Faber & Faber.

Billington, M. (2004, May 29). Review of *The history boys*. *The Guardian*. Retrieved from https://www.theguradian.com/stage/2004/may/29/theatre

Derrida, J. (1967). *Of grammatology* (G. C. Spivak, Trans.). Baltimore, MD: John Hopkins University Press.

Jacobi, M. (2006). The sad reception of classical education in Alan Bennett's *The history boys*. *South Atlantic Review, 71*(3), 76–99.

Kelleher, J. (2005). Sentimental education at the National Theatre. *PAJ: A Journal of Performance and Art, 27*(3), 45–54.

Loveridge, L. (2004, May 26). Three visits to *The history boys*. Curtain Up. Retrieved from http://www.curtainup.com/historyboys.html

Stansky, P. (2009). Simon Schama: A history of Britain. *The American Historical Review, 114*(3), 684–691.

Vineberg, S. (2006). Theater for grown-ups: *Sweeney Todd* by Stephen Sondheim, Hugh Wheeler and John Doyle; *The history boys* by Alan Bennett and Nicholas Hytner. *The Threepenny Review*, (107), 19–20.

Why are You Doing This? Negotiating the Gift of Education in Development Work in Nepal through *Kathmandu: A Mirror in the Sky*

Ruth Hol Mjanger, in dialogue with Bibek Shakya,

Reiny de Wit, & Meena Subba Karki

Introduction

The film *Kathmandu: A mirror in the sky* (Bollaín, 2011) sets the scene for a discussion about the paradoxes connected to the gift of education in a globalized world. What motivates a single western foreigner to voluntarily initiate educational change in a local community in a developing country? What does it mean to act ethically in such a context? This chapter analyzes the film from the perspective of "gift exchange theory," a socio-economic theory for valuing relations. Our chapter looks at the implications of the gift exchange, for the giver and the receivers, influenced by both self-interests and generosity (Nicholson, 2005).

This chapter is a reflection of the close cooperative relationship between educators from Nepal, the Netherlands, and Norway, who, in institutional partnership since 2008, have established and developed preschool and primary teacher education in Nepal. De Wit, one of the authors, has a similar starting point as the main character in the film. In the 1980s, she left the Netherlands for teaching in Nepal. In 2001, she founded the Early Childhood Education Centre, which today is a leading teacher education institution in Nepal (ECEC, 2017).

Kathmandu: A Mirror in the Sky – *A Synopsis*

The film is an award-winning Spanish movie freely inspired by the autobiographical book *A teacher in Kathmandu* by Victoria Subirana (2015) (see also EduQual Foundation, 2011). We emphasize that we base our analysis on the characters portrayed in the film. The director's main aim was to present a good story for an audience within the limitation of a ninety-minute film. In addition, we acknowledge that the director and crew might have lacked depth of cultural knowledge, and this may have influenced the production.

The main character in the film is Leia, a young woman who moves alone from Spain to Kathmandu, the capital of Nepal, in the 1990s. As a teacher, she volunteers in a local school and witnesses a system of rote learning, corporal punishment, and a management that focuses on profit (Bhatta, 2009). Leia feels a strong need to help the children, especially the neediest Dalit children in the slum – children without any school. Dalits, or untouchables, inhabit the lowest status in the Hindu Social System. Even though the caste system was abolished in 1963, most Dalits suffer in extreme poverty with a lack of social and economic mobility (Prasad, 2012). Leia is visionary, and challenges the local school authorities, but struggles in her lack of cultural knowledge. Leia regularly seeks guidance from a Buddhist monk, who helps her to focus on her tasks. Still, she remains emotionally unstable. After a while, she manages to start a slum school, and next a non-governmental organization (NGO) supported by international aid agencies. The film portrays Leia's personal journey to adapt her Spanish mind-set towards Nepal and to find her home there, her "mirror in the sky."

The film has two other important characters: Sharmila, the female Nepalese teacher, who works together with Leia, and Tsering, the young man Leia marries to get an extended visa to stay in Nepal. These two characters put Leia's "gift of education" in perspective, and exemplify the interwoven connections between the professional and private in a foreigner's life.

Sharmila is Leia's teacher colleague and acts as her lingual and cultural translator. Sharmila has a strong voice in the film, but Leia does not always listen carefully. Despite a loving husband, Sharmila has great obligations and duties to her family-in-law (Chetri, 2013; Kaushik, 2012), but Leia does not fully understand Sharmila's complex situation. Their friendship grows stronger, and after the first challenges, Sharmila chooses to stand by Leia to start a slum school. She explains that she wants to leave the dark, the cultural traditions that limit her, and enter the light Leia brings with her gift of education. After a while, the need for economic support grows, and Sharmila urges Leia to go for fundraising to Spain. First, they seek a Hindu fortune-teller and he reads their palms; he reveals that Sharmila will have a long-desired son and that Leia has special gifts and will succeed with all her visions.

Tsering, Leia's husband of convenience, is Leia's opposite. As a Buddhist, Tsering takes over the monk's position by her side. He is stable. He respects his family. He is willing to help her, without gaining anything in return. When she asks him what he wants in return for marrying her, he says he is happy as he is. She doubts his answer. He cooks food, obtains the school licence, and helps her in many ways. In the beginning, Leia wants to give him something in return by joining him at his sister's wedding in the remote mountain area of Mustang. During this journey, they become more intimate and their love for each other grows. However, during the film she becomes totally focused on her school project and neglects him more and more. Towards the end of the film, when Tsering asks Leia to go with him to his family, he discovers that she has already chosen her family – the slum school community.

The Metaphor of the Gift: An Introduction

Anthropologist Marcel Mauss presented the basics of gift exchange theory in an essay in 1924 (Mauss, 2002). He focused on the negative aspects of the gift, such as self-interest, referring to the linguistic German origin "gift," meaning "poison" (Nicholson, 2005, p. 160). Mauss managed to problematize the relationship between givers and recipients, questioning assumptions about altruistic, unselfish motives of the giver. Another aspect, developed by Mauss, is that "a gift carries an obligation to reciprocate" (Gullestad, 2007, p. 273). Gift exchange has three obligations: to give, to receive, and to return, and is important to establish social solidarity in a society (Martin, 2013). In a local community where there is an imbalance of power and/or material wealth between donors and recipients, both foreign teachers and local staff will benefit from discussing such a nuanced, critical perspective. In development work deep gratitude in return might be the most desirable expectation, but the receivers do not necessarily feel gratitude. The cultural differences also make it possible to overlook the returned gifts from the local community. The foreign worker needs to be aware of how to do gift exchange without leaving the receiver with feelings of debt or humiliation (Gullestad, 2007).

Later, several researchers criticized Mauss for neglecting the positive attributes of a gift (Martin, 2013). Among these voices was the philosopher Jacques Derrida (1992), who claimed that a gift could be given voluntarily and unconditionally, as an ethical alternative to self-interest (cited in Nicholson, 2005). The problem, according to Derrida, is that this theoretical assumption is practically impossible to do in real life. The reason is that as soon as a gift is identified as a gift, it becomes a symbol and enters into a system of *value*, shared and understood in a community. This means it is not possible to have a purely altruistic motive, since there will always be uncertainties and a mixture of self-interest and selflessness related to a gift. In intercultural relations, the risk is high for misunderstandings, since the knowledge about, and the interpretation of the system seldom is shared at a deep level between the giver and receiver (Jandt, 2013).

Gift exchange is not always logical, safe, and rational. Sometimes it is spontaneous, risky, and emotional (Nicholson, 2005), and this describes most of Leia's acts of giving. The film shows many examples of gift exchange, but our focus is on the motives and ethics related to the *gift of education*. In the next section, we analyze Leia's motives for giving.

"Why are You Doing This?" Or Motives for Giving the Gift of Education

When Tsering asks Leia directly, "Why are you doing this? For politics? Or religion?" she does not answer him. To look at Leia's conceivable motives, we focus on four factors: first altruism, second the need to do something significant, third the underlying theme in the film – in search for a home, and finally mutual affection.

Altruism

Foreign development workers often receive the label "altruistic person;" it is presumed they are "unselfishly concerned for or devoted to the welfare of others" (Altruistic, 2010, para. 1). In which way does Leia show signs of altruism? She left her own culture and sacrificed physical comfort and stability to live in Nepal. She even married an unknown man to be able to stay in the country. When she chooses the children before her husband, she also sacrifices the possibility of her own biological family. In a scene at the end of the film, Leia is crying in the rain, all by herself. Tsering has left and Sharmila has passed away. Even if the children like Leia, they are not her supporters, as she is for them. Therefore, Leia needs to handle the situation alone. Leia has sacrificed her personal happiness for fulfilment of her vision. At first sight, these factors imply an unselfish attitude; she has real passion for offering the children a better future, motivated by her own bad childhood experiences in Spain.

The need to do something significant

According to gift theory, altruism is seldom the only motive. Talking to the monk, Leia expresses her wish for doing something significant, rather than being one out of many teachers back in Spain. When Tsering asks Leia to stay with him instead of prioritizing the children, Leia tells Tsering she has to continue to work, because she has never done something as profound and important. These scenes reveal self-interest – the good feeling of doing something significant.

A research project about homemade aid initiatives in Norway, learned that such personal initiatives are an alternative to giving to established aid agencies, which fulfil the initiators' needs for doing something good – to do it themselves and be in direct contact with the receiver instead of sending money. The study also reports an interest for operating in far-away countries motivated by a desire for having new adventures and exploring cultures (Haaland & Wallevik, 2015). The researchers consider it important to nurture such grassroots engagements, as they represent a "do-it-yourself" democracy. They encourage a broader cooperation between the experienced aid agencies and the aid amateurs, such as in the case of Leia when Sharmila urges her to get external funding.

In search for a home

The subtitle provides a clue about another important motive. In the beginning, Leia does not know where her home is – her "mirror in the sky." The film describes the strong forces involved in her search for a home and a family. Short flashbacks portray Leia's background in Spain: a strict Catholic school, a dysfunctional home, an unsatisfying relationship with a man, and being a young pregnant student teacher seeking an abortion. These scenes from Spain provide an interesting backdrop for analyzing self-interest in Leia's need for helping others. One interpretation could be that Leia is leaving her home country to find a place where she can fulfil her calling for teaching underprivileged children. When she arrives in Nepal, the strong impressions awaken her own bad memories as a neglected child and her inner child starts searching for a home. Leia therefore works hard to create this home by giving poor children education, food, and love. In return, she expects the gift of love, deep gratitude, and a community – a home.

Tsering's mother offers Leia a home after his sister's wedding, and Tsering invites her to settle with him. She hesitates. When she goes back to Spain to fundraise, she writes to Tsering and says she really misses him, and that her "mirror in the sky" is Nepal. It seems it is easier to promise something from a distance. When she returns, she continues to focus at work. In the end, Tsering says to her, "You have chosen your family," referring to the school community. She builds her home on her own terms. When Tsering and Sharmila leave her, she begs them not to leave her alone. Her focus is on herself, not on them, nor their families.

Mutual affection

What is the role of emotions in gift exchange? The film portrays Leia as passionately interested in her students, especially in a girl called Kushila. In the opening scene, Leia and a class are playing learning games in the schoolyard. Kushila manages to name the provinces of Nepal, and Leia gives her a big hug. In many western cultures, hugs are a sign of love, and therefore a strong visual signal of who the director chooses to be the most caring person in the film. Leia hugs the students very often, but the Nepalese do not hug, due to cultural codes.

Next, Kushila gives Leia a handmade notebook, where she has painted her wish for becoming a teacher. This is an effort to deepen their personal relationship. This situation is a gift exchange and can be named as an "empathetic dialogue," where there is mutual affection between the giver and receiver (Fennel, cited in Nicholson, 2005, p. 164). A teacher–student relationship built on trust is important for learning. Nevertheless, it is vital to highlight the asymmetry in power and the teacher's responsibility for maintaining the relation (Mjanger & Steinhovden Wathne, 2012). Leia shows an example of this responsibility when Kushila stops coming to school. Leia searches for her, together with Sharmila and Tsering. When they figure out that the girl is a victim of trafficking to India, Leia is devastated. When Kushila later returns, Leia overwhelms her with hugs and comfort, and offers to take care of her, since the family rejects their girl.

The Need for Cultural Awareness to Act Ethically

Leia's main mistake in her efforts to give the gift of education is her lack of cultural awareness. Leia's ignorance of the local culture causes both her and the other people involved trouble. A strong impression in the film is her disrespect for Nepalese adults. In Nepal, respect for authorities is crucial, and humiliation of adults is not appreciated. When Leia several times shouts at teachers, the principal, and local authorities, she neglects the cultural code for social interaction and respect. After a while, she incidentally learns that the principal has raised the school fees because of her presence, resulting in children leaving school. Leia considers this as exploitation of her expertise and presence, whereas the situation might look different from the principal's perspective. As a way to take control over the feeling of humiliation triggered by the foreign gift-giver, some receivers (such as the principal) might see themselves as "crafty takers" and the foreigners as "foolish givers" that can be taken advantage of (Gullestad, 2007, p. 276). Over time, the acts from both sides consolidate a contradictory relationship.

Another example of Leia's lack of cultural awareness, is when she discovers lice in the children's hair, and asks Sharmila to call for the barber. Sharmila questions her request, but Leia answers, "Just call, Sharmila, please." On Leia's command and in the presence of the whole school, the barber starts cutting children's hair. After a while, Sharmila asks, "Is this what you do in your country when children have lice?" "No," Leia answers puzzled. "So why do you do it here?" Sharmila replies and leaves the schoolyard. This is an important, but also problematic question, because cultural awareness is often *not* to do as you usually do (Jandt, 2013). This scene, situated in the beginning of the film, could give the impression that Leia should just transfer her cultural norms to Nepal. The scene that follows gives nuance to this first thought. Sharmila expresses the reason why cutting hair is so bad. To give a child a bath and cut his/her hair on their day of their birth signifies bad luck. This is core of cultural knowledge; actions may have very different motivations and repercussions across cultures.

When Leia visits Tsering's village, she is more culturally sensitive. She is not in charge of the actions and therefore has the time to observe and listen. Throughout the film, Leia adjusts herself more to the cultural codes, and manages to interact more smoothly with other adults. Also, on a number of occasions we see Leia acting in contrast to the values she brings from her own culture. To feel the pressure to act against your own values might be, for some, a challenging part of cross-cultural relations. When Leia does not manage to get an extended visa in a country with strict boarder control, she is forced to marry for convenience. Leia follows Sharmila to a Hindu fortune-teller, though she feels uneasy facing this religious practice. To obtain the school licence, Tsering helps her by offering bribes, which is an act against her own values. Pressure over a longer period may destabilize a person's inner compass. This might result in alienation from one's own values, or it can offer a liminal zone for changing some of one's values and adopting values from the new culture. The person gets individually assimilated or integrated in the new culture (Eriksen, 2015).

The Foreign Teacher as the Saviour?

The film, in many ways, leaves the impression of Leia as a saviour – even if she is a miserable one, which is expressed through the metaphors of *light* and *dark*. Sharmila introduces the metaphor, referring to her first experience of the still living tradition of menstrual huts in some Hindu communities in Nepal. When the monthly period arrives, the female leaves the house and enters isolation in a dark shelter (Crawford, Menger, & Kaufman, 2014). Sharmila wants to leave these *dark* traditions and enter the *light* of education that Leia brings to her doorstep. This metaphor has strong religious connotations, in which a saviour is often part of the picture. In addition, popular culture often uses light and dark as visual signs of good and evil (Meier, Robinson, & Clore, 2004). It is a problematic metaphor in the film, because Leia is always connected to the light and Nepal to the dark.

To emphasize the "divine" backdrop of Leia's life, the director has chosen to highlight the presence of the Buddhist monk and the fortune-teller's forecast about Leia's future success. This adds a cultural link that strengthens the trustworthiness of Leia's reasons to come and stay in Nepal: It is God's will and her destiny. This way of portraying Leia makes it harder for the viewer to question her presence and ethics in Nepal. When someone claims to do God's will, and it influences others in a bad way, it is important to ask questions.

One scene shows Leia teaching the children about personal development skills. She is fostering individuality, with limited knowledge about the importance of group culture in Nepal (Kaushik, 2012). Leia as an individual is represented by the light, who tries to change what the film presents as a dark community. In the end, Sharmila commits suicide, because she is expecting an unwanted girl, leaving Leia a letter telling her to continue to spread the light for the children in the dark. However, we question if it is ethical to represent Leia as always in the light and Sharmila, the children, and the rest of the community in the dark.

Conclusion

The aim of this chapter is to raise an ethical awareness about the paradoxes of the gift of education in foreign voluntary work in developing countries. Visual popular culture such as films strongly influences our understanding of other cultures. Films based on true stories present a strong visual impact, but sometimes leave out facts in favour of a good story. The real "Leia" was a trained teacher and studied Nepalese culture and language at the state university in Kathmandu. Therefore, it is important to question if the director of this film presents an impression that it is Nepal's destiny to put incompetent volunteer foreigners in the front row of educational transformation. With 100,000 to 200,000 personal aid organizations in Europe alone and little research on the phenomena (Fylkesnes, 2016), continual negotiation and reflexivity around teacher portraits in films related to personal initiatives in educational development around the globe are vital.

After Sharmila's death, there is still hope in the film. The last scene pictures Kushila leading other children in singing. This presents the forecast of a slow transformation from sex-abused victim to becoming a future teacher. The last scene visualizes the need for Nepalese teachers taking Leia's front-line position. This is what we work for: establishing mutual trust between partners and raising cultural awareness in developing teacher education that equips the Nepalese schools, teachers, and society to serve their children (ECEC, 2017; Mjanger, 2014).

REFERENCES

Altruistic. (n.d.). Dictionary.com. Retrieved from http://www.dictionary.com/browse/altruistic

Bhatta, P. (2009). 60 years of educational development in Nepal. In P. Bhatta (Ed.), *Education in Nepal: Problems, reforms and social change* (pp. 1–16). Kathmandu, Nepal: Martin Chautari.

Bollaín, I. (Director). (2011). *Kathmandu: A mirror in the sky* [Motion picture]. Spain: Savor Ediciones S.A. Trailer retrieved from https://www.youtube.com/watch?v=ktxLyOTAkOQ

Chetri, N. K. (2013). Understanding the status of Nepali women. In B. C. Upreti and U. P. Pyakurel (Eds.), *Contemporary Nepal* (pp. 230–242). Delhi, India: Kalinga Publications.

Crawford, M., Menger, L., & Kaufman, M. (2014). "This is a natural process": Managing menstrual stigma in Nepal. *Culture, Health & Sexuality, 16*(4), 426–439.

Derrida, J. (1992). *Given time: Counterfeit money*. Chicago, IL: University of Chicago Press.

Early Childhood Education Center (ECEC). (2017). Teaching trainers shaping future. Retrieved from www.ecec.org.np

EduQual Foundation. (2011). Victoria subirana. Retrieved from http://eduqual.org/wordpress/?page_id=12290&lang=en.

Eriksen, T. (2015). *Small places, large issues: An introduction to social and cultural anthropology* (4th ed.). London, UK: Pluto Press.

Fennel, L. A. (2002). Unpacking the gift: Illiquid goods and empathetic dialogue. In M. Olsteen (Ed.), *The question of the gift* (pp. 85–102). London, UK: Routledge.

Fylkesnes, L. (2016). *Small streams make big rivers: Exploring motivation and idealism in Norwegian personalised aid initiatives in the Gambia* [Master's thesis]. University of Agder, Kristiansand, Norway. Retrieved from https://brage.bibsys.no/xmlui/bitstream/id/455802/Fylkesnes,%20June.pdf

Gullestad, M. (2007). *Picturing pity: Pitfalls and pleasures in cross-cultural communication – Image and word in a North Cameroon mission*. New York, NY: Berghahn Books.

Haaland, H., & Wallevik, H. (2015, September 26). Global solidaritet og hjemmelaget humanitær bistand (Global solidarity and homemade humanitarian aid). *Fædrelandsvennen*, p. 29.

Jandt, F. (2013). *An introduction to intercultural communication: Identities in a global community* (7th ed.). Thousand Oaks, CA: Sage.

Kaushik, A. (2012). Women in transition in Nepal: Challenges and prospects. In B. C. Upreti, & U. P. Pyakurel (Eds.), *Contemporary Nepal* (pp. 187–194). Delhi, India: Kalinga Publications.

Martin, K. (2013). Gift exchange. In R. L. Warms, & R. J. McGee (Eds.), *Theory in social and cultural anthropology: An encyclopedia* (pp. 323–326). Thousand Oaks, CA: Sage Publications, Inc.

Mauss, M. (2002). *The gift: The form and reason for exchange in archaic societies*. London, UK: Routledge.

Meier, B. P., Robinson, M. D., & Clore, G. L. (2004). Why good guys wear white: Automatic inferences about stimulus valence based on brightness. *Psychological Science, 15*(2), 82–87.

Mjanger, R. (2014). Playing with shadows, playing with words: Exploring teachers' ownership through poetic inquiry in a Norwegian-Nepalese preschool teacher's education project. *Research in Drama Education: The Journal of Applied Theatre and Performance, 19*(3), 296–312.

Mjanger, R., & Steinhovden Wathne, A. K. (2012). Prøverommet – bruk av estetiske læreprosesser i faget pedagogikk og elevkunnskap i grunnskolelærerutdanningene (A room for exploring – Use of esthetical learning processes in the course pedagogy and student knowledge in primary and secondary teacher education). In J.-B. Johansen (Ed.), *Skapende og kreativ læring (Creative learning)* (pp. 175–200). Trondheim, Norway: Tapir Akademisk Forlag.

Nicholson, H. (2005). *Applied drama: The gift of theatre*. London, UK: Palgrave.

Prasad, C. (2012). Exclusion of excluded Dalits in Nepal. In B. C. Upreti, & U. P. Pyakurel (Eds.), *Contemporary Nepal* (pp. 175–186). Delhi, India: Kalinga Publications.

Subirana, V. (2015). *A teacher in Kathmandu* [Kindle Edition version].

Learning with Brecht: Exploring the "Learning to Read and Write" Scene in *The Mother*

Stig A. Eriksson

Introduction

In looking at situations on stage and in film portraying teachers and teaching, an implicit anticipation is the presence of tension between teaching and learning, and an expectancy that the learning approach is theoretical, tedious, and removed from real life. Bertolt Brecht is a dramatist who has a keen eye for such dialectics, and possesses the gift for setting up simple, down-to-earth situations that can model change. In fact, Brecht devised a dramatic genre – *the Lehrstück*,[1] for discussing issues suited for contributing to societal transformation. Even though Martin Esslin labelled Brecht's language in his learning-plays as austere and functional (1971, p. 118), my claim is that Brecht was a creative and innovative pedagogue in a true sense of the word. Brecht's work comprises much more than his famous theatre plays. A red thread of great pedagogy runs across all his rich contribution to theatre theory and practice, his political and cultural theory, and his poetry. Brecht can in fact be viewed as a pioneer of drama pedagogy through his learning-plays, for which the German scholar Reiner Steinweg created a learning-play-theory-and-practice based on Brecht's scattered notes on the subject (1972, 1995). Brecht is probably even the first in the educational theatre field to use the now common term *applied theatre*, in his *Journals 1934–1955*, as early as 1942 (see Brecht, 1994). One of the leading exponents of Brecht's learning-play genre in both theory and practice, Gerd Koch states that "[Brecht] as a producer of literature is a pedagogue, and as a producer of entertainment, he never fails to teach; and as a producer of art he is first and foremost involved in societal production" (1988, p. 3, my translation). This view that dramatic art and art pedagogy has a productive value, a societal use, steeped in an interest in marrying entertainment and education, is a main thrust of this chapter.

The Mother *as Pedagogy*

In order to perspectivize some main interchanges of the play, I have chosen to insert parts of Brecht's (1950/1976, p. 424) theatre poem entitled "Looking for the new and the old," as a kind of meta-text to the actual teaching-scene for the context of this chapter. I hope to induce in the reader a resonance between the educational journey of a mother living in difficult political times almost a hundred years ago, and the situation of refugees and immigrants in the world today. The old working woman, the workers, the teacher, and his brother in the poem are characters in *The mother* (Brecht, 1931/1965).

> When you read your parts
> Exploring, ready to be surprised
> Look for the new and old. For our time
> And the time of our children is the time of struggles
> Between the new and the old.
>
> (Brecht, 1950/1976, lines 1–5)

On one level the whole play embodies a portrayal of education. The Lehrstück genre is generically and conceptionally about teaching and learning, and represents a vision of a theatre of the future that Brecht termed "The Major Pedagogy," in which the traditional separation of audience and actors is erased and they all take part as percipients[2] in a common process of exploring and investigating significant themes for raising consciousness and learning: "The Major Pedagogy completely changes the role of acting. It abrogates the system of actors and spectators. It only recognises actors who are simultaneously students" (Brecht, 1930/2003, p. 88). Brecht's Lehrstück often (but not necessarily) takes on the quality of *parable*, i.e., an allegorical or metaphorical saying or narrative (a comparison, a similitude). In Brecht's words, "the purpose of a 'parable' is to clearly demonstrate the relations of men to and among each other and their attitudes towards each other" (in discussion with W. J. Jerome, see Brecht, 2012b[3]). First performed in 1932,[4] *The mother* can be said to portray the stages of an educational journey (*Bildungsreise*[5]) of a mother going through an awareness process and becoming a revolutionary. In the play, the protagonist Pelagea Vlassova develops from being an uneducated worker and housemother to becoming a committed union agitator. Within a time frame of twelve years, the play takes us through the stages of Vlassova's education – from her being a self-effacing widow, caring for her son, to becoming a strong leader with personality, caring for her fellow workers and the revolution. It should be observed, however, that within this metaphorical frame of the Lehrstück itself, the individual scenes can work as parables too; because what happens can take place in many countries, everywhere, and today, where conditions and movements like the ones portrayed in the play occur. With this in mind, let us now focus on just one of the scenes, with the intention of identifying some characteristics of Brecht's pedagogy.

The Mother Learns to Read

> The cunning of the old working woman
> Who relieves the teacher of his knowledge
> Like a pack too heavy to carry, is new
> And must be shown as new. And old
> Is the fear of the workers in wartime
> Reluctant to take the leaflets which will teach them; it must
> Be shown as old.
>
> (Brecht, 1950/1976, lines 6–12)

In this scene the protagonist and her fellow workers – all illiterate, poor, and out of work – learn spelling and concepts, motivated by the opportunity this learning will give them to become equal citizens in a future democratic society that they hope their common fight for revolution will provide. The lesson provides an entertaining opportunity to see pedagogy in relation to curriculum orientations (Eriksson, 2009b),[6] examples of teacher roles (Wagner, 1979),[7] and Brecht as a (drama) pedagogue[8] from a broader educational perspective. First of all, however, the lesson functions as an *example*: a core educational situation of teacher and student interaction. The use of example is by itself a pedagogic device, and illustrates the former claim that Brecht is a pedagogue and a teacher even if he writes drama. The example is also a device that points beyond itself and raises new questions, for instance: Who is a Pelagea Vlassova of today – and what kind of teaching and learning does she need? With such questions in mind, let us now look at Brecht's classroom lesson as it stands in the play:

TEACHER (*before a blackboard*): All right, you want to learn to read. I cannot understand why you need it, in your situation; you are also rather old. But I will try, just as a favor for Mrs. Vlassova. Have you all something to write with? All right then, I will now write three easy words here: "Branch, nest, fish." I repeat: "Branch, nest fish." (*He writes.*)

THE MOTHER (*who sits at the table with three others*): Must it really be "Branch, nest, fish"? Because we are old people we have to learn the words we need quickly!

TEACHER (*smiles*): I beg your pardon; but the reason you may have for learning to read is a matter of total indifference.

THE MOTHER:	Why should it be? Tell me, for instance, how do you write the word "Worker"? That will be of interest to our Pavel Sostakovich.
SOSTAKOVICH:	Who needs to know how to write "Branch"?
THE MOTHER:	He is a metal worker.
TEACHER:	But you will need the letters in the word.
WORKER:	But the letters in the words "Class Struggle" are needed too!
TEACHER:	Possibly; but we must begin with the simplest things and not at once with the hardest! "Branch" is simple.
SOSTAKOVICH:	"Class Struggle" is much more simple.
TEACHER:	Now listen, there is no class struggle. We must become clear on that subject at once.
SOSTAKOVICH	(*getting up*): I can learn nothing from you, if you don't want to know anything about class struggle!
THE MOTHER:	You're here to learn reading and writing. And that's something you *can* do here. Reading, too, is class struggle.
TEACHER:	What nonsense. What is that supposed to mean; reading is class struggle? What kind of talk is that? (*He writes.*) All right; this means "Worker." Copy it.
THE MOTHER:	Do you want to know what "reading is class struggle" means? It means we can put together our own pamphlets and read our own type of books, once we can read and write. Then we can be leaders in the class struggle.
TEACHER:	Look here; although I am a teacher, and for twelve years I have taught reading and writing, there is something I want to tell you: I know that everything, at bottom, is nonsense. Books are nonsense. They only help men to become worse and worse. A simple peasant is a better man for, very simply, not having been spoiled by civilization.
THE MOTHER:	Now how do you write "Class Struggle"? Pavel Sostakovich, you must put your hand down firmly; otherwise it trembles, and nobody can read your writing.
TEACHER:	"Class Struggle." (*to SOSTAKOVICH*): Be sure to write in a straight line, and not over the edge. Whosoever overwrites the margin also oversteps the law. Knowledge has been heaped upon knowledge for generations and generations now, and book after book has been written. As for technical knowledge, we never before had so much. Of what use is it all? We have never been so confused. The entire lot ought to be hurled into the sea at its deepest point – all the books and the machines, into the Black Sea. Let us raise a resistance against knowledge! Have

SOSTAKOVICH: you finished? At times I sink into a deep melancholy. At these moments I ask myself, what have the really great thoughts, thoughts that concern not merely the here and now, but rather the eternal, lasting and universal man, what have these to do with class struggle?
SOSTAKOVICH: Ideas like that are useless. While you're so busy sunk in melancholy, you are exploiting us.
THE MOTHER: Pavel Sostakovich, be quiet! Please, can you tell me, how do I write "Exploitation"?
TEACHER: Exploitation. That is a thing you find only in books. Do you imagine I ever exploited anybody?
SOSTAKOVICH: You say that only because you don't get any of the loot.
THE MOTHER (*to* Sostakovich): Look; the "e" in exploitation is just like the "e" in worker.
TEACHER: Knowledge is of no help. Knowledge helps not at all. What helps is to be good.
THE MOTHER: Well, you just let us have your knowledge if you don't need it.

Who is the Teacher? Who is the Learner? The Pupil Transforms Herself into Teacher

The teacher's willingness to teach
Is overlooked by his brother, but the stranger
Sees it.
Check over all the feelings and actions of your characters
For new and old features.
Reading your parts
Exploring, ready to be surprised
Rejoice at the new, be ashamed at the old!
(Brecht, 1950/1976, line 21–25 and 34–36)

At the start there is the traditional teacher role of the one who knows: *the dissemination model*. However, during the course of the lesson, the situation changes and in effect the student becomes instructor alongside the teacher: *the dialectic model*. In fact, we also discern a change in the teacher, who begins to contemplate – at least a reflection process seems to start in him – what education is essentially about. Teacher and pupils embark on a formative journey together: *the dialogue model*. On one hand, Pelagea applies a kind of motherly wisdom for herself and the other learners as a form of revolutionary weapon for change. It is not driven by individual interest but is primarily socially motivated. On the other hand, the teacher in teaching the group reading and writing acquires for himself new awareness, new knowledge. The way I read the scene, it exemplifies Brecht's political–cultural pedagogy (Koch, 1988) as well as his poetic–didactic strategy of *making strange*, which is the core quality of distancing, applied as a procedure in everyday life:

> The achievement of the A-effect[9] constitutes something utterly ordinary, recurrent; it is just a widely-practised way of drawing one's own or someone else's attention to a thing, and it can be seen in education as also in business conferences of one sort or another. The A-effect consists in turning the object of which one is to be made aware, to which one's attention is to be drawn, from something ordinary, familiar immediately accessible, into something peculiar, striking and unexpected.
> (Brecht, 1940/2001b, p. 143)

The scene also illustrates Brecht's effort to try to marry the theatrical and the educational (entertainment and learning): "theatre remains theatre even when it is instructive theatre, and in so far as it is good theatre it will amuse" (Brecht, 1936/2001a, p. 73).

The Mother *as Lehrstück*

In Brecht's notes to the play, he states: "*The mother* was written in the style of a *Lehrstück* ('play for learning'), although it requires professional actors" (Brecht, 1931/1965, p. 133). This might seem to be a contradictory statement, because Brecht's conception of Lehrstück as an educational theatre genre is one to be performed for and with the participants themselves:

> We learn from the learning play by playing it, not by watching it. In principle, the learning play needs no audience, although it may of course make use of an audience. The learning play takes as its basis the expectation, that the player can be socially influenced by practicing certain actions, partaking of certain attitudes, reproducing certain manners of speaking, etc.
> (Brecht, 1937/1963b, p. 78, my translation)

In *The mother*, Brecht (1931/1965) keeps quite strictly to the epic style (short finished episodes), using the idea of parable as a structural element, and breaking with traditional linear dramaturgical development:

The play's dramaturgy is anti-metaphysical, materialistic and non-Aristotelian. Thus it declines to assist the spectator in surrendering himself to empathy in the unthinking fashion of the Aristotelian dramaturgy [...]. Its concern is to teach the spectator a most definite practical conduct that is intended to change the world, and for this reason he must be afforded a fundamentally different attitude in the theatre from that to which he is accustomed.

(Brecht, 1931/1965, p. 133)

I do not know why Brecht felt that this learning-play required professional actors and an audience. Compared to being a passive spectator, the active partaking in exploring a theme, an issue, or an event potentially provides the participant with a broad and tangible register of learning possibilities.

Brecht's Lehrstück project is an epistemological project. The mere term for it: Lehrstück/learning-play, characterizes this intent quite well. It is also a project of critical pedagogy – and a pioneering one as such, which formed a basis that later Augusto Boal (1976) could build on and adapt in his own way. Seen from the perspective of critical pedagogy, it is reasonable to view Brecht's ideas of an "instructional and entertaining" theatre as, broadly speaking, a new Enlightenment project: "Brecht placed the theatre in a new enlightenment project not paralleled since the advancement of the bourgeois theatre of the 1700s" (Gladsø, Gjervan, Hovik, & Skagen, 2005, p. 167). The dialectics of entertainment and instruction, realized in the form of the epic theatre, "through a process of alienation: the alienation that is necessary to all understanding" (Brecht, 2001a, p. 71) is a visible commitment for Brecht in most of his plays and theoretical writings. As in modern drama pedagogy, in which "distancing" – mistakenly often translated as "alienation" – also plays a significant rational and poetic role (Eriksson, 2009a); the activation of percipients (O'Toole, 1992) within the same learning process constitutes epistemological dynamics.

I question Esslin's (1971) perception that *The mother* (and other learning-plays) is dominantly didactic, in a negative sense, because it seems to be based on the preconception that pedagogy should be placed outside the world of art. (Moreover, even based in the prejudice that politics, and particularly leftist politics, should be expelled from the art world.) In the case of Brecht, this is missing the point. Brecht's learning-plays were devised particularly to explore and discuss political issues, and he often set up disturbing dichotomies, like questioning the individual's right in relation to the interests of the collective (e.g., in *The Decision*, Brecht, 2012a). There is not enough space within the context of this chapter to discuss this further; however, the new interest within contemporary pedagogical literature with concepts such as *Bildung* (Biesta, 2002) does create resonances with both Brechtian educational philosophy and contemporary forms of drama education, in which the notion of "theatre and Bildung" is present (Heggstad, Eriksson, & Rasmussen, 2013).

Conclusion

From the whole play emerges Brecht's view of how humans learn, but the scene in which the mother learns to read and write in company with her equals encapsulates both the very practical approach Pelagea Vlassova takes to the situation and at the same time her gift in thinking dialectically. Dialectics is hers (and Brecht's) theoretical platform – one that blends so well with the sense of the useful. "Brecht lets the conditions speak for themselves, so that they confront each other dialectically" (Benjamin, 1998, p. 8). This positive consideration of the useful is what schooling often fails to convey to the learner. For the uneducated in *The mother* the useful is precisely what they are after, and for the percipients of the play that insight is very much disseminated by the interplay of the "entertaining" and "educational" concepts. One will think that this basic situation might not be very different for a contemporary Pelagea seeking education and the skills of reading and writing – be it in emigration to a new country or as a representative of a new feminist order in her old country. In this respect, the play has kept the same allegorical actuality it has had since it was first written eighty-nine years ago.

REFERENCES

Benjamin, W. (Ed.) (1998). What is epic theatre?. *Understanding Brecht* (A. Bostock, Trans.) (1st ed.) (pp. 1–13). London, UK: Verso Books. (Original work published 1931)

Biesta, G. (2002). Bildung and modernity: The future of Bildung in a world of difference. *Studies in Philosophy and Education, 21*(4/5), 343–351. Retrieved from https://link.springer.com/article/10.1023%2FA%3A1019874106870

Boal, A. (1976). *De förtrycktas teater* (M. E. og Loreta Valadares, Trans.). Södertälje, Sweden: Gidlunds Förlag.

Bradley, L. (2006). *Brecht and political theatre: The mother on stage*. Oxford, UK: Clarendon Press.

Brecht, B. (1963a). Über Stoffe und Form. In W. Hecht (Ed.), *Schriften zum Theater* (Vol. 1) (pp. 224–227). Frankfurt am Main, Germany: Suhrkamp Verlag. (Original work published 1929)

Brecht, B. (1963b). Zu den Lehrstücken. Zur theorie des Lehrstücks. In W. Hecht (Ed.), *Schriften zum Theater* (Vol. 4) (pp. 78–80). Frankfurt am Main, Germany: Suhrkamp Verlag. (Original work published 1937)

Brecht, B. (1965). *The mother* (L. Baxandall, Trans.). New York, NY: Grove Press. (Original work published 1931)

Brecht, B. (1976). Looking for the new and the old. In J. Willett, & R. Mannheim (Eds.), *Bertolt Brecht: Poems 1913–1956*. New York, NY: Methuen. (Original work written 1950)

Brecht, B. (1994). 10 Oct 42 In M. Esslin (Ed.), *Bertolt Brecht journals 1934–1955* (H. Rorrison, Trans.). New York, NY: Routledge.

Brecht, B. (2001a). Theatre for pleasure or theatre for instruction. In J. Willett (Ed.), *Brecht on theatre: The development of an aesthetic* (pp. 69–77). London, UK: Methuen Publishing Ltd. (Original work published 1936)

Brecht, B. (2001b). Short description of a new technique of acting which produces an alienation effect [Appendix]. In J. Willett (Ed.), *Brecht on theatre: The development of an aesthetic* (pp. 136–147). London, UK: Methuen Publishing Ltd. (Original work written in 1940)

Brecht, B. (2003). Theory of pedagogies. In T. Kuhn, & S. Giles (Eds.) *Brecht on art and politics* (pp. 88–89). London, UK: Methuen. (Original work published 1930)

Brecht, B. (2012a). *The decision*. In J. Willett (Ed.), *Brecht collected plays: 3* (pp. 65–81). London, UK: Bloomsbury.

Brecht, B. (2012b). Discussion Jerome/Brecht/Eisler. In J. Willett (Ed.), *Brecht collected plays: 3* (pp. 270–276). London, UK: Bloomsbury.

Eriksson, S. A. (2009a). *Distancing at close range: Investigating the significance of distancing in drama education*. Vasa, Finland: Åbo University Academy.

Eriksson, S. A. (2009b). Looking at the past for stepping into the future: Background reflections for drama in the curriculum of the 21st century. In J. Shu, & P. Chan (Eds.), *Planting trees of drama with global vision in local knowledge* (pp. 371–384). Hong Kong: IDEA Publications.

Esslin, M. (1971). *Brecht: The man and his work*. New York, NY: Anchor Books.

Gladsø, S., Gjervan, E. K., Hovik, L., & Skagen, A. (2005). *Dramaturgi. Forestillinger om teater*. Oslo, Norway: Universitetsforlaget.

Hecht, W. (1962). *Brechts Weg zum epischen Theater. Beitrag zur Entwicklung des epischen Theaters 1918 bis 1933*. Berlin, Germany: Henschelverlag Kunst und Gesellschaft.

Heggstad, K. M., Eriksson, S. A., & Rasmussen, B. (2013). *Teater som danning*. Bergen, Norway: Fagbokforlaget.

Koch, G. (1988). *Lernen mit Bert Brecht: Bertolt Brechts politisch-kulturelle Pädagogik*. Frankfurt, Germany: Brandes & Apsel.

O'Toole, J. (1992). *The process of drama: Negotiating art and meaning*. London, UK: Routledge.

Steinweg, R. (1972). *Das Lehrstück: Brechts Theorie einer politisch-ästhetischen Erziehung*. Stuttgart, Germany: J. B. Metzlersche Verlagsbuchhandlung.

Steinweg, R. (1995). *Lehrstück und episches Theater: Brechts Theorie und die theaterpädagogische Praxis*. Frankfurt am Main, Germany: Brandes & Apsel.

Wagner, B. J. (1979). *Dorothy Heathcote: Drama as a learning medium*. London, UK: Hutchinson.

NOTES

1. Brecht himself has translated this as "the learning-play."
2. The term "percipience" is used by John O'Toole to describe the particular feature of the drama education genre, where there is no audience, as such, and several of the ordinary functions of theatre are combined: "Accordingly, the word 'participants' will be used for those who are actively engaged in making the drama [...] while the word 'percipients' will be used throughout to denote *all* those who take part in a drama, [...] who all have their proper *perceptions*" (O'Toole, 1992, p. 9).
3. Discussion Jerome/Brecht/Eisler (Brecht, 2012b). Admittedly, during this discussion Brecht asserts that he is not using "parable" as a device in *The mother* (p. 271). I think this comes from the fact that Brecht had a major fall-out with the Theatre Union in New York about the staging of the play there in 1935. The Theatre Union insisted on a naturalistic, Stanislavskian approach, and did not understand what were the basics of epic theatre.
4. A main reference of the production history of *The mother* is Laura Bradley (2006).
5. The concept of *Bildung* brings together the aspirations of all those who acknowledge, or hope, that education is more than the simple acquisition of knowledge and skills, that it is more than simply getting things "right," but that it also has to do with nurturing the human person, that it has do with individuality, subjectivity, in short, with "becoming and being somebody" (Biesta, 2002, p. 343).
6. In the referenced article, I differentiate between four core educational paradigms: (a) The dissemination model, (b) the development model, (c) the dialogue model, and (d) the dialectic model.
7. Wagner (in reference to Dorothy Heathcote) refers to teaching registers: (a) the one who knows, (b) the would you like to know?, (c) I have no idea, (d) the suggester of implications, (e) the interested listener, (f) I'll get what you need, (g) it's no use asking me, (h) the devil's advocate, and (i) the going along.
8. Already in 1929 Brecht asserted that a new purpose is needed for art, and that only the new purpose can make the new art happen: "The new purpose is called: Pedagogy" (Brecht, 1963a, p. 227). In this process of converting theatre in the direction of education, Brecht proceeds to develop a theatre-based knowledge-pedagogy by conducting Lehrstück experiments. The experiments were interrupted, however, and a comprehensive theory was never completed, owing to the political happenings in Nazi Germany, which forced Brecht into exile in 1933 and a continuous moving around for 15 years. Nevertheless, enough fragments exist to evidence that core issues in Brecht's learning-play philosophy represent appropriate instrument(s) for inquiry. In my doctoral work from 2009, I investigated various forms of *distancing* as a most active ingredient in effecting new knowledge (Eriksson, 2009a), and identified Brecht's Lehrstück project as "an epistemological project" (p. 50). For the German Brecht scholar, Werner Hecht, distancing was for Brecht "the condition for cognition" (Hecht, 1962, p. 104).

9. Alienation-effect. This unfortunate choice in translation of the term Verfremdung (which creates unwanted associations to Marx's conception of "alienation" = Entfremdung) has contributed to weaken its core meaning of "making strange" (Eriksson, 2009, pp. 103–110).

Teaching, Fantasy, and Desire:
Me and *Mona Lisa Smile*

Kate Bride,[1] edited by Elizabeth Yeoman

Introduction

The film *Mona Lisa smile* (Johanson & Newell, 2003) tells the story of a young feminist art history professor beginning her career in the 1950s, teaching young women to question and challenge the traditional roles for which they seem destined. In this chapter, I explore the ways in which the film constructs notions of teaching and learning through the fantasy of the teacher as hero, and simultaneously consider my own attachment to *Mona Lisa smile* as a particular rendition of the teacher as hero fantasy. I discuss what a reading of *Mona Lisa smile* offers in terms of my own attachments and desires in teaching and learning, and how learning to examine such attachments critically can lead to more open and democratic teaching.

Attaching to Stories: The Hero Fantasy

Most educators can recall a teacher or teachers who offered generous mentoring and guidance, who taught us how to teach and whose philosophies and approaches continue to steer our own. When I teach I draw on the teachings of those who guided me; the excitement of engaging with new ideas, the challenge and exhilaration of impassioned intellectual debate, and the patience and humility of those teachers whose discipline, integrity, and love for their students continue to inspire me. It is not just our own teachers who provide models and examples for new teachers to follow; representations of teaching and learning in popular culture abound. Many of the most powerful of these representations, especially in film, centre on the notion of the teacher as hero.

In Hollywood representations of teaching and learning, while the teacher hero is meant to represent a revolutionary and emancipatory model of teaching, the portrayal of the teacher as hero – the rare, charismatic, inherently talented, enlightened maverick – is a fundamentally conservative one, because, as Moore says, the teacher is seen as working alone:

> the solutions they offer their students to social problems are at the level of individual experience and are dependent on the interrelations of a very small group of people [...] they suggest a route out of the problem as experienced rather than an attack on the problem itself: we might say, a conservatively *symptomatic* rather than socialistically *causal* reading of and response to the issues.
> (2004, p. 62, emphasis original)

Of course, from a post-structural perspective, this view of the teacher as an essential unified subject is an impossibility. Nevertheless, for those teachers who do not see themselves as heroes but who ascribe to this portrayal, the effects can be devastating, replete with feelings of not measuring up, loss of confidence in their work, and failure. Yet, while it is clear that the construction of the hero teacher can make trouble for teachers, this does not preclude that we teachers do love to attach to these kinds of stories. Exploring these attachments, I contend, is vital in terms of teaching for social change.

To explore attachments to *Mona Lisa smile*, I am informed by Lynne Joyrich's (1995) exploration of her response to the film *The Prime of Miss Jean Brodie* (Cresson & Fryer, 1969). Through her own identifications with the film, Joyrich examines the "mobility of identifications, and therefore of knowledges, that the film makes possible" (1995, p. 47) for her. In my discussion, I work through my own attachment to the film as a particular rendition of the hero teacher fantasy. For as Joyrich so poignantly suggests, "the pedagogical significance of *The prime of Miss Jean Brodie* [and *Mona Lisa smile*] does not simply lie in what it says about teaching" (1995, p. 59), but what it illuminates about the history of ourselves and the complexity of our identifications.

Mona Lisa Smile

One way to view this film is to say that it is a story about women (teacher and students alike) struggling to define themselves when White, middle-class American women were expected to be beside their man and in the kitchen. To deviate from this path was often seen as morally questionable. The main character in the film, Katherine Watson, moves from California to New England to teach art history at Wellesley College in the fall of 1953. There she finds a climate of conformity and conservatism on campus that is in line with the mainstream or power elite views of women's lives in the early 1950s. The administration at Wellesley is depicted as extremely conformist, resisting modern art and other "subversive" acts. During Watson's first art history class, we see in the background an older man leaving the lecture hall, having just sat in on what has appeared to be a miserable failure of a class. In the next scene, Watson is reprimanded for her lack of discipline with students.

Recovering from her failed first lecture, Watson tosses the assigned curriculum aside to give the students a lesson in independent thinking. Here we see the beginnings of the good and heroic teacher, the one who liberates the students by "defying the official school rules and curriculum" (Mitchell & Weber in Moore, 2004, p. 57). In the end, Watson's "unorthodox" teaching methods and her connections with students are met with an ultimatum that she either subscribe to past teaching syllabi or leave Wellesley. Watson decides to leave after her year at the college, but not before she has transformed students' lives and taught them how to think for themselves.[2]

Popular cultural texts about and in educational settings mark and leave traces on their viewers and readers in terms of constructing their understandings of what it means to be a teacher. In the following section I explore these questions: What are the different ways that teachers are figured as "liberating" or "enlightening"? What are the implications and consequences of such representations of teachers? And what was it that I became so attached to? Robertson (1997) suggests that "beginning teachers' engagement with screen images of [idealized versions of teaching] demonstrate discourses of mastery that both reveal and conceal knowledge of the self and others in teaching" (p. 123). If unaccounted for, she says, "fantasy can work to obstruct the thoughtfulness of education" (1997, p. 123). What does my relationship to *Mona Lisa smile* tell about my fantasies of teaching? How does my attachment to the film speak to my attachment to teaching?

Me and Mona Lisa Smile: *Fantasy, Desire, and Epistemic Rupture*

One evening in the late fall of 2003, early in my teaching career, I was watching television and saw a trailer for *Mona Lisa smile*. I made an immediate connection with the story that this film would tell from watching the trailer alone. Part of this had to do with the narrative, but another part had to do with Julia Roberts, the actress who plays Katherine Watson. I have seen all of Julia Roberts' films, and perhaps I could say that I developed a little crush on her and on the characters that she played – vulnerable yet strong, careful yet a little bit wild, funny and serious, beautiful, and almost always an outsider. And, perhaps it is also the case that my identification with the qualities of Roberts' characters (which I also imagined

Roberts had herself) was an overidentification – a desire (and wish) to have those characteristics myself. Days later I went to the theatre and revelled in the story of *Mona Lisa smile*, delighted by its representation of a young teacher who overcomes adversity to enlighten and guide her students. I felt strong connections between myself and the character of Watson; I wanted to teach like she taught, I wanted to be like her, I wanted to *be* her. I went on to see *Mona Lisa smile* twice more in the theatre in the coming weeks, and then added a personal copy of the film to my small collection of inspiring stories about teachers. By now, I have watched *Mona Lisa smile* too many times to count – I have a fascination with this film that is unlike any other film I have encountered. It takes its place in this chapter as an object of my affection, and, as a site of struggle in relation to my fantasies and desires of becoming a teacher.

When I began to consider writing about my relationship to *Mona Lisa smile*, I revisited it to remind myself of the details of the story. I watched the film armed with the script and recited the parts along with my favourite characters. My reading along was performative of my own teaching identity. In introducing the notion of performativity in terms of gender, Butler (1999) suggests that all bodies are gendered and that there is no "natural body" that exists before the body is culturally inscribed. In other words, gender is not something one *is*, rather, we are always "doing" it. Similarly, we are not born to teach, but through "a set of repeated acts within a highly rigid regulatory frame" (1999, p. 25), as Butler puts it, we *perform* teaching. The concept of performativity highlights the instability of the subject and ruptures the possibility of a true and authentic self. My attachment to *Mona Lisa smile* certainly draws on what are held up to be characteristics of "good" teaching; expertise in subject area, challenging students, critical thinking, being articulate.

Although teaching and learning scripts that popular culture promotes tend to shape how we might "perform" the teacher, there is also a tension between the scripts of teaching to which we aspire and the felt effects of teaching and learning (recalling Gardner & Kelly, 2008; Moore, 2004). And perhaps this is why I have always loved going to the movies, entering the dark and quiet space of the theatre, settling into the seat and getting lost in an (idealized and scripted) story, escaping for a few hours.[3] I had always formed attachments to the strong heroes of rescue fantasies, perhaps because I myself longed to be rescued, and I saw Katherine Watson as just such a hero. Many films about teachers present specific isolated classrooms (occupied by loved and heroic teachers) as places where socially and economically disadvantaged youth get a second chance at leading a fulfilling life. *Mona Lisa smile* departs from these scripts to the extent that the students in the film are represented as some of the most privileged in the country. They do not need saving in the same way. But the themes of liberation and the teacher as hero are still vividly present.

Watson's view of education is that it ought to liberate. Yet the film is fraught with tensions and contradictions in relation to the best-known film narratives about teaching, pushing normative ideals, and disrupting them at the same time. The most obvious middle-class ideal that the film supports *and* disrupts is that of the woman as good wife and mother. Joan, a straight-A student who wants to apply to Yale law school at the beginning of the film, decides to get married and have babies instead. Her best friend, Betty, has the same priorities. Watson challenges and disrupts such a status quo with her feminist ideals, presenting a message of independence and success. The film challenges the Wellesley girl's traditional pursuit of the day, as does Betty's failed marriage as the film progresses. Watson, in tossing aside the old curriculum for a set of critical questions for students to think about, disrupts the widespread view of learning as a promise of progress, linearity, and certainty. In her eagerness to teach her students about life and choice, Watson, however, shows great disappointment when Joan chooses not to go to law school but to accompany her husband to Pennsylvania. Watson's liberatory pedagogy is rooted in freedom from the modern expectations of femininity and women, which Joan's choice undermines. While the film does not portray Watson pondering her reaction to Joan's choice, it does indirectly raise a critique of feminist rescue fantasies.

Like Watson, I too felt disappointed that Joan decided to decline admission to law school. A part of my disappointment might be read as my need to be loyal to the teacher (an unconscious wish relating to my desire to be loved through identification with the "good" or heroic teacher) – and therefore, loyal to my fantasy of the teacher as hero, to Watson and her ideals (and perhaps mine) to enlighten and liberate. This loyalty disavows the conflicts that provoke Joan's decision. In the film, Joan makes a case for her choice, which seems to be thought out and clear. My response evoked my fantasy of education's transformative effects, education as freedom, which is intimately tied up with my attachment to the emblematic "teacher as hero." How can the teacher be the hero if education does not transform? This incident raises several questions then: Who is being liberated in the film? Who is the liberator? Watson's fixed understanding of liberation is called into question. Perhaps at the core of my disappointment with Joan is that I saw liberation as fixed, not fluid.

What is also at stake in my initial reaction to Joan's decision is my own feminist rescue fantasy – one that Watson and I seem to share. However, a critique of this fantasy reveals a flaw in the inherent logic. When Joan suggests that she might be open to law school, Watson stages what I might call a feminist assault on her desire to get married and have a family, inundating her with lectures and law school applications. Watson's behaviour stems from first-wave feminism's belief in the promises of shared experience based on gender, and the benefits through social reforms (education, child care, health, reproductive technologies, pay equity, etc.). First-wave feminism hoped to transform women in general to become politically astute and active, equal citizens. But, as Penny Russell suggests,

> Such aspirations ring hollow at the turn of another century, ones we must inevitably face with anxiety, if not deep foreboding. The ideals of citizenship, empire, and progress those women lived and breathed, and which were inseparable from their feminism, seem in the twentieth century also inseparable from total war, technologies of mass destruction and environmental degradation.
> (2002)

Since the period depicted in the film, feminism has evolved in a multitude of ways (and, indeed, is generally conceptualized as "feminisms" in the plural), exploring new ways of thinking about politics, sexuality, race, ability, representation, spirituality, ecology, and much more. I am not making an argument that certain feminisms have nothing to offer in response to Russell's concerns, but that the narrow notion of women's progress as described and enacted in *Mona Lisa smile* in the 1950s is inadequate.

For instance, in the film Watson constantly reiterates to the "Wellesley girls" that they can "have it all," a career, a family, and supper on the table by five p.m. But, as we have seen in the past five decades, many women with successful careers are exhausted and frustrated as they try to raise a family and have a career at the same time. Others who have opted to follow successful careers, but do not have children, may deeply regret this decision. Incidentally, Watson does not "have it all," and her hopefulness for her students might be read as hopefulness for herself, that she, too, can "have it all." This favoured tale of the feminist rescue fantasy plays itself out in the film in Watson's response to Joan, presuming Joan not to have been reflective about her decision or, simply not to have made the right one. A feminist rescue fantasy of progress and movement out of the grips of the patriarchy positions Watson, the feminist teacher, as the one who speaks the truth and renders Joan as the submissive housewife who has "sold her soul."

The character of Betty, the upper-class and newly married student in her final year of college, also highlights the difficulties of attaching deeply to idealized notions of the world (of women's roles, of the place, and use of education, etc.). But in Betty's case, "having it all" is not a possibility, nor a wish. Unlike Joan, Betty believes that her destiny is to get married and have babies, a "role that she was born to fill." Whereas Joan is positioned as making thoughtful and reflective choices about the trajectory of her life even if they defy the feminist rescue fantasy that Watson's teachings advance, Betty is an upper-class snob (with a domineering mother) who resists Watson's "subversive teachings" and feminist ideals. Betty questions the authority (the hero status?) of the teacher and establishes her own by resisting and undermining Watson's teachings through a series of scathing editorials in the college newspaper. Betty and Watson struggle throughout the film, confronting each other's views and beliefs and are remarkably similar characters for it, both investing heavily in right and wrong ways of doing and being. However, as Betty's anger escalates due to news of her husband having an affair and the pressure her mother puts on her to "fix" her marriage, she has a breakdown that illuminates her new-found respect and admiration for Watson's "subversive" teachings. In her final editorial, she writes:

> My teacher, Katherine Watson, lived by her own definition and would not compromise that, not even for Wellesley. I dedicate this, my last editorial, to an extraordinary woman, who lived by example and compelled us all to see the world through new eyes. By the time you read this, she'll be sailing to Europe, where I know she'll find new walls to break down, and new ideas to replace them with. I've heard her called a quitter for leaving and an aimless wanderer. But not all who wander are aimless, especially those who seek truth beyond tradition, beyond definition, beyond the image. I'll never forget you.

As the film ends, we see Betty and Joan on bicycles chasing the taxi that Watson is riding in, as she presumably departs for Europe. Betty is dumped by her husband and her mother only to be rescued by the hero teacher at the end of the film. The feminist rescue fantasy is enacted – feminism rescues Betty; Watson saves her.

In *Mona Lisa smile*, the characters of Betty and Joan illuminate something more about Watson's fantasies of teaching. Both women, in their differences, are meaningful, representative characters and it is important that both see Watson off in the end. While Betty defies Watson's teachings (until she is saved), Joan is more open-minded, and though she is contemplating an engagement with her boyfriend Tommy, she is also considering law school. Betty and Joan highlight Watson's own struggle to sort out her identity as a teacher. As Watson pulls away from the school grounds in the taxi, tears streaming down her face, her struggles and successes at Wellesley point to some questions about teaching. What about being a teacher fulfills me or gives me some sense of my identity? Why do I want to teach and what does it mean to me? If teaching can be thought of as a "helping profession," what drives any of us to want to teach? Let us not kid ourselves – there is something about being a teacher that is more than helping. Teaching is also about trying to resolve, undo, or redo something. In part, teaching is about resolving something in the self; it is about a practice of self. And perhaps we can imagine that Watson's leaving Wellesley is her own kind of return to the self where she must then reflect on her own investments in what teaching means to her.

Holding On and Letting Go

What I learned from this reading of my relationship to *Mona Lisa smile* are the ways that popular cultural texts not only reinforce, but shape our views and beliefs about teaching and learning. My identification with Watson – the beautiful, independent, smart teacher, has influenced my own perceptions of the work of teaching and learning. Teaching meant offering students particular kinds of knowledge that I was attached to with high expectations that students would take what I offered and be transformed by it. The film highlights that when students learn what we want them to learn, we are reinforced and seen. As with Watson, however, my attachments to understanding teaching in this way foreclosed the possibility of asking questions about student choice and direction. In addition, such a narcissistic understanding of the self in teaching and learning has the potential to close off the possibilities for more open and attentive teacher–student relations. Watson highlights this point when she says to Joan: "I give up. You win."

My unconscious story of coming to teaching includes feelings of emptiness, absence, and invisibility, and a longing for something I did not know how to recognize or ask for: love. Through teaching I could feel visible and loved. Perhaps this is the strongest connection I can make between myself and Watson: watching her character gradually break down as she refuses to explore her own desires. When we attach to stories like *Mona Lisa smile* that inform and sustain our fantasies of teaching and learning without question, those attachments do little to allow for other kinds of understandings and possibilities in teaching and learning. Letting go of such attachments enables us to rethink our dearly held ideals about teaching and learning. While our attachment to narratives such as that of the teacher as hero offers historical continuity and certainty, such attachments prevent and foreclose new understandings. An interrogation of knowledge-making practices such as viewing films about heroic teachers, a reckoning with our attachments to knowledges, and an engagement with the felt effects of letting go of them, hold the possibility of imagining more open and democratic ways of teaching.

REFERENCES

Butler, J. (1999). *Gender trouble: Feminism and the subversion of identity*. New York, NY: Taylor & Francis.

Cresson, J., & Fryer, R. (Producers), & Neame, R. (Director). (1969). *The prime of Miss Jean Brodie*. UK: Twentieth Century Fox.

Gardner, M., & Kelly, U. (2008). Narrating transformative learning in education. In U. Kelly, & M. Gardner (Eds.), *Narrating transformative learning in education* (pp. 1–9). New York, NY: Palgrave MacMillan.

Johanson, F. (Producer), & Newell, M. (Director). (2003). *Mona Lisa smile* [Motion picture]. USA: Revolution Studios and Columbia Pictures in association with Red Om Film Productions.

Joyrich, L. (1995). "Give me a girl at an impressionable age and she is mine for life": Jean Brodie as pedagogical primer. In J. Gallop (Ed.), *Pedagogy: The question of impersonation* (pp. 46–63). Bloomington, IN: Indiana University Press.

Moore, A. (2004). *The good teacher: Dominant discourses in teacher education*. New York, NY: Routledge Falmer.

Robertson, J. P. (1997). Fantasy's confines: Popular culture and the education of the female primary school teacher. *Canadian Journal of Education, 22*(2), pp. 123–143.

Russell, P. (2002, February 8). Feminist echoes. *Australian Review of Public Affairs (Digest)*. Retrieved from http://www.australianreview.net/digest/2002/02/russell.html

Spark, M. (1999). *The prime of Miss Jean Brodie*. New York, NY: Harper Perennial.

Sprengnether, M. (2002). *Crying at the movies: A film memoir*. St. Paul, MN: Greywolf Press.

NOTES

1. Kate Bride completed her Ph.D. thesis, *Learning to love again: Loss, self study, pedagogy and women's studies,* at Memorial University in education in 2009. Kate was a dear friend to many of us, a gifted and beloved teacher, an original and promising researcher, a vulnerable, searingly honest, generous, funny, kind person. She died in 2012 of a sudden devastating illness. We still miss her dreadfully. This chapter is an abridged version of a chapter from her thesis. I (Elizabeth Yeoman) discussed the possibility of including a version of her thesis chapter in this book with Kate's mother, Mary Kay Bride, who approved of the project. With her approval and the help of editors Diane Conrad and Monica Prendergast, I edited the chapter and cut it to an appropriate size for their book. The original chapter was much longer and discussed a much wider range of characters and concepts. The thesis is available online via Memorial University's research repository at http://research.library.mun.ca/id/eprint/9192.

2. Recalling Moore, the representation is of a solitary act between Watson and her students that does little to transform the systemic structure of schooling.

3. And perhaps this desire to escape is one that is rooted in a disavowal of loss. For as Madelon Sprengnether (2002) asserts, "For years, I cried, not over my own losses, but at the movies. When bad things happened to me in real life, I didn't react […]. Yet in the dark and relative safety of the movie theater, I would weep over fictional tragedies, over someone else's tragedy" (p. 2).

PART V

Destabilizing Perspectives of Teachers and Teaching

Wrestling with Vulnerabilities and the Potential for Difference: The Pedagogy of Drug Use in *Half Nelson*

Diane Conrad

Introduction

The half nelson is a wrestling hold in which a wrestler pins their opponent to the mat by wrapping one forearm under their opponent's underarm pulling up, while pushing down on the back of their head with the other hand. This move of opposing forces effectively debilitates the opponent. In the film *Half Nelson* (Boden, Patricof, Howell, Orlovsky, Korenberg, & Fleck, 2006), white teacher Dan Dunne (Ryan Gosling) teaches history at a Brooklyn public junior high school to African-American students. He teaches history from the perspective of dialectics (Dialectic, n.d.) – about how history works as change over time brought about by opposing forces pushing against one another. Change happens when one force gains strength to overpower the other. We see this dynamic of opposing forces at play in the social context of the film and in the characters' personal lives. Caught up in these dynamics within the setting of the film is the contentious issue of the illegal drug trade, which is particularly contentious within the context of education. In this chapter I examine details of the film, in particular the characters' vulnerabilities, to explore the pedagogy of drug use – how and what drug use, in this instance, might teach us and what the experience of drug use has to offer teaching and learning.

Half Nelson: *The Film*

Half Nelson (Boden et al., 2006) is about education and the broader social context in which it is set. The film alludes to Brown v. Board of Education, the 1954 supreme court case that ended legal racial segregation of schooling in the United

States, a major victory in the civil rights movement. As such, education is revealed as a rich context for discussion of social justice issues broadly. Set fifty years later, *Half Nelson* is ostensibly about the interminable frustrations around racial justice in the United States, and the complexities and struggles these have engendered, such as the state of the illegal drug trade. These complexities are portrayed through the life experiences of Dunne, a white middle-class teacher, and his 13-year-old African-American female student Drey (Shareeka Epps). The unconventional relationship that is forged between them offers a glimmer of hope against pervasive disillusionment. Having this scenario unfold in an educational setting allows the writers to focus in on some of the opposing forces or dichotomies at play in the larger social context, including categories of identity – e.g. youth/adult, power/powerless, black/white, good/bad, and suggest that it is in such a micro-political setting where hope may lie.

At the beginning of the film we meet Dunne, a teacher by day, and a drug user leading a self-destructive, solitary life. Early in the film his student, Drey, catches him in the locker room after basketball practice, smoking crack cocaine. The typical power relations between teacher and student begin to shift as Drey tends to Dunne almost passed out on the locker room floor – his secret exposed. It is the unusual tenderness of the relationship that develops between Dunne and Drey throughout the film, around the sharing of each other's pains and vulnerabilities that prompts me to question the educative value of drug use in this instance.

As a teacher, Dunne is inspiring. In teaching the kids about class struggles and the civil rights movement, he goes above and beyond the expectations of the approved "core curriculum." For example, he shows his class a 1964 news clip of a student activist speech, which I surmise is representative of Dunne's perspectives:

> There is a time when the operation of the machine becomes so odious, makes you so sick at heart, that you can't take part; you can't even passively take part, and you've got to put your bodies upon the gears and upon the wheels, upon the levers, upon all the apparatus, and you've got to make it stop.
> (Mario Savio, University of California, cited in Boden et al., 2006)

Dunne's self-destructive drug use can be seen as putting his body upon the gears. Through dialogue with his students Dunne elicits their understandings of the school as part of the dreaded machine, in which he as their teacher and even the students themselves more or less willingly participate. This is heady subject matter for 13-year-olds.

Drey's life is also entangled in social conditions not of her making. Her older brother is in jail on drug charges. He is doing time related to his work for a mid-level drug dealer, Frank (Anthony Mackie), portrayed as a level-headed, caring individual, who happens also to be a drug dealer. Frank provides money for Drey's family in exchange for her brother's loyalty, which Drey's overworked mother, a paramedic who works night shifts, accepts with a mixture of reluctance and gratitude. The play of opposing forces is evident on many levels within the film.

The relationship between Dunne and Drey unfolds as the film progresses. Drey's curiosity about her drug-using teacher, Dunne, leads to various afterschool interactions. One day Drey asks him for a ride home and then feigns having lost her house keys. She goes with Dunne to his apartment to wait for her mother's return from work. Following some playful banter while they are preparing dinner, Drey takes the opportunity to ask Dunne the question she has been waiting to ask him: "What is it like when you smoke that stuff?" Dunne cannot answer her.

Sometime later when Dunne learns of Drey's family connections to Frank, he goes to Frank in a fury. He warns Frank to stay away from Drey in an effort to protect the girl from what he sees as the negative influences of the drug world. Frank counters that he is family and a friend to Drey. He accuses Dunne of perpetuating a "what's white is right" mentality. Dunne is left directionless: "What am I supposed to do?" He feels the responsibility to do something for Drey, from his position as teacher and adult in her life, but he is immobilized from knowing the right response. His ambivalence is reflective of the treatment of illegal drug use throughout the film. Frank invites him in for a soft drink.

Dunne's mental state deteriorates as the film progresses. Near the end of the film, Drey, now working to deliver drugs for Frank, delivers to Dunne at a seedy motel room party. She returns to the motel room the next day to rescue him, after Dunne has missed a day of school. Here the tables are fully turned; Drey, from a position of strength, reaches out to Dunne, who is defenseless. In this scene, it is through his total relinquishing of his defenses and exposure of his vulnerabilities that Dunne is potentially saved.

Drug Use Portrayed in Half Nelson

Dunne struggles with his vulnerabilities throughout the film. He is both a good guy, an inspiring teacher and coach, a passionate advocate for social justice, and also a bad guy, with a drug habit that leads him to make bad choices and model behaviours he abhors. It is these internal contradictions that tear him apart.

Dunne's drug use is linked to his disillusionment with his leftist politics. During his interactions in the classroom he is animated and enthusiastic to share his passion with his young students. In his off hours he is even working on an illustrated children's book that explains dialectics, but his personal life engulfed by the drugs gets in the way of his good intentions.

In one scene, at a family dinner, we learn that Dunne's parents were anti-war activists in the 1960s/70s. They thought they were going to change the world, his mother says. When Dunne comments that they *had* stopped the war, her benign response of "that's nice," suggests they had long since abandoned those ideals – replaced, perhaps, by the bottles of wine that flow freely throughout the family dinner. In a moment of nostalgia his mother puts on a record; the song "It's alright to cry" is from an album from his childhood: *Free to be, you and me* (Hart, Lawrence, & Hart, 1972). As the song hailing liberal idealism plays in the background, the disillusionment in Dunne's face and his inability to express the distress he feels is palpable.

Dunne's personal relationships with women in the film exemplify his inability to show emotion or connect. At one point his ex-girlfriend turns up, but she is now clean having gone through drug rehabilitation, and so any connection with her has been lost. The morning after a casual sexual encounter with a fellow teacher at his school, he treats the woman with indifference. On another occasion he turns up at her home stoned and forces himself on her. After she hits him and locks herself in her bathroom, he is filled with awkward remorse. It is only to a woman picked up at a bar, who is as stoned as he is, that he can open up. He tells her that he uses drugs to get by. He insists that it is his students who keep him focused and keep him sane.

For Dunne, drugs perhaps serve an aesthetic function – a desire for an experience of the sublime, through an altered or non-ordinary state of consciousness (Addiction Info, 2008), in the short term, to replace the exhilaration of his thwarted ideals. More significantly, it seems, they serve an anaesthetic function (Buck-Morss, 1992) – a kind of self-medication, to numb the pain of disillusionment, the lack of gratification, the meaninglessness and hopelessness of his life. This is, perhaps, his sacrifice of the self, his symbolic throwing of his body onto the gears of the machine, responding to the call of the death drive (Freud, 1920/2011).

Our synesthetic system, Buck-Morss (1992) describes, is open as it relates to the world through our sense-perceptions – our senses, our brain, the environment, and memory. To numb the impoverishment of our lives in today's post-modern reality, to numb our painful emotions that make us vulnerable, to endure the shocks of life without pain, we often choose to dull the synesthetic experience (e.g., through drugs of one kind or another) (Brown, 2010; Buck-Morss, 1992). Drugs, as an *anaesthetic*, block the openness of the synesthetic system; they block present consciousness from the past and memory. According to Brown (2010), however, we cannot numb our emotions selectively. When we close off to bad feelings, we simultaneously numb our capacity for feeling joy, happiness, and connection with others. It is such connection with others, Brown believes, that life is all about. Buck-Morss concurs that the subject only exits through its relationship with others. When we are closed off from others, our shame and fear of disconnection further inhibit our ability to connect, leading to further alienation of the self. Rather, we need to feel a full range of emotions and embrace our vulnerabilities. We must allow ourselves to be seen with our vulnerabilities exposed in order for connections to be authentic. This describes the circumstances of Dunne's life in the film. His drug use has taken him on a downward spiral of self-destruction, and yet, it is his drug use, which leads to the chance encounter with Drey in the locker room that opens up other possibilities.

Beyond Dunne's personal struggles with drug use, the film also clearly illustrates that drug use by individuals, and the drug trade, does not exist in a vacuum, but is deeply embedded within a particular social–political context. Maran (2003), journalist and mother, whose teenage son also experienced drug use, for her book *Dirty: A search for answers inside America's teenage drug epidemic,* followed three teens through drug rehabilitation programs. Maran reveals that while just as many white people as black people in the United States admit to drug use, most of the drug trade occurs in black neighbourhoods. She cites David Simon, journalist and writer/producer of the HBO series *The wire* (Simon et al., 2008), who specializes in criminal justice and urban issues. Simon's (Rothkerch, 2002) contention is that the US government's War on Drugs has done as much damage to communities as the drugs themselves. These are communities whose only hope for economic survival is the self-perpetuating drug trade. The government's efforts to eradicate the drug trade without viable alternatives in place, he suggests, is naïve.

The Pedagogy of Drug Use

My aim in looking at the portrayal of drug use in *Half Nelson* (Boden et al., 2006) is in seeking its potential for teaching us something relevant to teaching and learning. In exploring this pedagogy of drug use, based on the discussion above, I now draw on Deleuze and Guattari's "tool box" of concepts via Malins (2004) re-thinking of drug use. Congruent with my aims, Malins searches for alternative ethical interpretations of drug use – its creative and productive potentials, specifically the potential for drug use to enable a body's *becoming-other*. A number of Deleuze and Guattari's concepts are useful in such an endeavour. An *assemblage* in Deleuze and Guattari's ethico-aesthetics is the connections that *bodies* form with other bodies, be they human or otherwise (e.g., animal, plant, machine, phenomenon, body of knowledge). Malins explains that the body is not "a stable, unified, bounded entity [...] [rather] a body's function or potential or 'meaning' becomes entirely dependent on which other bodies or machines it forms an assemblage with"

(p. 85). Malins notes that each assemblage, taken as an event, can be examined for the ethical and aesthetic relations it creates. The connection Dunne forms with drugs (his symbolic throwing of his body onto the gears of the machine) is such an assemblage.

Another Deleuze–Guattarian concept relevant to my exploration is the notion of "lines of flight"; these are the particular *affects* (states of mind and body) or movements that various assemblages produce. Positive lines of flight are those that allow new flows, new becomings, new relations, the opening a body up to difference/variation and multiplicities (becoming-other), and increasing the capacity for life.

Dominant dichotomous ways of thinking and morality condemn drug use as "bad," and particularly reprehensible for a teacher. Deleuze and Guattari's "rhizomatic" thinking, which allows for an infinite network of connections with multiple possibilities or lines of flight, suggests otherwise. Rhizomatic thinking allows for a body to be multiple with multiple potentials depending on the assemblages it forms (Malins, 2009). Drug use, then, is not intrinsically good or bad, but dependent on its affects. A body can be both a good teacher and a drug user. The drug trade can be both an economically viable option for families and a social problem. Malins explains that good or bad are dependent on, "whether a particular assemblage enhances or harms each body's life force; in other words, whether it increases or reduces each body's power to act and its potential to go on forming new relations" (p. 97). She continues: "an assemblage becomes ethical or unethical depending on the affects it enables and the potentials it opens up or blocks. It becomes ethical when it enables the body to differentiate from itself and go on becoming-other" (p. 102).

Relating the film to Malin's (2009) Deleuze–Guattarian re-thinking of drug use, it is evident that both Dunne and Drey have formed assemblages to drugs. Dunne is a consumer/user of drugs. Drey's brother is in jail on drug-related charges; her family receives money from the drug dealer Frank, upon which their survival depends; and by the end of the film Drey is delivering drugs for Frank. Both Dunne and Drey also connect to the socio-economic context of the drug trade as consumers or dealers and through living and working in a community where the drug trade is prominent. Their individual assemblages form a shared assemblage through the meeting in the locker room when Drey catches Dunne smoking crack. This inexorably connects them and opens up a *line of flight*.

Prior to the inadvertent meeting with Drey in the locker room, Dunne's relation to the body of knowledge he teaches at school is already altered. In part, I would suggest, as an effect of the context in which he finds himself teaching and his personal history, which includes his drug use. I concur with Jeroenn's (2009) astute evaluation of Dunne's teaching:

> Also well portrayed [in *Half Nelson*] is Dan [Dunne]'s character as a teacher who tries to encourage the students to really understand underlying structures of history instead of just throwing dates at them that are either right or wrong (he gets told off by the principal for not following the school curriculum). He tries to eliminate his presence in class as a hierarchical figure that tells his students the way things are, and rather pushes them to think for themselves. As Deleuze writes in *Difference and Repetition* . . . teachers should not say "Do as I do," but shout "Do with me!" An exploration of problems as *possibilities* for new concepts, not equations that come with answers in the back of the book.
>
> (para. 5, emphasis original)

Dunne is not the heroic teacher so often portrayed in films, who saves his students; rather, Dunn's downward spiral through the course of the film shows that he is the one in need of saving. The incident in the locker room with Drey initiates a line of flight that offers potential for difference in his relations with his students – or at least with one particular student, and for renewed possibility in his own life. Teacher as drug user disrupts the traditional binaries, the dichotomous categories of identity – teacher/student, drug user/clean, good/bad, and others – that limit possibilities for difference, and rather opens a space for difference, for possibilities of *becoming-other*.

Conclusion

In the last scene of the film, Dunne and Drey sit silently at opposite ends of the decrepit couch in Dunne's apartment. The image is one of temporary balance, though we do not know what the next moment might bring. Dialectics aims for reconciliation of paradoxes to arrive at truth, however tentative. In this final scene, we see the contradiction, in the coming together of these two individual disparate lives in the way that they have, both embroiled in a culture of drug use and racial injustice, and we see the potential, as a starting point for imagining different sorts of relations.

The defensive move against the half nelson hold in wrestling is for the overpowered opponent to keep their head up strong and make their way to a sitting position. To counter that defensive move the offender wrestler keeps their body weight forward and pins their opponent's head down to the ground with their own forehead.

REFERENCES

Addiction Info. Humans need to alter consciousness: Alternatives to 12-step treatment. Retrieved from http://www.addictioninfo.org/articles/183/1/Humans-Need-To-Alter-Consciousness/Page1.html

Boden, A. Patricof, J., Howell, L., Orlovsky, A., & Korenberg, R. (Producers), & Fleck, R. (Director). (2006). *Half nelson* [Motion picture]. USA: ThinkFilm.

Brown, B. (2010, June). The power of vulnerability [Video]. TedxHouston. Retrieved from https://www.ted.com/talks/brene_brown_on_vulnerability?language=en

Buck-Morss, S. (1992). Aesthetics and anaesthetics: Walter Benjamin's artwork essay reconsidered. *October, 62*(Fall), 3–41.

Freud, S. (2011). *Beyond the pleasure principle* (T. Dufresne, Ed.) (G. C. Richter, Trans.). Buffalo, NY: Broadview Press. (Originally published in 1920)

Hart, C. Lawrence, S., & Hart, B. (1972). *Free to be... you and me* [Recorded by Marlo Thomas and Friends]. [CD]. New York, NY: Bell Records.

Jeroenn (2009, February 8). *Half Nelson*: A poetics of confusions [Blog post]. Transversal inflections. Retrieved from https://transversalinflections.wordpress.com/2009/02/08/half-nelson/

Malins, P. (2004). Machinic assemblages: Deleuze, Guattari and the ethico-aesthetics of drug use. *Janus Head, 7*(1), 84–104.

Maran, M. (2003). *Dirty: A search for answers inside America's teenage drug epidemic*. New York, NY: Harper Collins.

Dialectic. (n.d.). University of Chicago: Theories of media – Keywords glossary. Retrieved from http://csmt.uchicago.edu/glossary2004/dialectic.htm

Rothkerch, I. (2002, June 29). What drugs have not destroyed, the war on them has. *Salon*. Retrieved from https://www.salon.com/2002/06/29/simon_5

Simon, D., Colesberry, R. F., & Noble, N. K. (Executive Producers), Thorson, K., Burns, E., Chappelle, J., Pelecanos, G., & Overmyer, E. (Producers). (2008). *The wire* [Television series]. Los Angeles, CA: Warner Bros; HBO.

The Seductress in the Classroom: The Female Teacher as Erotic Object and Fantasy in *The Piano Teacher*

Melissa Tamporello

Introduction

I typed "sexy teacher," "sexy passionate teacher," and "passionate teacher" into my Google search bar just to see what kind of curious entries might come up. Unsurprisingly, the first two entries produced pages and pages of "XXX" videos listed on pornography sites and YouTube. They included titles such as "Sexy teacher and student hot romance!," "Fourth grade teacher dubbed the sexiest teacher alive!," "The hottest teachers caught sleeping with students," and "Private passionate teacher." When I searched "passionate teacher," a list of articles about teachers' dedication and commitment appeared. These articles listed things teachers should do to be *more committed.* Based on this dichotomy, there seem to exist either teachers who are superhuman (Scull & Peltier, 2007) or teachers who are just *too sexy* to teach because they "distract students" and deviate from teacher norms (Robinson-Cseke, 2012).

In the film *The piano teacher* (Heiduschka & Haneke, 2001), Erika Kohut (Isabelle Huppert) embodies both teacher depictions. She is a passionate piano teacher at a Vienna conservatory who has dedicated and sacrificed her entire life to the piano. Yet, she has a deep need to express her sexuality. There is a difference, however, between Erika's character and the many other characters in films that depict female teachers as having sexual relations with students. Throughout the movie Erika is not depicted as being typically sexy, nor does she seem to have the desire to express sexuality in her dress and body language. Her sexual desires are displayed privately through her voyeurism and sadomasochistic fantasies of physical pain and restraint for pleasure that ultimately lead to an abuse of power.

Erika Kohut appears to be an everyday schoolmarm, yet somehow we (the audience) do not dislike her as we would many of her counterparts in

American teacher films, for instance, Miss Trunchbull in *Matilda* (Dahl, DeVito, Shamberg, & Sher, 1993), Kitty Farmer in *Donnie darko* (Fields, Juvonen, & McKittrick, 2001), or Barbara Covett in *Notes on a scandal* (Fox & Rudin, 2006). Typically, the schoolmarm is the villain pitted against the protagonist teacher who is trying to save the students from self-destruction. Rather, Erika's passion for the piano overtakes her stern attitude. The audience is able to sympathize with her in trying to understand her dark fantasies, while also feeling the pain she experiences because of her overbearing mother (arguably the root of her mental illness/sexual fetishism[1]) and destructive love affair, which establishes a rationale for the complexity of sexual expression in the film. Erika's mother lives vicariously through her daughter's life by controlling her career, her activities after work, and even the clothes she is allowed to buy. She is able to wield this amount of control because they live in the same apartment that creates strong tension in the film.

Female teachers are encouraged and oftentimes mandated to deny and mask desires by being modest in dress, behaviour, and by having impersonal relationships with their students (Johnson, 2005). Most often, the "schoolmarm image" of teachers in film masks the erotic culture and taboo surrounding female teachers as sexual objects. This culture exists not only in popular films, but in an entire category of the porn industry. Why is it that female teachers are so often characterized as being sexually frustrated, isolated, and easily seduced by their students? Johnson (2005) argues that a teacher's sex appeal is not primarily informed by society's standard of beauty, but in conjunction with a teacher's passion and ability to relate passion to students. How can this sexy passion then be used in positive ways, rather than abusively – as it is in *The piano teacher*, so that students are motivated to do better in their classes and strive harder to learn? Should we conclude that teachers are inherently sexy when they express great passion? My interest is to understand if and how sexual passion can be used in positive ways in classrooms through the exploration of how it is negatively portrayed in *The piano teacher*. I do not condone manipulation or abuse of students under any circumstances; however, I do hope to open the door for discussion surrounding this taboo subject within educational communities.

The Piano Teacher

The piano teacher (Heiduschka & Hanecke, 2001) was adapted from the novel of the same title by Elfriede Jelinek (1983), an Austrian writer. The film provokes many themes that touch not only on student–teacher relationships, but also on mother–daughter relationships, on mental illness and its relationship to classical music, on high and low culture in a bourgeois society, and on female sexuality expressed through sadomasochistic desires as a taboo subject viewed through a Freudian lens (Johnson, 2009; Sharrett, 2002; Wrye, 2007).

The first fifteen minutes of the film reveal Erika's unhealthy relationship with her mother and who she is as a teacher. Her teacher identity is initially conveyed by her interactions with three of her students in the small piano studio where she conducts her private lessons. Erika is painted as a negative, sarcastic, and harsh piano teacher. Her studio is a small, soundproof room with a window, a piano, and two portraits of her favourite classical composers: Schubert and Schumann. These two composers are the foundation of Erika's passion and symbolically create a link between her own and the composers' mental illnesses. Arguably, her student Walter Klemmer's (Benoît Magimel) susceptibility to her desires is the basis for Erika's obsession and love for him.

We first meet Walter arriving at his aunt and uncle's piano recital where Erika will perform. Erika and her mother walk into an old elevator that has a barred sliding door. Erika closes the door just before Walter is able to enter the elevator with them, thus he takes the winding stairs that circle around the elevator. The camera is situated behind Erika and her mother, which allows us to see him pass as they ascend each floor. This scene is metaphorical for Erika's relationship with her mother and her soon to be relationship with Walter. She is literally in a cage with her mother, representing her mother's overbearing control. Walter is seen running up the stairs with vigour, energy, and male assuredness that we experience later in the film.

At the recital, Walter watches Erika perform a piece by Schubert. His growing admiration for her is evident in his incessant applauding and through camera shots that move back and forth from Walter's eyes to Erika's hands and body. We are voyeuristically watching him watch her. After Erika's performance, Walter reveals his talent as a pianist by playing a piece by Schubert, inspired by an earlier conversation with Erika. There is a major difference in the way they play the compositions. Erika plays with seriousness and passionate bodily movements, while Walter performs more playfully; he appears to be trying to seduce her with his playfulness. After this moment early in the film, Erika and Walter's relationship begins to form in her studio classroom where, despite being an engineering student, he has a talent for the art. We learn more about Erika's mental illness, her sexual passions, and ultimately we see the breakdown of her schoolmarm teacher cloak that she uses to mask her feelings, which leaves the viewer just as lost and empty as she seems.

The Sexy Schoolmarm

In pop culture films, the schoolmarm teacher is typically the villain and a physically unattractive teacher with male characteristics. For example, in *Matilda*

(Dahl et al., 1993) the villainous teacher is Miss Trunchbull, the head teacher and principal of the school, whose motto is "Use the rod. Beat the child." She is tall, burly, constantly red in the face, yelling and seemingly never happy. She smiles only when she is inflicting physical or verbal pain upon the students. In comparison, in *The piano teacher*, Erika is perhaps not as extreme as Miss Trunchbull, yet she hides under many of the cold, unsmiling, strict characteristics of a typical schoolmarm teacher. Before her love affair with Walter, she dresses very conservatively, styles her hair tightly pulled back, and wears very little makeup. One might wonder what attributes of this schoolmarm would attract a teenage boy to become sexually obsessed with her. This attraction addresses the taboo subject of teacher sexuality and presents a counter-narrative to the typical trope in films that involves a physically attractive female teacher and male student.

Erika's ability to seduce lies in her passion for piano, musical composition, her strong sexual desires, and the mystery surrounding her mental illness that is implied through her actions in the film. When Erika plays the piano she uses her entire body; she plays with a vigour and self-assuredness that is incredibly attractive. The first time Walter sees her play at the recital, a conversation ensues about Schubert's mental state, a parallel to Erika's:

> Erika: He knows he's losing his mind. It torments him but he clings on, one last time. It's being aware of what it means to lose oneself before being completely abandoned.
>
> Walter: I'd say you are a good teacher. You talk about things as if they were yours. It's rare. And I think you know it.
>
> (Heidushcka & Haneke, 2001)

There are strong power differentials that exist between Walter and Erika. At the beginning of their affair, Erika exerted her control by giving Walter a laundry list of masochistic acts that she wanted him to perform on her including hitting her, bondage, and other physical restraints. Her demands made it seem like she desired to be powerless. Walter is initially repulsed by the idea of sadism, yet bends to Erika's desires by giving her some of what she wants. The lines between the beholders of power become incredibly blurred, when Walter becomes the seducer whose "seduction is stronger than power because it is reversible and mortal, while power, like value, seeks to be irreversible, cumulative and immortal" (Baudrillard, 1979, cited in McWilliam, 1996, p. 6). Walter begins to vilify Erika because of her power as seducer and it escalates towards the end of the film when he accuses her of giving him her mental illness after he had stood under her window and publicly masturbated. There is a connection between the characters, but there is a lack of clarity about the nature of this connection because both parties are blinded by their vision of fetishized romance. Had Erika maintained control of the situation, she could potentially have used the energy and passion Walter was pouring into their affair towards an educational goal.

Paraphilia as a Teacher Cloak

In *The piano teacher*, as viewers, we experience Erika's fantasy and pain in our own bodies (Johnson, 2009) because we can see her where other characters cannot. Her sadomasochistic fantasies correlate to Lacan's theory of the Real that "represents a lack of something desired by the self [and] also the paradoxical painful pleasure that the self experiences in attempting to fill that lack" (Robinson-Cseke, 2012, p. 255). Erika lacks intimacy and healthy relationships in her life – her model being that of an overbearing mother, and she attempts to fill this lack with physical pain when, for example, in one scene she cuts her genitals in the bathroom which results in a painful pleasure. Erika has kept her fantasies secret until she admits to Walter what she desires, which leads to a breach in the teacher–student barrier that maintains a respectful relationship. At times, it can be beneficial for a teacher to be relatively open with a student to create a bond of friendship and trust that would lend to the student respecting the teacher and hopefully respecting the overall classroom experience. Obviously, Erika's trust in Walter led to an unfortunate misuse of this bond.

Erika also takes on the role of pornographic voyeur and we participate in her voyeurism. She explores voyeurism in adult store peep booths and in a drive-in movie theatre parking lot where she watches a young couple having sex. In the latter instance, Erika squats next to the couple's car and upon their climaxing, she urinates and is caught by the couple and publicly humiliated for her actions. Two more voyeuristic scenes unfold in public spaces, this time involving Walter. They attempt to have intimate moments, but both are ruined through Erika's naivety of intimacy and Walter's male ego. In these voyeuristic scenes, the viewer's gaze is exploited, making us aware of our roles as voyeurs in these situations (Landwehr, 2011).

Erika's conflicted attitude to pornography is brought to the classroom after an incident in which she catches one of her students in a store looking at pornographic magazines and making crude remarks about a woman advertising for a sexual partner. She watches him look at the magazines with his friends then sidles up beside him, looks over the magazines herself and continues into the store. This is an awkward moment for the viewer because we expect her to reprimand or publicly humiliate him, but instead she continues on as if nothing had happened.

Later, in her piano classroom she confronts the student about the incident. She harshly tells him he has meagre talent, that he should take a job playing in a strip joint and to stop wasting her time. The student apologizes, but is unable to say what he is sorry for, thus Erika asks, "What are you sorry for? Sorry for being a pig? Sorry because your friends are pigs? Or because all women are bitches for making you a pig?" In this moment Erika is cloaked by her schoolmarm identity; she is harsh with the student and threatens to tell his mother if he cannot say why he is sorry. Yet underneath her cloak, Erika is also the "pig" who revels at pornography and fantasizes about such sexual encounters. In this instance, Erika is not wrong to reprimand the student and is very brave for breaching the taboo topic of sex inside her classroom studio. It is difficult to know if what she is saying is genuine, however. Her tone of voice and concern seem very genuine, but her actions outside of the studio are so contradictory. This begs the question: Is it less pig-like of her to participate in pornography than her male student because she is a woman, because she is a teacher, or because she seeks pornography to appease her lonely desires, which only alienate her further from other people, her family and Walter?

The Erotic Classroom and Its Repercussions

I argue that the relation between teaching and eroticism can be beneficial in the learning process to both the teacher and the student. When a teacher exhibits passion and knowledge about a subject, a student may become more engaged because of that teacher's ability to engage. Walter was immediately engaged by Erika's ability to play the piano and her passion for the subject at his aunt and uncle's recital, which presumably lead to him enrolling in the rigorous piano programme at his school. Through this type of engagement, an erotic bond may be formed where the teacher is able to see her/himself mirrored in the student and the student is able to gain gratification and satisfaction from the teacher (Maher, 2004). Erika forms an erotic bond with Walter based on the desires she projects on him; however, this passion quickly turns into an abusive relationship by both parties. Erika never had any interest in Walter becoming a good piano player; she was overtaken by Walter's seductive capabilities and her own sexual desires. Maher (2004) notes that as a female college professor she does not often experience an erotic bond with her students. She says, "some of my best teaching works by a means of seduction. But such seductions, with or without cultural consent, work differently for male and female students, for reasons beyond simple sexual desire" (p. 45). Perhaps Walter's seduction of Erika is simply sexual and he only enrolled in her piano course to attempt to achieve his goal of having sex with her. Or maybe his attraction to Erika is about her passion and obsession for the piano, which leads him to desire such a passion for himself and in attempting to reach that goal, finds himself sexually attracted to Erika, the possessor of passion, as well. The possible perspectives reflect the idiosyncratic positions of the viewers.

I believe that Walter's desire for Erika goes beyond the single goal of sex – he makes the mistake of conflating passion for the piano with sexual passion, and this has larger implications for his learning. He is attracted to her position of authority, as a woman who initially seems in control and who has sacrificed so much for her passion, by living through the work of Schuman and Schubert in a way that is sexually charged as well (Johnson, 2005). A combination of attraction and passion delineates Walter's desire to further his knowledge of piano. During his classes he tries to woo her instead of playing, but she is insistent that her classroom is for the piano only. If only she had stuck with her convictions. At this point, Walter's sexual urges may have overtaken his ability to learn anything from Erika; we do not explicitly learn if his piano playing progresses, or not. The ambiguity between teaching/learning and sexuality becomes a key device in the film that allows multiple interpretations based on the viewer's own orientation. This ambiguity shows the failure of a teacher–student erotic relationship, when it goes too far and the teacher–student barrier is breached. Any positive potential of eroticism in teaching in the relationship between Walter and Erika fails miserably in this film.

In an ideal scenario, Walter and Erika's relationship would have existed only inside the piano studio where they could have utilized each other's desires to strengthen Walter's learning and Erika's teaching. Johnson (2005) iterates a conducive teaching-learning relationship: "I think teachers can be sexy without being seductresses; they can enjoy the erotic element of teaching without being abusive" (p. 139). Erika and Walter's relationship was abusive, not only because of their perverted teacher–student dynamic brought on by Erika's mental illness and her traumatic family history, but because of the psychological manipulation that occurs in the film via the potential powers of passion. Here we see "a female teacher as a figure of desire for her male students [with] violent or potentially violent repercussions" (Maher, 2004, p. 46). Towards the end of the movie Walter goes to Erika's house, locks her mother in her mother's room, and beats and rapes Erika. Upon raping her, Walter says,

> I do realize that all of this isn't very nice of me. But you have to admit you are partly responsible. I'd appreciate it if you told no one. Anyhow it's for your own good. You can't humiliate a man that way, it's not possible.
> (Heiduschka & Haneke, 2001)

In this moment we see Erika's sexual fantasies shredded to pieces. The pain inflicted by Walter was not the kind of mutual pleasurable pain she had imagined. In this scene, the male sexual ego superseding the female sexual ego takes precedence over the teacher–student relationship. In the last scene of the movie, Erika goes to her recital where she is supposed to perform in place of one of her students, but after seeing Walter enter the concert hall, pretending like nothing had happened the night before, she takes a knife out of her purse and stabs herself in the shoulder near her heart. She exits and we watch her walk briskly into the night as blood drips down her blouse. We are left staring at the concert hall.

Conclusion

To be blunt, the film does not have a happy ending. It is a negative example of the kind of erotic education I am advocating. The first time I watched the film I was left deflated and could not help but wonder to where Erika was running. Would she quit her job or would she go home to commit suicide? Ultimately, what was Erika's fate as a human being? The ambiguous ending left me with a space to self-reflect and to reflect upon Erika's teacher identity in relation to those of other teachers portrayed in pop culture and teachers in my everyday life. The film is truly a work of cinematic art; however, its approach to the cultural taboo subject of teacher–student sexual relationships leads to yet another film portrayal of a female teacher unable to control her sexual desires around her students, leading to almost fatal consequences. The film's strength and its redemptive quality is in its capacity to provoke reflection on the challenging issues it raises.

The possibility of erotic teaching leading to an abuse of power is clearly demonstrated in *The piano teacher*. The tragedy of the film is that the erotic educational potential – the passion that Erika displays in her piano playing – is perverted. Sexual abuse in the classroom certainly happens and has serious implications. Yet, I think that teachers, students, parents, and school administrations need to recognize and talk about this topic. Masking the sexiness of teaching under cold attitudes will not solve any problems or conflicting understandings of the public and private selves of teachers, nor the projection of our teacher identities comprised of personal experiences inside and outside of the classroom. Avoidance will not harness the positive, nor the negative potential of sexy-passionate teaching. If we are able to embrace the relationships that occur between teachers and students, where there is a positive exchange of knowledge through erotic passionate attraction, then teachers might be able to open a new space for learning as a kind of erotic intellectualism.

REFERENCES

Baudrillard, J. (1979). *Seduction*. Hampshire, TX: Macmillan.

Dahl, L., DeVito D., Shamberg M., & Sher, S. (Producers), & DeVito, D. (Director). (1993). *Matilda* [Motion picture]. USA: Sony Pictures Entertainment.

Fields, A., Juvonen, N., & McKittrick, S. (Producers), & Kelly, R. (Director). (2001). *Donnie darko* [Motion picture]. USA: Flower Films.

Fox, R., & Rudin, S. (Producers), & Eyre, R. (Director). (2006). *Notes on a scandal* [Motion picture]. UK: Fox Searchlight Pictures.

Heiduschka, V. (Producer), & Haneke, M. (Director). (2001). *The piano teacher* [Motion picture]. Austria: Kino International.

Jelinek, E. (1983). *Die klavierspielerin*. Reinbek, DE: Rowohlt Verlag.

Johnson, T. S. (2005). The "problem" of bodies and desires in teaching. *Teaching Education, 16*(2), 131–149.

Johnson, B. (2009). Masochism and the mother: Pedagogy and perversion. *Angelaki: Journal of Theoretical Humanities, 14*(3), 117–130.

Landwehr, M. J. (2011). Voyeurism, violence, and the power of the media: The reader's/spectator's complicity in Jelinek's *The piano teacher* and Haneke's *La pianiste, caché, The white ribbon*. *International Journal of Applied Psychoanalytic Studies, 8*(2), 117–132.

Maher, J. (2004). Hot for the teacher: Rewriting the erotics of pedagogy. *Bitch: Feminist Response to Pop Culture, 24*, 42–48.

McWilliam, E. (1996). Seductress or schoolmarm: On the improbability of the great female teacher. *Interchange, 27*(1), 1–11.

Robinson-Cseke, M. (2012). What not to wear: Exposing the g(host) in art education. *Studies in Art Education, 53*(3), 246–259.

Scull, W. R., & Peltier, G. L. (2007). Star power and the schools: Studying popular films' portrayal of educators. *The Clearing House: A Journal of Educational Strategies, Issues and Ideas, 81*(1), 13–17.

Sharrett, C. (2002). The piano teacher. *Cineaste, 27*(4), 37–40.

Wrye, H. K. (2007). Perversion annihilates creativity and love: A passion for destruction in Haneke's *The piano teacher*. *Psychoanalytic Inquiry: A Topical Journal for Mental Health Professionals, 27*(4), 455–466.

NOTE

1. There is no agreement in the world of psychiatry as to which unusual sexual interests stem from or comprise mental illness. While I am not a psychiatrist, in my interpretation, Erika's behaviours, as displayed in the film in regards to her student, go beyond a healthy sexuality towards mental illness.

Knowing Where We Came From: An Examination of the One-Act Play *Education is Our Right*

Carmen Rodríguez de France

Introduction

Without a doubt, the 1990s was an important decade in the history of humanity: Germany was reunified, the Hubble Space Telescope was launched, and the human genome project was born. In the political arena, important events coloured the media with the resignation of Margaret Thatcher as leader of the United Kingdom, Nelson Mandela being released from prison, and Gorbachev serving as the last leader of the Soviet Union, which dissolved in 1991. The decade also witnessed the birth of "Archie," the first Internet search engine developed in Montreal in 1990. Paradoxically, not far from Montreal, Aboriginal people were experiencing history in the making when the proposal for creating a golf course on the burial grounds of the Mohawk people living in Oka, Quèbec led to conflict and a violent dispute due to disregard for the beliefs, history, spirituality, and worldviews of the original inhabitants of the land. The 1990s was also the decade when the Royal Commission on Aboriginal Peoples was created, culminating in 1997 with a report that contained recommendations on education and training, health and healing, arts and heritage, economic development, the advancement of social equity, and the need for capacity building. To this day, some of those recommendations are yet to be considered by federal and provincial governments in Canada, the need for education and training being one of the most urgent goals.

Earlier documents had offered similar recommendations with regard to education: the *Hawthorne report* in 1967, *Indian control of Indian education* in 1972, and *Tradition and education* in 1988 – the last two produced by the

National Indian Brotherhood and the Assembly of First Nations respectively, which emphasized Aboriginal people's inherent right to decide on their education. Despite these recommendations and articulations, in 1990 the federal government proposed a 2% cap on post-secondary education funding for Aboriginal students. That same year, Ojibway playwright Drew Hayden-Taylor (1990) wrote *Education is our right*, a one-act play, where, borrowing from Charles Dickens' (2009/1843) classic story *A Christmas carol*, past, present, and future are woven together. The aim was to educate audiences about government policy and the sociocultural components that promoted social injustice, inequality, and lack of opportunity in the funding of education for Aboriginal people due to racist policies, and dismissive government practices. The play uses humour and tension as vehicles to illustrate (and educate about) the challenges Aboriginal people have faced regarding self-governance, opportunities to participate in decision-making processes, and development of policies, all of which have affected education causing disparity in graduation rates between Aboriginal and non-Aboriginal youth, which prevail to this day. Consequently, Hayden-Taylor's play is as relevant now as it was then; perhaps even more so now as we attempt to restore, repair, and honour Indigenous ways of knowing and being, in a time of truth and reconciliation between Aboriginal and non-Aboriginal peoples and their diverse communities.

Technically speaking, the staging of *Education is our right* (Hayden-Taylor, 1990) is not challenging: it requires simple props, clothing, and sceneries, which make it easy to perform on almost any stage or in any condition. However, the lessons to be learned require an understanding of the historical legacies of colonization, the assimilationist policies of the time, the agents implicated in the perpetuation of stereotypes, and the ways in which racist attitudes and discrimination towards Aboriginal people have unfolded through oppression. Consequently, Hayden-Taylor portrays real past and present events, including those that occurred during the late 1980s and early 1990s, in various parts of the country when funding for education for Aboriginal people was restricted. He chooses to imagine the future with vignettes that offer two sides to a story: contexts in which Aboriginal people continue to be oppressed and lack opportunities to succeed, and contexts in which hope and optimism abound.

This chapter will present vignettes from the play to illustrate how teaching belongs not only in a classroom, but also outside of it in our everyday contexts. The play itself is a teacher, as are various characters portrayed. Through analyses of the vignettes, readers and audiences alike can become more educated in regards to topics of racism, discrimination, and stereotypes about Aboriginal people, and discover that teaching is all but a one-way path.

The Education of Ebenezer Cadieux

Ebenezer Cadieux,[1] Minister of Indian Affairs, appears in the first scene to reveal his decision to put a cap on funding for post-secondary education for Aboriginal people. When this is questioned by a young woman, who ascertains education is an inherent right and one within the Treaties, Cadieux justifies his decision affirming that education within the Treaties meant on-reserve, and adds that treaties are left to interpretation, and that they change over time. Soon after, the Spirit of Knowledge enters the room to confront Cadieux who is irritated, confused, and "late for other appointments." The Spirit of Knowledge declares that the Minister needs to learn and therefore, he will be a student who will be visited by three spirits: those of Education Past, Present, and Future in order to realize how government decisions have damaged Aboriginal people throughout history. The portrayal of the Spirits as teachers and Cadieux as student in this first vignette humorously turns the tables – evoking an educational context to examine an important educational issue. It illustrates the need to re-consider distorted historical accounts in order to learn about the social injustices towards Aboriginal people.

The Spirit of Education Past

The Spirit of Education Past takes Cadieux on a "trip" back in time where he sees an old television set (which happens to have been his own) where he used to watch "cowboys and Indians," and characters such as Tonto, who in Cadieux's view "spoke funny" just like the Spirit of Education Past. The Spirit explains that this was the way his people were portrayed, and no one cared to correct that. In fact, the opposite was true; these views and voices were reinforced over and over in film, books, advertisements, and other media. In another vignette, they both see an Elder telling a story to a girl and other children illustrating the ways in which children used to learn from the land around them, from their elders, and from their parents. Cadieux explains that such life style is no longer possible because times change. The Spirit of Education Past nods in agreement, and takes Cadieux on another trip. This time, they both witness the abuses suffered by a girl at a Residential School who, in an attempt to escape, loses a foot due to frostbite. The Spirit of Education Past explains that the girl is now a grandmother who has many grandchildren. Cadieux's reaction is dismissive when he declares that he had nothing to do with those schools, and that they were not his fault. The Spirit agrees but adds that it is the people like him, who are in power, who have been making decisions on behalf of the Indigenous people without consulting them or caring about what they need. By then, Cadieux's attitude is sarcastic saying that unlike Aboriginal people's ways of feeling and thinking, for people in government decisions of the heart and the mind do not go hand-in-hand. The Spirit of Education Past slowly retreats making room for the Spirit of Education Present.

The Spirit of Education Present

With an attitude that is less than friendly, the Spirit of Education Present introduces herself to Minister Cadieux announcing she will now take him on a trip to the present, where a young student is willing to go on a walk to Ottawa to claim his rights to education, fearing that if he does not go, there will be no opportunities for him to advance his life and aspirations for the future. The boy is seen talking to his father who initially discourages him from walking but ends up joining him to have their voices be heard. Cadieux tells the Spirit that "her people" are never satisfied with what they have or with what they get. He further defends his position saying that "White people don't always get what they want either." The Spirit of Education Present adds that she will not discuss philosophical viewpoints, but would be happy to direct him to the Spirit of Race Relations because she cannot stand white people and racism or unacknowledged privilege. At one point, two young children emerge from under the shawl of the Spirit of Education Present. She acknowledges them as want and ignorance, and tells Cadieux that her hope is that one day those two will not hover around her.

The Spirit of Education Future

As the Spirit of Education Present departs, Cadieux is left with too much on his mind. While immersed in thought, a guard representing the Spirit of Education Future, announces himself from behind Cadieux reminding him they have an appointment. Through various vignettes, the future is revealed in a time and place where, due to the limitations on funding for post-secondary education, Aboriginal people are seen experiencing the same lack of opportunity and uncertainty as their ancestors did, with the exception of the woman called "the Integrator" who comfortably walks in "two worlds." Cadieux is then forced to reassess his decision, but adds that the final decision is not up to him but up to the people of Canada to decide the policy of the country.

Frameworks for Examining Social Complexities

In a humorous yet resolute way, Hayden-Taylor's (1990) scenarios serve as adequate examples to examine and explore the sociocultural complexities that have led to social injustice, discrimination, racism, and even exploitation of Aboriginal people. Social justice theorist Maurianne Adams (2000) offers ways in which these social complexities can be examined. Using two frameworks, socio-historical conditions and intergenerational legacies, Adams explains that it is paramount that we understand our socio-historical legacies in order to move towards change. She adds that it is important to understand that we have inherited stereotypes as well as our own group's privilege and disadvantage as part of intergenerational legacies. Within the first framework, she explains that social group identities have been used historically to justify and perpetuate the advantages of privileged groups at the expense of the disadvantages of marginalized groups based on location and difference in social identity. This can be seen in the play when Cadieux declares that he is making decisions on behalf of the Aboriginal people because that is his role as Minister. In this process, he is not really caring about consultation. By dismissing the voices of those who are directly affected by policy, Cadieux perpetuates paternalistic practices, which in turn continue to oppress and marginalize people.

Adam's (2009) second framework contends that these social identities together with their different positions resulting in inequality have been socially constructed within specific historical conditions; she adds that the notions of privilege and disadvantage are also socially created. This is evident when the Spirit of Education Past revives the old television set to show Cadieux the portrayal of "Indians" in shows and films. Stereotypical figures, images, landscapes, and even forms of accented and "incomplete" speech are portrayed as accurate representations of who "Indians" are, thus confirming Adams' notion of socially constructed identities. Consequently, as Adams argues, we unconsciously absorb prejudices as part of our socialization from the people who surround us and whom we trust to know what is right and correct (such as our parents, caregivers, and teachers). In a vignette from the play, also from the past representing residential schools, Cadieux justifies his ignorance saying he learned about such schools only recently, and that he had nothing to do with them. He claims that he thought schools and education were good, and that those who created such schools had good intentions. He is suddenly interrupted by the Spirit who says that the road to hell is paved with good intentions. Within these views, Adams (2009) contends that it is only through an examination of what constitutes oppression that one can appreciate and understand the complexities that lead to social injustice. The Spirit of Education Past proposes the utilization of a problem-posing approach to education (Freire, (1973) that considers "peoples' historicity as the starting point" (p. 75). To that end, one could consider feminist scholar Judith Butler's (2009) notions of *representability* of life, and the construct of *responsibilization*. Within the former, she asks us to ponder on how life is represented, what allows life to become visible, and what keeps us from seeing or understanding certain lives as (dis)similar to our own. Within the construct of *responsibilization,* Butler asks us to consider how we make our moral judgments and think: When is a life grievable? Under what circumstances? Where do we draw the lines that tell me whom I am responsible for?And whose lives are worthy of protection? Butler contends that our moral responses to different forms of social injustices (and thus the answers to these questions) depend on how affect is regulated, given that what we feel is conditioned in part by how we interpret the world around us based on our prior knowledge, history of upbringing, choices made in the past, and so forth.

Looking at Ourselves through Theatre

In order to effectively examine our own historicity and how it affects our understanding of the world, the inclusion of anti-oppressive, anti-racist, and culturally relevant pedagogies becomes paramount in teacher education. St. Denis and Schick (2003) maintain that anti-oppressive and anti-racist education are challenging but necessary approaches to developing understanding and awareness of Indigenous worldviews, perspectives, and traditional modes of education, which have been disrupted due to colonization, racist policies, and oppressive practices, some of which prevail to this day. St. Denis and Schick contend that within Teacher Education programs, pre-service teachers tend to respond in defensive ways when learning about the history of oppression and racism against Indigenous people for the first time in their courses. Their experiences are similar to those of other scholars (Fitznor, 2005; Rodríguez de France, 2010; Scully, 2012) who report similar responses from non-Indigenous students in diverse contexts in Canadian universities. Consequently, self-location becomes the first necessary step to begin to understand how our inherited legacies and privileges have shaped the way in which we see the world around us. There are many ways to explore one's own location (see Johnson, 2001; Tatum, 2013; Woodger & Anastacio, 2013) using diverse paradigms, techniques, and approaches that when non-threatening or non-confrontational tend to yield better and longer lasting results than approaches that are confrontational or hostile. In that sense, theatre can offer a gateway through which oppression, colonization, and racism can be explored. Augusto Boal (2002) said that theatre "is the art of looking at ourselves" (p. 15). As a social activist and creator of Invisible Theatre and Forum Theatre, he contended that theatre allows community members to remember significant periods in either personal or sociopolitical history, and consequently reflect upon the theatrical experience allowing for a unification of past and present.

Drew Hayden-Taylor's (1990) play *Education is our right* invites us to do precisely this, to unite past and present and in this case, learn from difficult and painful experiences in order to prevent them from happening in the future. His play is also a tool to imagine and envision positive outcomes when working towards dismantling colonial mind-sets. Morrissette, McKenzie, and Morrissette (1993) maintain that colonization efforts included "the devaluation of traditional spirituality, knowledge, and practices through the actions of missionaries, the residential school system, the health system, and the child welfare system; and the imposition of artificial legal distinctions among Aboriginal peoples" (p. 94). Even though the play was written in 1990, social inequities and disparities still prevail in the life experiences of Indigenous people who pursue an education. While the graduation rates and educational attainment of Indigenous people have increased in the past five years (Gordon & White, 2014), the same has happened for the non-Aboriginal population, indicating that the gap between these two groups especially for those between the ages of twenty-five and fifty-four continues to widen despite more opportunities for access. What then is needed to achieve equality and equity in education? How can one bring attention and awareness to social issues where racism and discrimination need to be explored and understood in order to move forward as a Nation? How can one engage in enacting the calls to action from the Truth and Reconciliation Commission (2015) in relevant and meaningful ways? How do we nurture what Dr. Marie Battiste (2013) calls "The Learning Spirit?"

Conclusion

As an educator working mostly with future teachers, I am aware that the pathways to creating opportunities and possibility rest in part on the shoulders of those of us who work in teaching and learning contexts, be they schools, universities, museums, art galleries, libraries, recreation centers, or any other spaces where there are opportunities to become more aware, more knowledgeable, less critical and judgmental, more compassionate, and more patient. To Indigenize is to educate; the creation of new stories is what we need. In the words of late Ojibway writer Richard Wagamese (cited in Poling, 2017, para. 9), "[w]hat comes to matter then is the creation of the best possible story we can while we're here; you, me, us, together. When we can do that and we take the time to share those stories with each other, we get bigger inside, we see each other, we recognize our kinship – we change the world, one story at a time."

REFERENCES

Adams, M. (2000). Conceptual frameworks. In M. Adams, J. Blumenfeld, C. Castaneda, H. Hackman, M. Peters, & X. Zuniga (Eds.), *Readings for diversity and social justice* (pp. 1–21). New York, NY: Routledge.

Assembly of First Nations. (1988). *Tradition and education: Towards a vision for the future.* Ottawa, ON: Author.

Battiste, M. (2013). *Decolonizing education: Nourishing the learning spirit.* Vancouver, BC: University of British Columbia Press.

Boal, A. (2002). *Games for actors and non-actors.* London: Routledge.

Butler, J. (2009). *Frames of war: When is life grievable?.* London, UK: New Left Book.

Dickens, C. (2009). *A Christmas carol: A ghost story of Christmas.* Auckland, NZ: The Floating Press. (Originally published 1843)

Fitznor, L. (2005). Aboriginal educational teaching experiences: Foregrounding Aboriginal/Indigenous knowledges and processes. Retrieved from http://www.cst.ed.ac.uk/2005conference/papers/Fitznor_paper.pdf

Freire, P. (1973). *Education for critical consciousness.* New York, NY: Seabury Press.

Gordon, C. E., & White, J. P. (2014). Indigenous educational attainment in Canada. *The International Indigenous Policy Journal, 5*(3). Retrieved from http://ir.lib.uwo.ca/iipj/vol5/iss3/6

Hawthorn, H. B. (1967). *A survey of the contemporary Indians of Canada* (Vols. I and II). Ottawa, ON: Indian Affairs Branch.

Hayden-Taylor, D. (1990). *Toronto at dreamer's rock and Education is our right: Two one-act plays.* Markham, ON: Fifth House.

Johnson, A. (2001). *Privilege, power, and difference.* Mountain View, CA: Mayfield Publishing Company.

Morrissette, V., McKenzie, B., & Morrissette, L. (1993). Towards an Aboriginal model of social work practice. *Canadian Social Work Review, 10*(1), 91–108.

National Indian Brotherhood (1972). *Indian control of Indian education policy paper.* Ottawa, ON: National Indian Brotherhood. Retrieved from http://www.avenir-future.com/pdf/maitrise indienne de l%27éducation ang.pdf

Poling, J. (2017, March 16). We are story. *The Minden Times.* Retrieved from http://www.mindentimes.ca/we-are-story

Rodríguez de France, C. (2010). Reflective practice and reflexive praxis: Teaching Indigenous pedagogy at the University of Victoria. Camosun College, Victoria, Australia. Retrieved from http://camosun.ca/aboriginal/pdf_files/stenistolw-defrance.pdf

Scully, A. (2012). Decolonization, reinhabitation and reconciliation: Aboriginal and place-based education. *Canadian Journal of Environmental Education, 17,* 148–158.

St. Denis, V., & Schick, C. (2003). What makes anti-racist pedagogy in teacher education difficult?. Three popular ideological assumptions. *The Alberta Journal of Educational Research, 49*(1), 55–69.

Tatum, B. (2013). The complexity of identity: Who am I? In M. Adams, W. J. Blumenfeld, R. Castaneda, H. W. Hackman, M. L. Peters, & X. Zuniga (Eds.), *Readings for diversity and social justice: An anthology on racism, anti-Semitism, sexism, heterosexism, ablism, and classism* (pp. 5–9). New York, NY: Routledge.

Truth and Reconciliation Commission of Canada. (2015). Honoring the truth, reconciling for the future. Summary of the final report of the Truth and Reconciliation Commission of Canada. Retrieved from http://www.trc.ca/websites/trcinstitution/File/2015/Honouring_the_Truth_Reconciling_for_the_Future_July_23_2015.pdf

Woodger, D., & Anastacio, J. (2013). Group work training for social justice. *Groupwork*, 26(2), 26–47.

NOTE

1. Pierre H. Cadieux, Minister of Indian Affairs and Northern Development, in 1989, announced the cap on post-secondary education spending.

Art School Confidential: Profound Offence or Just Good Fun?

Anita Sinner & Thibault Zimmer

In a recent graduate course for art educators entitled "Portrayals of teachers' lives in pop culture," we (and our pop culture alter-egos, Mr. T and Wonder Woman) surveyed how teachers are represented in a broad range of historic to contemporary films and television shows. In this chapter we deliberate on the implications of one film, in particular, *Art school confidential* (*ASC*) (Hall & Zwigoff, 2006). This film was presented in our first class meeting, and that viewing set the tone for critical considerations and deliberations on the role of pop culture in our academic context, but in ways that could not be foreseen. In this chapter, we map our reading of the film in relation to the class response, and highlight key dimensions from among many possible dimensions offered by the film that address teacher–student dynamics.

To set our scene, this satirical comedy operates as a sociocultural material object where hyperised[1] stereotypical portrayals provoked responses of profound offence by some members of the class. Young (2010) borrows from Feinberg to define profound offence as "an offence to one's moral sensibilities […] such an offence strikes at a person's core values or sense of self" (p. 130). In turn, our embodied perceptions, aesthetic preferences, and historical moments were juxtaposed with our preferred reading of this film as just good fun. Just good fun is in jest and meant to invoke laughter. But the rift begs the question: why such a polarized response? And, what are our diverse investments in the image of a teacher that provoke such responses?

Cameras Rolling: Opening Conversations

Because of our shared ethics of practice, we feel an obligation to bring forward this incident as a pedagogic pivot in the classroom that encourages further consideration of reception, response, and rumination upon *ASC*. Such reflection is intended to serve as an opening of possibilities that brings forward our deliberations on what unexpectedly emerged as a deliberative prompt. As an expression of intellectual exchange, in which we are both learner–teacher and fan-critic operating within a didactic space, we "stop," as our colleague Lynn Fels (2009) states, in response to an "ah-ha" moment. The rupture in our emotional and intellectual contexts around *ASC* raises questions about the leaky dialectic boundaries of film (Hall, 1980) in relation to subject positions that mobilize desire, and the ways in which viewers are influenced to respond to dominant themes within an aesthetic–ethical–political value framework (Dalton, 2010).

Informed by Deleuzian (2001a) cinematic theory, we examine how *ASC* functions as a third space in a graduate class to assess how we append understandings onto characters in film through our affection for them, and where movement-space has nomadic intent. Such lines of flight are passageways for sensations to occur, and we argue that as viewers, we are always in a process of collaging the actual (real lives) and the virtual (cinema) together to translate meanings. In this chapter, we demonstrate these theoretical underpinnings through self-reflective life writing alongside the storyline of the graduate course. We write in a conversational mode as a means to interrogate the renderings of *ASC* teacher–student archetypes and to deliberate on the graduate student responses to how the characterizations, contexts, and issues embedded in the layered narratives of this film contribute to the construction of polemical attitudes about art, art students, and art teachers in society. Films like *ASC* reveal how identity construction of teachers with, in, and through film is a vital form of pedagogic intent (Giroux, 2008). Viewing this film in our class was a threshold, a point of entry, and as reflective practitioners of curriculum studies we regard this film as a site of mediated ecologies that generate intensities of observation and encounters as *more-than-human* (Deleuze, 2001b).

And... Action!

ASC is based on a four-page comic book written by Daniel Clowes,[2] who also wrote the movie screenplay (2006) in which he parodies art school students, teachers, staff, and the post-secondary institutions through scenes of in-class critiques and out-of-school hijinks in ways that lampoon the politics of space. The main character, Jerome (Max Minghella), is a first-year student at what he presumed was a prestigious school, Strathmore Academy. Jerome has dreams of becoming a great success, but instead he realizes the pretentiousness of the art world during his time studying at Strathmore, resulting in his loss of innocence. Over the course of the film he becomes a darker and darker character, smoking, drinking, stealing another's artwork (that of the Strathmore Strangler, played by renowned actor Jim

Broadbent) and presenting it as his own, resulting in his growing cynicism along the way. With rich irony, Jerome is eventually implicated in murder, and although he is not guilty, a manipulative art dealer exploits his imprisonment to advance Jerome's cachet. Thus, he becomes a famous and wealthy artist, and yes, he gets the girl (Sophia Myles, aka Audrey) in the end too.

From a pedagogic perspective, what does this all mean? We suggest that *ASC* moves beyond the typical Hollywood portrayals of teachers and students as singular (teachers who are rebels in schools, or heroes to students, or other single stereotypical roles) by exposing art teacher and students as multiple, "whilst highlighting a morsel of bitter truth," as Mr. T would say. Relating the film to moments from our everyday lives, we find a number of points of convergence with stories we have heard and/or lived ourselves. For example, Professor Sandiford (John Malkovich) is a college faculty member depicted as – to extend the idiom of "those who can't do, teach" – in this case, an artist who cannot succeed as an artist. He teaches art while still trying to advance his specialization of twenty plus years: painting triangles. After all, he was "one of the first." This subtheme in the storyline is just one of many that depicts a sharp-witted rendering of art school in the film. In turn, the teacher–student relationship undergoes repeated strains when Sandiford tries to explain to the class that "[Jerome] is attempting to achieve the impossible [when making art]. He is trying to sing in his own voice using someone else's vocal cords" (Hall & Zwigoff, 2006). This metaphor resonated with members of the graduate class, as it did with individuals in the fictional *ASC* class, providing a worthy entry point to conversation among our cohort by generating opinions on a continuum from humorful to offensive.

From specific teacher–student scenes we argue that *ASC* provides a quite realistic account of the realm of experiences art students in postsecondary settings may encounter, where some students envision becoming "one of the greatest artists of the 21st Century," as Jerome proclaims is his goal (Hall & Zwigoff, 2006). In the screenplay (Clowes, 2006), the notion of critique is also exploited as being a painful experience for the presenting artists. In one particular scene, Jerome finds himself in a competitive stance with another student whose works are far different than his regarding techniques, styles, and subject matter. The objective of the assignment was to create a portrait of Audrey, a model with whom Jerome falls in love. In his portrait, he renders a highly realistic and emotionally charged expression, and proudly presents it in hopes of receiving acknowledgement and praise. However, Jerome's positive assumptions falter when students, along with Professor Sandiford, focus their attention and praise on works of art by other students, which Jerome finds aesthetically inadequate in each case. Professor Sandiford persuades a reluctant Jerome, who is clearly upset and opts to say nothing, to explain his sentiments to the class by prompting, "nothing doesn't actually exist in this class" (Hall & Zwigoff, 2006). In that moment Jerome risks expressing himself, but by doing so he antagonizes his peers. Thus, he leaves one of his classmates in tears while turning the classroom ambience into a hostile environment, alienating an already disenchanted Jerome and his classmates even further. As a result of persistently chaotic artistic efforts and compromised social relationships, Jerome seeks guidance again from Professor Sandiford. He advises Jerome to create works in the "now-ness," leaving him to find alternative methods to explore his own "uniqueness" and creative artistic identity. The debate that emerged after part of the film was viewed in our art education graduate class was in tandem with this scene, and as a spoof on art school, this scene highlights many issues that are prevalent in today's art education culture. Indeed, what is a dedicated artist to do?

Writing Our Script in the Graduate Classroom

Mr. T

Although I pity the fool who does not stay in school, I remember several years ago being enrolled in a specific studio course as part of my art education undergraduate degree that was by no means like any other course. Much like my peers, and akin to Jerome, I was an eager third-year student who, simply put, loved to create, to be inspired, and to motivate others by giving constructive criticism during our monthly art critiques. After all, I was a proud art education student and always felt that understanding how to participate and meaningfully contribute to significant art critiques would sharpen my teacher skills in understanding how to assess student work. This notion better equipped me as an art educator, until I realized on a fateful day how intrinsically difficult it was to navigate through art critiques, let alone give and take criticism from someone who may or may not understand the art, or the message, that was so desperately the essence of what I was trying to convey.

On this critique day, I had witnessed the epitome of a pedagogical meltdown that was also embodied in the scenes of *ASC*. Perhaps the student was misunderstood, or maybe not able or willing to accept feedback on the work. Or perhaps, the fault was the instructor's. Certainly, there was a lack of communication. It was clear to me that whatever the reason or cause may have been, I witnessed an artless dialogue that had no beginning, no end, and seemingly no real purpose or value to the people involved. Everyone had given up trying to understand each other's points-of-view as a result. I sat watching this unfold before me and thought about the many contentious attitudes that were manifested in this instant. In turn, this moment exposed the true and fragile tensions embedded in the art critiques in this class and shaped my understanding of the vulnerable nature of the learner.

I left the studio that evening thinking about the event I had witnessed and I was quick to speak about it with a dear friend from my programme. My friend recommended I watch the movie *Art school confidential* (Hall & Zwigoff, 2006) to see how similar the narratives were on film and in the reality of the classroom. And so I did.

Wonder Woman

I spend a great deal of my time wondering. I wonder about what, who, where, when, but mostly I wonder about why and how. All this wondering is reflected in my advocacy for life writing, that is, our stories as the basis for curriculum. And I have long been inspired by bell hooks (2010), with attention to her arguments concerning the value of pop culture as a method of teaching and learning that resonates in meaningful ways with the lives of our students. How we receive pop culture, identify our various selves in relation to characters and situations, and then construct our narratives in response, has been central to my scholarly interests and at the heart of what I often wonder about. In most courses, I find ways to integrate pop culture as exemplars of practice, as openings to reflective writing, and, in particular, as a means to advance the breadth and depth of evolving teacher identities. This is something I regard as a life-long, life-wide, and life-deep practice.

These curricular possibilities left me very excited to bring together a special topics course for graduate students. In preparation for this course, Mr. T completed a comprehensive literature search for course readings, in addition to the body of work I had from a previous research project, and he provided consultation on the course outline. This was a great fit, for we both love movies and we collaborated on the course in ways that reinforced the integrity of hooks' (2010) philosophical stance. It was an opportunity for us to walk on an instructional journey together. Mr. T was completing a master's degree and embarking on his doctorate, so the opportunity to join forces in this way was most apropos. Our alignment was further reinforced through our views of *ASC*, a film we agreed was a superb portrayal of the reality of art school because it poked fun in ways that shaped our actual learning and teaching practices. We often laughed, recalling lines from the film and imagined how wonderful it would be to share this conversation with our community of learners.

Cut and Print, Together

Wonder Woman

When this film was shared in our first class, it became clear that some students were growing increasingly uncomfortable. Sensing the atmosphere of the classroom, the film viewing was stopped midway and instead we debriefed. Opening the floor to comments revealed that the film was too graphic in language, too mocking of the arts, too scathing in the portrayals of women, and in general, too sarcastic in its interpretation of art school as a whole. All of these concerns were aspects that inspired the genesis of the course and offered critical perspectives upon which to build conversations for the remainder of the term.

At the same time, as the instructor I was surprised, and responded that yes, this was all so, but (with the deflection of Wonder Woman's silver bracelets), I also suggested that this was the power of the film; to allow us to make fun of ourselves, to bring a humorous, tongue-in-cheek lens to experiences that were all too familiar. So I asked, how might we receive *ASC* both literally and rhetorically? Can we think about *ASC* as folding upon itself, where divergent interpretations of the film are provocative and productive to our thinking? Yet this ah-ha moment made me stop and wonder if I was out of step with students and if I needed a trip to Transformation Island to rethink the intent of *ASC*.[3]

Mr. T

Looking back on that class response, and thinking through the film today, it presents an unsettling reality about art education and teacher–student interrelationships, and confronts binary understandings of right/wrong, good/bad, humour/sarcasm. Dalton (2010) argues that typical Hollywood films are usually composed of a linear narrative and are often hero-centred, which is not so of *ASC*. To fully understand, we must uncover the sociocultural implications for teachers embedded in this particular film in relation to the typical genre of teachers in film, which serve as the reference points for both art educators and the public.

ASC encapsulates general practices of art education and raises questions about legitimacy of creative practice and educational outcomes and the performance of players in institutions. The film communicates those issues through stark portrayals in an effort to appeal to the masses. It spits up the art teacher–student archetypes and clichés that continue to shape public knowledge and the misrepresentations we assign to art education, pedagogy, and art institutions. Through a satirical aperture, *ASC* highlights the ramifications of the deskilling of art teachers as a direct outcome of employing a passive, teacher-centred model in the art classroom, and thus standardizing pedagogy (and art) in ways that are evidently revealed by Sandiford's lack of involvement, lack of commitment, and lack of dedication to his students.

Coming back to the "leaky boundaries" in film that allow narratives of social conformity and/or narratives of opposition (Dalton, 2010, p. 45), we swung back and forth on the issues that emerged in class, while pondering on the blatant and crude humour throughout the film as well as its negative sociocultural repercussions concerning art school and art students in society. After all, Giroux (2008) reminds us that "as a form of public pedagogy, films shape habits of thinking by providing audiences with framing mechanisms and affective structures through which individuals fashion their identities and mediate their relationship to public life, social responsibility, and the demands of critical citizenship" (p. 7).

Given the vitality of democratizing classrooms inherent in our teaching philosophies, we strove to address teacher–student power dynamics rendered in the film by opening up a horizontal approach of sharing authority in the graduate class to help articulate the differing responses to the film, while at the same time working to ensure multiple perspectives were equally considered and heard. Doubling back to the film, in the bigger picture, *ASC* showcases how students explore their agency of creative identity where they must negotiate their budding identities within a difficult, repressive, and competitive environment: school. In other words, the movie, and arguably the graduate class itself, displayed how educational institutions instil both doubt and certainty upon students as they perform and unveil their art and opinions to the world.

Wonder Woman

Extending Mr. T's argument, *ASC* operates on a number of psycho-social levels that reflect the staunch commitment we hold to our personal and professional identities. One such aspect is the characterization of the interloper; that is, one who is within the system of art school but a severe critic of that same system. Interlopers in film operate as self-reflective foils that challenge beliefs and values, and assumptions about ourselves that we may hold. Mr. T's discussion of performance captures this state very well, and the performance of identity by Jerome, the interloper, and how that might resonate with students, was a dimension I did not give full consideration in advance of showing *ASC*. The articulation of artist identity in a negative light could certainly spiral into profound offence and prove to be an affront. Although we may all share commonalities with the characters by virtue of being art students and art teachers, when recognition strikes a deep nerve, not all viewers may find that funny. I do not disagree that the language, the characterizations, and the status-seeking embedded in the plotline highlight our own ambitions in the extreme. But I do wonder, as members of the field of art education, can we find masked in the comical interloper the clichés and stereotypical characterizations of individuals and institutions of learning that help us see with both an insider and outsider point of view? Where the objective and subjective selves meet between interiority and exteriority in the field of art education (Deleuze, 2001a)? In this way, pop culture can fulfill the educative intent of the graduate course, operating as a self-reflective method of rethinking our artistic assumptions and our teacher expectations, and in turn, reshaping our curriculum in our classrooms.

Directors' Commentary: Looking Back...

The intent of showing ASC in the graduate class was not to generate profound offence, nor just to have good fun, but to attend to the pedagogic responsibility of not brushing past such moments. Instead, we endeavoured to attend with deep listening (Snowber, 2005) to then invite conversation that invigilates greater understandings of self-actualization. Our purpose was to concentrate attention on how as art students and teachers we live within the expectations of social stereotypes. How might we begin to change those perceptions through our acts and actions in relation to pop culture, as part of our commitment as artists, teachers, and researchers who dedicate our working lives to public service? We have an ethical, and arguably moral obligation to mindfully consider the context, the place, and the timeline as factors that may have a far greater role to play in pop culture as a pedagogic tool than we may have encountered in scholarly literature and in practice in university courses to-date.

The movie has evoked many thoughts concerning how we navigate through art school and graduate school while negotiating our teacher–student identity. Despite the hidden curriculum of unspoken competition that is instilled within most (if not all) educational settings, we must question how we come to understand education as a learning and sharing experience that can be mutually beneficial between all parties involved. Most importantly, we must question how we interpret subjectivity and critical understandings of art's complex nature as both students and teachers when cultivating artistic and educational practices. Films such as ASC help us to not only reflect as individuals, but also invite us to become the cultural change agents of society as we engage in a critical and pedagogical process that can result in transformative experiences for teachers and/as learners alike.

One thing is for certain: ASC has taught us that such movies can serve as points of entry to become critical of both the self and the other within art studio spaces as well as the classroom. We may often forget that as artists, teachers, and mutual learners, the picture may become blurry at times, and a potential source of discouragement, especially when navigating art school. Like watching a film that is out of focus, we may lose track of the sensitive nature and the goals, the purpose, the aims, the reasons, the love, the pain, and the palpitating passion that drives us to be artists, like Jerome, and hopefully to be another kind of art teacher than Sandiford. Significant to art education, we both came to understand that ASC was not only a comical flick to watch (if you like satires). Instead, it made present an underlying yet powerful rupture within the graduate class that left us wondering if we are all now bringing a more self-critical lens to bear on our field as well as our pedagogic and artistic practices. In either case, *ASC* demonstrated that there is still work to be done, and more films to watch as integral parts of pop culture and pedagogy of the arts for the betterment of our academic contexts, and more importantly, our society.

REFERENCES

Clowes, D. (2006). *Art school confidential: A screenplay*. Seattle, WA: Fantagraphics.
Dalton, M. (2010). *The Hollywood curriculum: Teachers in the movies*. New York, NY: Peter Lang.
Deleuze, G. (2001a). *Cinema 1: The movement-image* (H. Tomlinson, & B. Habberjam, Trans.). Minneapolis, MI: University of Minnesota Press.
Deleuze, G. (2001b). *Cinema 2: The time-image* (H. Tomlinson, & R. Galeta, Trans.). Minneapolis, MI: University of Minnesota Press.
Fels, L. (2009). Welcome to notes from the field. *Educational Insights, 14*(1). Retrieved from http://www.ccfi.educ.ubc.ca/publication/insights/v14n01/intro/welcome.html
Giroux, H. (2008). Hollywood film as public pedagogy: Education in the crossfire. *Afterimage, 35*(5), 7–13.
Hall, B. A. (Producer), & Zwigoff, T. (Director). (2006). *Art school confidential* [Motion picture]. USA: Sony.
Hall, S. (1980). Encoding/decoding. In S. Hall, D. Hobson, A. Lowe, & P. Willis (Eds.), *Culture, media, language* (pp. 128–138). London: Routledge.
hooks, b. (2010). *Teaching critical thinking: Practical wisdom*. New York, NY: Routledge.
Kroker, A., Kroker, M., & Cook, D. (1989). *Panic encyclopedia: The definitive guide to the postmodern scene*. New York, NY: St. Martin's Press.
Snowber, C. (2005). The mentor as artist: A poetic exploration of listening, creating and mentoring. *Mentoring and Tutoring, 13*(3), 345–353.

NOTES

1. In this case, "hyperised" is not slang for playing basketball, but it is used in reference to Kroker, Kroker, & Cook's (1989) argument that postmodern panic culture operates through a hyper-circulability of exchange, and the hyper-technological self is "falling, falling without limits" (p. 16). In this case, hyperised is the furthest point of movement to the extremity of character portrayals in the film.
2. For more on Clowes' graphic narrative see https://artinfiction.wordpress.com/2013/09/01/art-school-confidential1991-daniel-clowes/
3. In Wonder Woman comics and television, Transformation Island is the place of rehabilitation for villains. See http://dc.wikia.com/wiki/Transformation_Island

The Emancipatory Reaggregation of the *Irrational Man*: (Im)moral Possibilities of an Existential, Lived Curriculum

Sean Wiebe & Pauline Sameshima

Introduction

If "an identity is always articulated through concepts and practices made available by religion, society, school, and state; mediated by family, peers, friends" (Appiah, 2007, p. 20), how do critical pedagogues effectively move themselves and press students to imagine outside these confines? How are the immutable expectations challenged? In the movie, *Irrational man* (Aronson, Tenebaum, Walson, & Allen, 2015), directed by Woody Allen, philosophy professor Abe Lucas (played by Joaquin Phoenix) confronts his nihilistic academic frustrations. In this chapter, we examine the (im)moral, (ir)rational possibilities of an existential, lived-curriculum by examining the emancipatory reaggregation (Pinar, 2010) of the main character cast as an intriguing, inspirational, mysterious, troubled, alcoholic, dishevelled teacher disillusioned by the meaninglessness of the educative process and his inability to make a difference.

The movie grew out of the book *Irrational man: A study in existential philosophy* by William Barrett (1958), a philosopher touted as introducing existentialism to North America. Barrett discusses the advent and sources of existentialism in the western tradition, and provides commentaries on Kierkegaard, Nietzsche, Heidegger, and Sartre. He concludes by advocating for the imperfect integral whole being over the unreasonable scientific and rational sounding mask of human orderings.

Idealism vs Existentialism

Questioning the scientific mask is especially needed in education. Because of its social tendency towards idealism, education students are oftentimes wooed into the profession with the promise of a meaningful career of contributing to human progress. Consider, for example, the obvious propaganda embedded in recruitment practices of universities via print and media materials[1] that portray images such as the twenty-first-century teacher holding the future, the cliché image of the hands of the teacher planting a sapling with a child – both the student and the sapling will grow into a renewable resource of a thriving economy. Such unabashed idealism in education is problematic.

Idealism is troubling because it mortgages present living for a future hope. Whether it is an individual or an entire system, idealism sacrifices what could be enjoyed now for a yet-to-be realized investment in a presumably better future. A simple example is how end-of-year exams narrow curriculum experiences – the tested curriculum (exam preparation) takes precedence over the lived curriculum, student and teacher interests, concerns, and questions. Idealism is additionally troubling because as institutional agents, teachers are accountable to the social ideal that the institution projects. This curtails teachers' freedoms as human beings and citizens, restricting their morality to social norms. Speaking of the idealism so rampant in education, Christine Neider, in her autobiographical dissertation, writes about her divided soul, when she began to question what had previously made so much sense:

> Personally, I had begun to run up against previously unseen obstacles to reaching my adult ideals. The ugly side of religion, cracking marital ideals, infertility, addiction, voices in my head intensifying in the "shoulds" of a well-lived life. Because some of these began to surface, I began to "see" life differently than I had imagined it.
>
> (2016, p. 24)

The phenomenon is not new; historically, teachers have been restricted in their dress, their behaviour, their personal time (including bedtimes), their politics, and so on. A few recent cases will serve to illustrate the point: in Mississauga, Ontario, the Peel District School Board investigated a drama teacher for having students dramatize injecting crystal meth (Zing, 2017). Presumably, the dramatization was used to elicit discussion of a serious social problem under the guidance of a trained adult (critical pedagogue). But when a parent complained, the teacher was suspended and investigated. A different teacher took over the classes until the end of the year, one who would not risk involving the students in an education that could be relevant and meaningful. When it comes to idealism in education, students are the innocents that need protection from the world. Absurdly, such idealism does not consider how many students will then go on to learn about the abuse of drugs on their own, without any institutional support. If children are the innocents, then teachers will always be in the difficult situation of trying to bring children into the light without exposing them to any of the shadows. The examples of idealism are everywhere: in Florida, a teacher was recently transferred to a different classroom because she revealed to students that she was transgendered (Rozsa, 2017). In Britain, policy-makers are debating whether it is appropriate for teachers to have visible tattoos (Swain, 2017). In Canada, a professor at Laurentian University was removed from his class because he asked students to sign a waiver permitting him to use vulgar language in his lectures (Quan, 2016); his efforts to help students understand the social value of free speech was shut down by the University Provost. Morality is a seldom questioned social ideal. In education, where teachers are held up as society's moral representatives for children, actions that are protected by constitutions and charters of rights are brought into question by school authorities, who, as part of a so-called moral majority, cannot risk acceptance of difference and diversity in the classroom. Thus, under the scrutiny of the social norm, teacher values and community values become one and the same; a teacher's aspiration of being a critical pedagogue is thus undermined.

In relief against the background of educational idealism is the existentialist philosopher, the main character of *Irrational man* (Aronson, Tenebaum, Walson, & Allen, 2015), Abe Lucas. Because of its opposition to idealism, existentialism is a valuable philosophical system for teachers. Existentialism's base claim is to begin with nothing, that is, to doubt everything and then only dare to construct what is absolutely verifiable. Not surprisingly, under such a rigorous theory, where belief is stripped to only the fundamentals of existence, it is difficult to hold onto meaning, for, as with everything else, meaning needs to be questioned. According to Yalom (1980), for everyone who exists there are five basic struggles: One, there is the struggle with mortality. Because everyone dies, lives are filled with the anxieties of extending life, making the most of life, improving the quality of life, and so forth. Two, there is the struggle with meaning. Lives have no inbuilt design or purpose so one has the responsibility of making meaning and/or creating purpose. For some, the meaningless of life is so profound that the chief question of existence is why live? Three, there is the struggle with the lack of knowledge. Human beings are not fully knowledgeable creatures. They do not know the future; they do not know another's feelings, emotions, or thoughts; they do not know others' cultural norms; and what they do know fades, becomes fragmented, is erroneous, and subject to feelings, senses, assumptions, and a priori beliefs. Four, despite a lack of knowledge, lack of meaning, and a lack of lifespan through which one might come to learn things through trial and error, human beings are still responsible for making good choices. The communities that human beings belong to value good decision-making. Every day there are decisions, and with each one, no matter how small, human beings face the burden of deciding well. Five, human beings are alone. No one can fully know another human being, there is no hive-mind to connect the species. An intimate partner might intuit feelings or even guess at what a person might be thinking, but that guess is still a kind of fuzzy logic. Many spend their entire lives looking for partners who can provide intimacy, and even for those who do find such partners the intimacy is never fully complete. This is what it means to be an individual – to be in division from others. These five struggles combine to make the existential condition. They are, if you will, the key literacies for understanding human realities. The point is not to be negative, or offer disillusionment where there once was hope. Instead, the point is to describe as accurately as possible the human condition of existence.

The Film

At the outset of the film, and before his arrival to teach a summer course in continental philosophy at Braylin, an idyllic college town that has all the trappings of a small and closed community, Abe Lucas' reputation precedes him; he is brilliant but troubled, inspirational but unstable. Cast in these tensions, Lucas' persona falls outside the normative social expressions of the teacher as a moral touchstone. He is well-liked by his students, who respond to his otherness (Block, 1998; Greene, 1973), but his social critique lacks efficacy. In the first classroom scene of *Irrational man* (Aronson et al., 2015), Abe Lucas asks his students, "Why are you taking philosophy? What do you want to get out of it?" The same question might be addressed to teachers. "Why would anyone want to be a teacher?" asks Debra Britzman (2009, p. 385). She questions those who never leave the classroom; those who transition directly from student to teacher. What forgotten histories, values, and desires are teachers bringing into the classroom? These are critical questions because regardless of how much time is spent in the classroom, teachers always ever remain human beings who love, hope, hurt, fail, and desire. Abe Lucas is atypical, in that he has lived and done everything. The film is full of references to his social justice efforts, from serving in refugee camps to saving lives after Hurricane Katrina, but Abe is depressed. He has nothing to live for; he cannot write because he cannot breathe. At a key moment in the movie, Abe reveals the meaningless of the educative process: "I wanted to be an active world changer and I've wound up a passive intellectual who can't fuck" (Aronson et al., 2015). Wanting more than intellectual masturbation from himself and his students, Abe sinks deeper into nihilism. He says to Jill Pollard, a student who is fascinated with him, that he is no longer convinced by the reasons for living; the distractions have ceased to matter. Abe's existential malaise is also illustrated when Rita, a faculty member disillusioned in her marriage, brings him a bottle of his favourite single malt scotch late one night. Abe accepts her advances, but their sexual distraction still does not solve his writer's block.

Abe Lucas has lived so fully, so why would he be depressed? Barrett (1958), similarly, asks "how do philosophers exist in the modern world?" (p. 4). He suggests that,

> as a human being, functioning professionally within the Academy, the philosopher can hardly be expected to escape his own professional deformation, especially since it has become a law of modern society that man is assimilated more and more completely to his social function.
>
> (1958, p. 5)

In other words, Abe Lucas' depression largely results from following the social expectation to do good, to be all he can be, to help others, to be counted among those who have achieved success. With more than a dozen references to Abe's humanitarianism and good will, it is part of the running comedy of the movie.

Barrett (1958) goes on to explain that the teaching professions were not always so narrowed, that early Greek philosophers were seers and poets, their works unveiling the intuitive and mythological. Thinking, says Barrett, was a "passionate way of life" for Plato (p. 5). Illustrative of the early philosopher-teachers, Abe Lucas is clever, well-read, sexy, and depressed. Even factoring in his depression, his existentialism is a refreshing counter to the typical idealists in most teacher movies, such as Mr. Keating in *Dead poet's society* (Haft, Thomas, Witt, & Weir, 1989) or Erin Gruwell in *Freedom writers* (DeVito, Shamberg, Sher, & LaGravenese, 2007).

Hoping to restore his passion for living, his student, Jill Pollard, offers herself as a way to get Abe's creative juices flowing. She had heard that Rita could not, and suggests to Abe that she might be a more potent distraction. What follows are a series of scenes demonstrating Jill's increasing infatuation, and Abe's resistance. When they are in a diner together, Jill and Abe overhear a conversation about a Judge Spangler, who, in a family court decision, is going to unfairly award the children to the husband (Frank). As an aggrieved party, the wife (Carol) is at her wits end; she has no more money to pay the legal fees, and the judge is on friendly terms with Frank's lawyer. She wishes Spangler were dead. Wishing doesn't work, Abe thinks to himself; if you want him dead then you have to make it happen. In his speculations he gets excited about killing the judge on Carol's behalf. When he leaves the diner he is dizzy. Attributing it to anxiety, it is actually the beginning of a newfound wakefulness, and his slumber of meaninglessness is coming to an end.

Planning a murder genuinely rekindles Abe's energies. He feels a limitless freedom. Knowing that he can commit the ultimate immoral act, there is no normative behaviour that can hold him down. His zest for life has returned. Adding an overlay of comedy, Jill thinks Abe's newfound meaning is because of her affections. As Abe moves from planning the murder to executing it, what he finds exhilarating is the risk. He surveils the judge and learns the judge's routines; he steals keys from Rita to break into the chemistry lab; he steals some cyanide from the lab, and eventually carries out the murder. The risks energize him, and after the murder, it is the accomplishment Abe finds satisfying. He compares what he did to writing a journal article, thinking that a journal article about corruption in the legal system would have been a waste, doing nothing to make the world a better place. But the murder, he thinks, rids the world of an evil man, and tangibly improves the world, even if it is only an "infinitesimal percentage."

Existentialism as a Response to Educational Idealism

Beyond its comedy and weakly veiled whodunit motif, what are viewers to make of murder as a means to rekindle creativity? Like the unraveling of the murder itself, there are a few clues to how existentialism can be a legitimate response to educational idealism. Clue one: still fairly early in the plot, Abe is at a student party, and when a revolver is taken out of a parent's gun case and shown around, Abe grabs it for himself, loads it with a bullet, points it to his head, and plays three rounds of Russian roulette. He is the only one playing, and the students who are there to party are upset. Justifying his actions, Abe says to them that Russian roulette is an object lesson in existentialism, that the odds are better than the ones that life will give you. Clue two: Jill and Abe are at the fair together, and Abe tries his luck at a spin-the-wheel carnival game. He wins. Even though he does not believe in luck, it seems as though his luck has changed. Could his own intention, attitude, or choices have changed his luck? And in anticipation of clue three, the prize that Jill chooses for herself is a flashlight. Clue three: at the end of the movie, in the act of committing a second murder, Abe trips on the flashlight, falling to his death in an elevator shaft. A prize won by chance thus randomly changes the course of both of their lives. All three clues involve spinning: in the first, Abe does not care so he spins the revolver; in the second, Abe is on a roll, life is grand, so he spins his wheel of fortune; and in the third, Abe is desperate to maintain control, the secrecy of his crime, and he trips over a rolling flashlight. These three events remind the viewer of humanity's existential struggles, the lack of control one has over mortality, meaning and purpose, and the futile grasp of knowledge, decision making, and isolation.

Part of the suspense of the movie is whether Abe, after the murder, will go back to his depression. Two days after the murder, Abe does sleep with Jill. He says to her that he does not know what has come over him, and Jill replies that he is finally celebrating his life instead of being obsessed with death, as with his crazy Russian roulette. While it seems that an intentional and deliberate action of murder gives Abe his life back, will his life continue to have the same sense of adventure, meaning, and inspiration? Will he need something else to continue his high? In murdering the judge Abe makes a unique choice, and he feels that this is what makes him an authentic human being. That is, Abe makes a choice that does not fall within normative, social strictures. As a person who had done everything, had tried every way possible to be the ideal man, Abe could not stave off depression. The unique choice of murder gives Abe his passion back. In his philosophy class, Abe says to his students that life gives us existential choices, and such choices make us authentic human beings. Quoting Sartre, Abe says, "Hell is other people" and the viewer is left to reason that others' purposes, morals, beliefs, and systems are what keep a person from being authentic – freedom and moral responsibility requires individual choice and action outside of social expectations.

Given that existentialism is a description of the human condition and not, per se, a belief system, moralists will argue that immoral acts, such as Abe's committing of murder, demonstrate that moral indifference or silence is untenable. Is there an existentialist reply that justifies the possibility of a secular and amoral teaching profession? Looking to the film's treatment of the question, the first murder is justified while the second is not. This moral relativist position, where it is possible to advocate murder in one instance but condemn it in another, unseats morality from fixed normative structures. Teachers, however, are likely to face serious institutional threat were they to promote moral freedoms. Unlike doctors or lawyers, teachers are in a profession with a long history of claiming the role of moral example and guide. But this impossibility of belief is the very reason why it is needed in education. Untempered idealism, particularly in the realm of morality, has little room for creativity, experimentation, curiosity, and freedom.

For Abe, for the reasons outlined above, the first murder frees him, but the second is an act of control. What the ending of the film illustrates is that efforts to control our lives are fruitless against the fundamental randomness of the human condition. In the rationality of idealism, human beings strategically employ means to control ends. By contrast, in existentialism the ends are random. There is no object or point to the game of life. Such knowledge brings us to the existentialist choice, why play at all?

Chapter one of Barrett's (1958) book offers an illustration: "The story is told [by Kierkegaard] of the absent-minded man so abstracted from his own life that he hardly knows he exists until, one fine morning, he wakes up to find himself dead" (p. 3). Abe divines the ultimate plot: to supplant his own existential death by killing another. At a key point in the movie, in one of his philosophy classes, Abe quotes the following from Kierkegaard: "When making everyday decisions you have absolute freedom of choice. You can do nothing, or anything. And this feeling of freedom creates a sense of dread. Anxiety is the dizziness of freedom" (Aronson et al., 2015).[2] Freedom is awakened with the "release of imagination," Greene (2001) asserts, without which, "human beings may be trapped in literalism, in blind factuality" (p. 65). Thought of in terms of the lived-curriculum, Pinar (2011) would describe Abe's actions as the synthesis phase of a lived curriculum, explaining that Abe's emancipatory reaggregation of himself "constitutes the labor of subjective reconstruction and its consequence" (p. 99). Abe refashions himself and the redemptive possibilities of his imagination release him from his stupor. Pinar quotes Patrizia McBride (2006) as she explains the immanent purposiveness that accompanies an "intelligibility dawning" (p. 19), a novel sense of reality,

> In [Robert] Musil's account, the ecstatic experience triggered by aesthetic feeling favors a reshuffling in the individual's perception of reality and disrupts formulaic modes of experience, releasing the individual from the spell of established pictures of the world and opening up a space for the imaginative play with, and the emancipatory reaggregation of, given elements of experience.
>
> (Pinar, 2011, p. 99)

Human activity needs to be meaningful unto itself and not rendered meaningful according to the outcomes it produces.

Conclusion

The sheer volume of teacher films available suggests that one way teachers come to understand their classroom role is through film. Through film teachers might question their personal practical knowledge (Clandinin, 2013), their understanding of the ethics of the profession, or their purposes for wanting to be and remain teachers. Unlike most of the idealist teacher films that espouse a grand narrative of teacher agency and caring, *Irrational man* (Aronson et al., 2015) suggests that our motivations for wanting to make a difference ought to be tempered by a realistic assessment of what we are up against. As an existentialist film, *Irrational man* queries whether an existentialist praxis can support more theoretically robust approaches to teaching. The short answer is yes, for the normalized role of teaching limits teachers' ethical decision-making and an existentialist orientation counteracts that mind-set. Existentialism presents the possibility of an ontological commitment more than an epistemological one. It encourages us to pursue our questions and doubts with vigour. That is the way of freedom. Says Greene,

A teacher in search of his/her own freedom may be the only kind of teacher who can arouse young persons to go in search of their own . . . and children who have been provoked to reach beyond themselves, to wonder, to imagine, to pose their own questions are the ones most likely to learn to learn.

(1998, p. 4)

Existentialism encourages critical thinking through the pursuit of one's own freedom. It is an invitation to doubt common beliefs and practices. It is the persistence to search out histories to find out how things have come to be the way they are. Because existentialism commits one to fiercely imagine alternate possibilities, it is, quite possibly, a critical way to live one's life fully, even if the expense is that education becomes emptied of its value. Facing the hard truth that maybe formal education could be meaningless or not transformative is an important prerequisite for social innovation in educational ethical practice. An existential stance protects teachers' rights and freedoms as human beings and citizens, and allows for a more robust dialogue around the experiential and relational aspects of teaching that are immanent to its practice.

Existentialism allows greater consideration of the teacher's ethical imperative. Greene (1967) aptly notes that, "To say that man's essence is his rationality is to say nothing about the existing being, with all his shifting moods, feelings, impulses, fantasies, who is struggling to cope with the world" (p. 7). Whether in the social context of the classroom or some other public jurisdiction, the rights and responsibilities of teachers need a philosophical base that can justify and motivate right action outside the social bullying of normative ideals. Teleological systems of ethics have failed, relying on a priori values that are rarely defined or interrogated. Through an analysis of *Irrational man* (Aronson et al., 2015), we argue for an existentialist understanding of teaching and teacher education. Quoting Debra Britzman (2009) again, she asks Bachelor of Education candidates to look at the realities of teacher education more accurately, "Why would anyone want to be a teacher?" (p. 385). She points to the difficult working conditions, stress, the long work-day, and the low pay. Her question is a kind of electric shock to wake students out of their naivety. *Irrational man* performs the same service for teachers: For those whose gagging reflex is engaged when reading or watching teacher education university recruitment materials, *Irrational man* is a stimulating antidote.

REFERENCES

Appiah, K. A. (2007). *The ethics of identity*. Princeton, NJ: State University Press.

Aronson, L., Tenebaum, S., & Walson, E. (Producers), & Allen, W. (Director). (2015). *Irrational man* [Motion picture]. USA: Sony Pictures Classics.

Barrett, W. (1958). *Irrational man: A study in existential philosophy*. New York, NY: Anchor Books.

Block, A. (1998). "And he pretended to be a stranger to them": Maxine Greene and teacher as stranger. In W. F. Pinar (Ed.), *The passionate mind of Maxine Greene: "I am . . . not yet"* (pp. 13–28). Bristol, PA: Falmer Press.

Britzman, D. (2009). The poetics of supervision: A psychoanalytical experiment for teacher education. *Changing English*, 16(4), 385–396.

Clandinin, D. J. (2013). Personal practical knowledge: A study of teachers' classroom images. In C. J. Craig, P. C. Meijer, & J. Broeckmans (Eds.), *From teacher thinking to teachers and teaching: The evolution of a research community. Advances in research on teaching* (vol. 19, pp. 67–95). Basingstoke, UK: Emerald Group.

DeVito, D., Shamberg, M., & Sher, S. (Producers), & LaGravenese, R. (Director). (2007). *Freedom writers* [Motion picture]. USA: Paramount Pictures.

Greene, M. (1967). *Existential encounters for teachers*. New York, NY: Random House.

Greene, M. (1973). *The teacher as stranger: Educational philosophy for a modern age*. Belmont, CA: Wadsworth.

Greene, M. (1988). *The dialectic of freedom*. New York, NY: Teachers College Press.

Greene, M. (2001). *Variations on a blue guitar: The Lincoln Center Institute lectures on aesthetic education*. New York, NY: Teachers College Press.

Grenz, S. J. (2001). *The social God and the relational self*. Louisville, KY: Westminster John Knox Press.

Haft, S., Thomas, T, & Witt, P. (Producers), & Weir, W. (Director). (1989). *Dead poet's society* [Motion picture]. USA: Touchstone Pictures.

McBride, P. (2006). *The void of ethics: Robert Musil and the experience of modernity*. Evanston, IL: Northwestern University Press.

Neider, C. (2016). *I am not yet: Explicating Maxine Greene's notion of naming and being*. Unpublished Doctoral Dissertation. University of Pittsburgh, Pittsburgh, PA.

Pinar, W. F. (2010). Notes on a blue guitar. *Journal of Educational Controversy*, 5(1), 1–9. Retrieved from http://cedar.wwu.edu/jec/vol5/iss1/18

Pinar, W. F. (2011). *The character of curriculum studies: Bildung, currere, and the recurring question of the subject*. New York, NY: Palgrave Macmillan.

Quan, D. (2016, January 5). Laurentian University professor loses class after asking students to sign form allowing offensive language. *National Post*. Retrieved from http://nationalpost.com/news/canada/laurentian-university-professor-loses-class-after-asking-students-to-sign-form-allowing-offensive-language

Rozsa, L. (2017, September 29). Transgender teacher removed from classroom after some parents object to gender neutral prefix "Mx." *The Washington Post*. Retrieved from https://www.washingtonpost.com/news/post-nation/wp/2017/09/29/transgender-teacher-removed-from-classroom-after-some-parents-object-to-calling-her-mx/?utm_term=.fd1020323fcb

Swain, H. (2017, July 4). Should teachers be able to have tattoos? *The Guardian*. Retrieved from https://www.theguardian.com/education/2017/jul/04/should-teachers-have-tattoos-school

Yalom, I. D. (1980). *Existentialist psychotherapy*. New York, NY: Basic Books.

Zing, L. (2017, February 17). Mississauga mom distraught over grade 8 son's crystal meth assignment. *CBC News*. Retrieved from http://www.cbc.ca/news/canada/toronto/cooking-crystal-meth-assigned-to-grade-8-drama-students-1.3986359

NOTES

1. For example, see University of British Columbia's 2017 Faculty of Education promotional video (https://www.youtube.com/watch?v=oSl1l3rfmmI).
2. See https://www.youtube.com/watch?v=oRuQbuBdIZM

Biographies
(in order of appearance)

DIANE CONRAD is professor of drama/theatre education at the University of Alberta. Her teaching is in curriculum studies, teacher education, drama instructional methods, and participatory arts-based research. Her research using drama methods with marginalized youth includes publication of a play based on research with incarcerated youth entitled *Athabasca's going unmanned: An ethnodrama about incarcerated youth* (Sense, 2012). She is co-editor of *Creating together: Participatory, community-based and collaborative arts practices and scholarship across Canada* (Wilfred Laurier University Press, 2015) and co-editor-in-chief of the open access journal *Art/Research International: A Transdiciplinary Journal* (https://journals.library.ualberta.ca/ari/index.php/ari). She is also director of the Arts-Based Research Studio: https://www.facebook.com/groups/abrstudio/.

*****

MONICA PRENDERGAST is professor of drama/theatre education in the Department of Curriculum & Instruction, University of Victoria. Her research interests are varied and include drama-based curriculum and pedagogy, drama/theatre in community contexts, and arts-based qualitative research methds. Dr. Prendergast's books include *Applied theatre* and *Applied drama* (both with Juliana Saxton), *Teaching spectatorship*, *poetic inquiry*, *staging the not-yet: Drama, theatre and performance education in Canada* and *Poetic inquiry II*. Her CV includes over fifty peer reviewed journal contributions, numerous chapters, book reviews, and professional contributions. Monica also reviews theatre for CBC Radio Canada and writes a column on theatre for *Focus Magazine*.

BIOGRAPHIES

* * * * *

JAIME L. BECK completed her doctoral work in the Centre for Research for Teacher Education and Development (CRTED) at the University of Alberta. Her dissertation, "Teachers' experiences of negotiating stories to stay by," continued to explore themes taken up in her award-winning master's thesis, "Breaking the silence: Beginning teachers' shared pathways out of the profession" (completed at the University of British Columbia). Jaime's unique insights into the experiences of teachers have inspired her current commitment to developing/delivering professional learning supports around issues of teacher induction, mentorship, and teacher professional growth. Jaime's published works also explore her additional research interests that include research-based theatre, arts-based, and narrative methodologies.

* * * * *

PHIL DUCHENE has taught in the teacher education programme at the University of Victoria for twenty years. Prior to coming to Canada in 1989, he taught in the Caribbean after fifteen years in UK schools. Throughout, his interests have focused on the fine arts, specifically drama and its role in the curriculum for younger students; in particular, on improvisation, the use of story drama, and large-scale theatre-in-education projects. He teaches regularly in Vancouver Island schools in course-related workshops and projects from K-8. Most recently, he worked with Indigenous studies and applied theatre departments on an ongoing Canadian Residential Schools' project "No Stepping Back," shared at an international conference in Cambridge in 2018. Working with teacher candidates is a highlight of his year.

* * * * *

DOROTHY MORRISSEY has been a lecturer in drama education at Mary Immaculate College, University of Limerick, since 2002. She is course leader of the college's master's in education and the arts (META). She researches the arts, gender, and education through the lenses of arts-based, narrative, and performance methodologies.

* * * * *

JENNY OSORIO is a Ph.D. student in secondary education at the University of Alberta, where she also works as a French instructor. Originally from Colombia, she migrated to Canada where she graduated with a bachelor's degree in Hispanic studies and a master's degree in applied linguistics. Her research interests are literacy and reading comprehension in second language as well as the use of literature in beginners' language classes.

*****

CARL LEGGO (1953–2019) was a poet and professor at the University of British Columbia. His books include: *Come-by-chance: Lifewriting as literary métissage and an ethos for our times* (co-authored with Erika Hasebe-Ludt and Cynthia Chambers); *Creative expression, creative education* (co-edited with Robert Kelly); *Sailing in a concrete boat: Arresting hope – Prisons that heal* (co-edited with Ruth Martin, Mo Korchinski, and Lynn Fels); *Arts-based and contemplative practices in research and teaching: Honoring presence* (co-edited with Susan Walsh and Barbara Bickel); *Hearing echoes* (co-authored with Renee Norman); and *Poetic inquiry: Enchantment of place* (co-edited with Pauline Sameshima, Alexandra Fidyk, and Kedrick James).

*****

CLAIRE AHN is an assistant professor of multiliteracies in the Faculty of Education at Queen's University. Within the broad field of multiliteracies, Claire is interested in how visual information is mediated across different platforms. Specifically, as a former secondary English teacher, Claire is interested in the implementation of Hollywood films in the English classroom; the influence of film on teacher identities; how educators implement digital media in their classrooms; and how adolescents navigate and understand digital media.

*****

ANGELINA AMBROSETTI is an associate professor and head of course in the School of Education and the Arts at Central Queensland University, Australia. Angelina was a teacher in primary schools for sixtxeen years prior to her move to the university sector, where she works with undergraduate pre-service teachers during their initial teacher education training. Angelina's doctoral research focused on mentoring and mentoring relationships in pre-service teacher education. Her ongoing research interests include mentoring roles and relationships in initial teacher education, teacher identity, and professional development for teachers.

*****

NANCY CURRY, holds a master of music from the University of Southern California and is a Ph.D. candidate in applied theatre and curriculum studies at the University of Victoria. She is is a music educator, collaborative pianist, music theatre coach, and Suzuki method piano teacher. Her research interests are praxial music pedagogy, educational theory, literary theory, and arts-based education for autistic individuals.

BIOGRAPHIES

* * * * *

JEFFREY CURRY holds a master of music from the University of Southern California and a doctor of arts in music education from the University of Northern Colorado. He is a music educator and trombonist, whose career includes elementary classroom music, public school band, college and community band, and jazz band. His research interests are praxial music pedagogy, educational theory, the psychology of music learning, and the history of music, particularly pre-1700 instrumental works.

* * * * *

TAIWO O. AFOLABI is a theatre practitioner-researcher with a decade of experience in applied theatre/theatre for development in over ten countries across four continents. His research interests include public health/biomedicine, ethics, and theatre for civil engagement and social change. He is currently pursuing his doctoral studies at the University of Victoria and his research focuses on forced migration, mobility and displacement, and the ethics of conducting arts-based research among refugees and internally displaced persons in Africa for citizen participation. He is a research fellow with Border in Globalization at the Centre for Global Studies, University of Victoria, a research associate at the University of Johannesburg, South Africa, and the founding director of Theatre Emissary International, Nigeria.

* * * * *

STEPHEN OGHENERURO OKPADAH is a Ph.D. candidate in the Department of the Performing Arts, University of Ilorin, Nigeria. He holds a BA Hons degree in theatre arts from Delta State University Abraka, Nigeria, and a master's degree in performing arts from University of Ilorin. His areas of research include performance aesthetics, eco-performances, geopolitics, and film studies. He is a senior research fellow at Theatre Emissary International, Nigeria.

* * * * *

ANITA HALLEWAS is currently undertaking her Ph.D. at Griffith University, Australia, with a research focus in refugee theatre; specifically, how theatre might improve the quality of life for those living in refugee camps and the ethical implications related to that practice. She is an active applied theatre practitioner and is the founding artistic director of a theatre company specializing in applied theatre programming that encourages intergenerational collaboration. Anita has taught drama in high schools in several countries and is a learning consultant for a British

Columbia-based home-learning community where she mentors families in the benefits and challenges of alternative learning opportunities.

*****

PATRICIA JAGGER is a Ph.D. candidate at the University of Alberta in the Department of Secondary Education. Her research explores the use of participatory visual methodologies in educational contexts and is richly informed by her work both in film and television production and as a teacher. As an instructor to pre-service English language arts teachers, she has developed a passion for working with soon-to-be teachers as they embark on their careers in education and navigate the complexities of becoming teachers.

*****

CLAIRE COLEMAN began her career in education by working as a puppeteer in a disability awareness education programme. Teaching at both secondary and primary levels, she has developed her interest in drama in schools and community settings. Following a master's in education at the University of Sydney, she embarked upon her doctoral study. *Dancing through the fourth wall* examines the potential of process drama as an enactment of the philosophies of critical pedagogy. Claire currently lectures in drama education and innovative pedagogy at the University of Waikato.

*****

JANE ISOBEL LUTION is the head of the drama and dance faculty at a leading secondary college in New Zealand, where she teaches and directs several productions a year. Her Ph.D. in education involved a creative practice component in drama. She has toured in the UK, USA and Ireland with a theatre company performing and leading workshops in schools, military bases and prisons. As a drama teacher, she has co-authored the ESA NZ years 12 and 13 drama study guides and had articles and chapters published in international peer-reviewed journals and books. Jane has frequently led workshops and presented at conferences using dramatic performance.

*****

MITCHELL McLARNON is a gardener, course lecturer, Ph.D. candidate, and project lead of the several community gardens at McGill University. He is also sessional faculty at Bishop's University. Mitchell serves on the executive council for the Canadian

Association of Curriculum Studies and is on the editorial board of *Pathways: The Ontario Journal of Outdoor Education*. His research interests include: gender, social justice, homelessness, community-based, participatory and arts-based educational research methodologies, gardens, and environmental and democratic education. To learn more about Mitchell's work, please see: https://www.mcgill.ca/garden/.

* * * * *

MATTHEW KREHL EDWARD THOMAS, Ph.D. (University of Melbourne), is a lecturer in pedagogy and curriculum at Deakin University who specializes in organizational culture. He is a former secondary school teacher with a background in strategy, negotiation, and organizational development. Matthew's research is focused on relationships, human behaviour, and social engineering amidst surveillance cultures. He often draws from across multiple theoretical domains to create bespoke research designs with a specific focus on time, privacy, and risk.

* * * * *

BERNADETTE WALKER-GIBBS, associate professor, is recognized as an outstanding educator with an international reputation in research for her leadership of large-scale, longitudinal studies in teacher education and for international comparative studies in rural education. Her research focuses on place-based pedagogy, specifically alongside teacher identity and initial teacher education more broadly. Bernadette draws on post-structural and qualitative methods to enhance the capacity of graduate teachers for the diverse contexts in which they will teach.

* * * * *

MATTHEW "GUS" GUSUL is currently living in Edmonton, Alberta, working for the Alberta government in Indigenous relations. Previously, he worked with Frontier College as the Indigenous programme support coordinator and worked as a contract instructor teaching theatre in Maskwacis Cultural College. Gus obtained his Ph.D. from the University of Victoria in the Theatre Department. His research project focused upon the creation of an intergenerational theatre performance in rural Tamil Nadu, India, between seniors' community organizations and children's orphanages/schools.

* * * * *

RACHAEL JACOBS is a lecturer in creative arts education at Western Sydney University. She is a former secondary teacher (dance, drama, and music) and primary arts specialist. Her research interests include assessment in the arts, pre-service teacher education, and embodied learning. Rachael is a teaching-artist with the Sydney Theatre Company, and conducts drama and literacy projects with refugee communities in Sydney. In 2016, she was engaged by the OECD to contribute to the progress of the Sustainable Development Goals for 2030. She is currently the director of research for Drama Australia. Rachael is a community activist, a freelance writer, practicing dancer, and choreographer. She is the convenor of the community group Teachers for Refugees, and runs her own intercultural dance company.

*****

IAN TAN XING LONG is a Ph.D. candidate in English at the University of Warwick, focusing on philosophy and the poetry of Wallace Stevens. He is interested in the relationship between literature, philosophy, and film, and has written and spoken widely on these topics. He has published academic essays on James Joyce, Flann O'Brien, and directors such as Bela Tarr and Alexander Sokurov in the journals *Literary Imagination*, *Studies in European Cinema* and *Senses of Cinema*. He has written two student literary guidebooks.

*****

RUTH HOL MJANGER is associate professor in drama and coordinator for internationalization at NLA University College, Norway. Mjanger holds a master's in drama from Bergen University College. She has extensive experience from the field of teacher education in Norway. Since 2008, she has been involved in NLAs partnership with the Early Childhood Education Center (ECEC) for developing teacher education in Nepal. Thematically, there is considerable variation in Mjanger's work and she emphasizes the three-fold competence of being an artist, teacher, and researcher. Through art-based research and as a reflective practitioner, she investigates new approaches and methods on the border between art and applied science.

*****

BIBEK SHAKYA is a teacher trainer at the Early Childhood Education Center (ECEC), Nepal. He holds a master's in education with English as major subject from Kathmandu University. Prior to working in ECEC, he worked as a teacher at Living Stone Academy for five years. Currently, he is involved in curriculum development team at ECEC, which is developing active learning-based curriculum for pre-schools in Nepal. He intends to work on equipping the teachers to provide developmentally appropriate education for children, and brings about awareness on importance of practical aspects of education in what children are learning.

* * * * *

REINY DE WIT has been living in Nepal since 1985, working in the field of education. In 2001, she established the Early Childhood Education Centre (ECEC) where, in the past eighteen years, thousands of preschool teachers have been trained. Her academic background in early childhood development (ECD), plus ten years of experience in the Netherlands, qualified her to cooperate in developing best ECD practices in Nepal together with Nepali stakeholders and the government. In 2017, the daily management of ECEC was transferred to a Nepali manager and de Wit is currently the chair of the Board of Directors of ECEC.

* * * * *

MEENA SUBBA KARKI is a senior teacher trainer and branch manager of the Early Childhood Education Centre's (ECEC) Kathmandu office. She is originally from India, born and raised in Bhutan, but has been living in Nepal since 1999. She has a bachelor of science (India), a bachelor of education, a master's in sociology (Nepal), and has completed courses in mentoring and science in preschool (Norway). Subba has been working in the field of education the last eighteen years, including seven years as a grade 2 teacher at a private school in Kathmandu. Subba has been actively involved in bringing transformation in education and parental awareness in Nepal.

* * * * *

STIG A. ERIKSSON, (master's in elementary drama, University of Calgary, Canada, 1979; Ph.D. in drama education, Åbo Akademi University, Finland, 2009) is professor emeritus in drama education and applied theatre at Western Norway University of Applied Sciences, Bergen. Eriksson is an experienced drama teacher and educator, and has lectured and presented workshops in more than twenty-five countries. His research interests are related to historical and actual developments in the field of drama/theatre and education, including the broad field of applied drama/theatre. Eriksson was project coordinator of IDEA's 4th World Congress in 2001 in Bergen, Norway. From 2008–2010, he participated in the EU-funded international research project DICE. He was part of the project management of the research projects Theatre as Bildung (2011–2013, faculty) and Drama-Theatre-Democracy (2014–2017, national). His Ph.D. was titled *Distancing at close range: Investigating the significance of "distancing" in drama education* (Åbo Akademi).

*****

KATE BRIDE completed her Ph.D. thesis, *Learning to love again: Loss, self study, pedagogy and women's studies,* at Memorial University in 2009. She taught in education and women's studies at Memorial University and the University of Prince Edward Island. Kate was extraordinarily accomplished; artistic and musical; an original and promising researcher and writer on many topics – from the movie *Mona Lisa smile* to the 1914 *SS Newfoundland* sealing disaster; and a dedicated, insightful, gifted, and much-loved teacher. She was utterly reliable, calm, and competent, the kind of person you would want to be with in a crisis. She was wonderful with children and animals (most of all her faithful canine friend, Newman), and a brilliant conversationalist and companion. She was vulnerable and searingly honest. She was funny. She was kind. She died in 2012 of a sudden devastating illness.

*****

ELIZABETH YEOMAN is professor in the Faculty of Education at Memorial University. She writes and teaches about language, culture, walking, history, and memory from critical and arts-based perspectives. For the past few years, her main research project has been working with Innu elder and environmental activist Elizabeth Penashue on translating and editing a book based on Penashue's diaries in Innu-aimun (forthcoming from University of Manitoba Press). Another recently completed project is a film about winter walking and accessibility, *Honk if you want me off the road*, co-directed with Sharon Roseman.

*****

MELISSA TAMPORELLO is a digital artist and teacher working in Montreal, originally from New Orleans, Louisiana. She received her master's degree in art education from Concordia University, Montreal. Melissa has taught media art to a variety of different populations ranging from "at-risk" youth to seniors in a community setting. While teaching is a great passion of hers, she also enjoys making her own artwork using mediums such as film, experimental video, animation, and graphic arts. Melissa has presented her research and exhibited her artwork at various conferences and galleries in Montreal and New Orleans.

BIOGRAPHIES

* * * * *

CARMEN RODRIGUEZ DE FRANCE, of Kickapoo ancestry and Mexican heritage, has been a grateful visitor on the land of the Coast Salish people for twenty-two years. Born and raised in beautiful Monterrey, Mexico, her career spans thirty-four years with participation in a broad range of educational, community service, and research activities. Carmen teaches courses on Indigenous education, pedagogy, and epistemology in the Faculty of Education, and contributes in the social justice programme and the Latin American studies programme at the University of Victoria. Her most recent research involves partnerships with community organizations to support the enactment of the calls to action from the Truth and Reconciliation Commission Report.

* * * * *

ANITA SINNER is an associate professor of theoretical foundations of visual art curriculum and instruction at Concordia University. She brings transdisciplinary perspectives to research involving qualitative approaches and many forms of arts research in relation to curriculum studies and social and cultural issues in education. Her research interests are: arts research, a/r/tography, arts-based pedagogies, international art education, history of education, material culture, life writing, social fiction, spatial design of classrooms, curriculum theory, sociology of education, community art education, and pre-service and in-service teacher education.

* * * * *

THIBAULT ZIMMER is a second-year doctoral student in art education at Concordia University. With years of experience teaching community-based art education, Thibault has worked extensively with diverse populations across Quebec, Canada, and grounds his research in curriculum theory, arts-based methodologies, innovative approaches to teaching art, museum education, aesthetics, and youth work. He currently works as an educational resource designer at the Montreal Museum of Fine-Arts.

* * * * *

SEAN WIEBE, an associate professor of education at the University of Prince Edward Island, teaches courses in multiliteracies, curriculum theory, and critical pedagogy. He has been the principal investigator on four Canadian Social Sciences and Humanities Research Council-funded projects exploring the intersections of creativity, the creative economy, language and literacies, and arts informed inquiries.

*****

PAULINE SAMESHIMA, professor and Canada research chair in arts integrated studies at Lakehead University, utilizes multi-modal methodologies to catalyse thinking, dialogues, and social innovation. She is editor-in-chief of *The Journal of the Canadian Association for Curriculum Studies* and curates the Lakehead Research Education Galleries. Website: solspire.com.